First World War
and Army of Occupation
War Diary
France, Belgium and Germany

31 DIVISION
Divisional Troops
Royal Army Medical Corps
93 Field Ambulance
1 March 1916 - 24 May 1919

WO95/2354/1

The Naval & Military Press Ltd
www.nmarchive.com
Published in association with The National Archives

Published by

The Naval & Military Press Ltd

Unit 10 Ridgewood Industrial Park,

Uckfield, East Sussex,

TN22 5QE England

Tel: +44 (0) 1825 749494

www.naval-military-press.com

www.nmarchive.com

This diary has been reprinted in facsimile from the original. Any imperfections are inevitably reproduced and the quality may fall short of modern type and cartographic standards.

Contents

Document type	Place/Title	Date From	Date To
Heading	WO95/2354/1		
Heading	95 Field Ambulance War Diary For March 1919 Is Missing		
Heading	31st Division Medical 93rd Fld Ambulance Mar 1916-1919 May		
Heading	93 F.A.M.C. Vol I		
War Diary	H.T Knight Templar	01/03/1916	08/03/1916
War Diary	Marseilles	09/03/1916	12/03/1916
War Diary	Wanel	13/03/1916	25/03/1916
War Diary	Flesselles	26/03/1916	26/03/1916
War Diary	Beauval	27/03/1916	27/03/1916
War Diary	Vauchelles	28/03/1916	31/03/1916
Heading	93rd Field Ambulance 75. Evacuations Nil B. Cornell Lieut Col Commanding 93rd Field Ambulance 31st Division		
War Diary	Wanel	13/03/1916	14/03/1916
War Diary	Vauchelles	01/04/1916	30/04/1916
Heading	May 1916 31st Div. No. 93. F Amb.		
War Diary	Vauchelles	01/05/1916	31/05/1916
Heading	June 1916 No. 93 F.A.		
War Diary	Vauchelles Les Authie	01/06/1916	11/06/1916
War Diary	Sarton	13/06/1916	30/06/1916
Heading	31st Division Vol VII War Diary Of 93rd Field Amb. 1st July To 31st July 1916		
War Diary	Sarton	01/07/1916	06/07/1916
War Diary	Beauval	07/07/1916	07/07/1916
War Diary	Candas	07/07/1916	09/07/1916
War Diary	Busnes	10/07/1916	15/07/1916
War Diary	Zelobes	16/07/1916	31/07/1916
Heading	31st Div. War Diary Of 93rd FA Ambulance Aug 1916 Vol VIII		
War Diary	Zelobes	01/08/1916	31/08/1916
Heading	War Diary 93rd Field Ambulance 31st Division September 1916 Vol 9		
War Diary	Zelobes	01/09/1916	17/09/1916
War Diary	Bethune	18/09/1916	30/09/1916
Heading	War Diary 93rd Field Ambulance 31st Division October 1916 Volume X		
War Diary	Bethune	01/10/1916	04/10/1916
War Diary	Annezin	05/10/1916	05/10/1916
War Diary	Busnes	06/10/1916	08/10/1916
War Diary	Lillers	09/10/1916	09/10/1916
War Diary	Amplier	10/10/1916	10/10/1916
War Diary	Louvencourt	11/10/1916	18/10/1916
War Diary	Bois Laleau	19/10/1916	31/10/1916
Heading	War Diary 93rd Field Ambulance 31st Division November 1916 Volume XI Vol 9		
Heading	93rd Field Ambulance		
War Diary	Bois Laleau	01/11/1916	30/11/1916

War Diary	War Diary 93rd Field Ambulance 31st Division December 1916 Volume XII Vol 10		
War Diary	Bois Laleau	01/12/1916	31/12/1916
Heading	War Diary 93rd Field Ambulance 31st Division January 1917 Volume XIII Vol XI		
War Diary	Bois Laleau	01/01/1917	22/01/1917
War Diary	Le Meillard	22/01/1917	31/01/1917
Heading	War Diary 93rd Field Ambulance 31st Divisional February 1917 Vol XIV Vol 12		
War Diary	Le Meillard	01/02/1917	18/02/1917
War Diary	Beauval	19/02/1917	19/02/1917
War Diary	Le Meillard	01/02/1917	09/02/1917
War Diary	Beauval	19/02/1917	19/02/1917
War Diary	Bois Laleau	20/02/1917	28/02/1917
Heading	War Diary 93rd Field Ambulance 31st Division March 1917 Volume X Vol 13		
War Diary	Bois Laleau	01/03/1917	10/03/1917
War Diary	Bus	11/03/1917	18/03/1917
War Diary	Beauval	19/03/1917	19/03/1917
War Diary	Rebreuve	20/03/1917	20/03/1917
War Diary	Gauchin	21/03/1917	21/03/1917
War Diary	Floringhem	22/03/1917	23/03/1917
War Diary	Bourecq	24/03/1917	24/03/1917
War Diary	Calonne	25/03/1917	31/03/1917
Heading	War Diary 93rd Field Ambulance 31st Division April 1917 Volume XVI Vol 14		
War Diary	Calonne	01/04/1917	09/04/1917
War Diary	Annezin	10/04/1917	11/04/1917
War Diary	Ruitz	12/04/1917	13/04/1917
War Diary	Frevillers	14/04/1917	28/04/1917
War Diary	Ecoivres In The Field	29/04/1917	29/04/1917
Miscellaneous	Summary Of Medical War Diaries For 93rd F.A. 31st Divn. 13th Corps. 1st Army 3rd Army From 11/4/17 Western Front April May 17		
Miscellaneous	93rd F.A. 31st Divn. 13th Corps.	11/04/1917	11/04/1917
Heading	War Diary 93rd Field Ambulance 31st Division May 1917 Volume XVII Vol 15		
War Diary	A.D.S. H. I.C. 3.8 (map Ney 51 B)	01/05/1919	04/05/1919
War Diary	A.D.S.	05/05/1919	06/05/1919
War Diary	St. Catherines	07/05/1919	20/05/1919
War Diary	Cambligneul	21/05/1919	31/05/1919
Miscellaneous	B.E.F. Summary Of Medical War Diaries For 93rd F.A. 31st Divn. 13th Corps. 1st Army. 3rd Army From 11/4/17 Western Front April-May 17		
Miscellaneous	B.E.F. 93rd F.A. 31st Divn. 13th Corps.		
Heading	War Diary 93rd Field Ambulance 31st Division June 1917		
War Diary	Cambligneul	01/06/1917	10/06/1917
War Diary	St. Catherine	11/06/1917	11/06/1917
War Diary	M.D.S. ST. Catherine	11/06/1917	30/06/1917
Heading	War Diary 93rd Field Ambulance 31st Division July 1917 Volume IX Vol 17		
War Diary	M.D.S. St Catherine	01/07/1917	04/07/1917
War Diary	Cambligneul	05/07/1917	15/07/1917
War Diary	Villers Au Bois	16/07/1917	31/07/1917
Heading	93rd Field Ambulance 31st Division August 1917		

War Diary	Villers Au Bois	01/08/1917	31/08/1917
Heading	War Diary 93rd Field Ambulance 31st Division September 1917		
War Diary	Villers Au Bois	01/09/1917	04/09/1917
War Diary	Rollincourt	04/03/1917	30/03/1917
Heading	War Diary. 93rd Field Ambulance 31st Division October 1917		
War Diary	Rollincourt M.D.S.	01/10/1917	04/10/1917
War Diary	Rollincourt	05/10/1917	31/10/1917
Heading	War Diary 93rd Field Ambulance 31st Division November 1917		
War Diary	Rollincourt	01/11/1917	30/11/1917
Heading	War Diary 93rd Field Ambulance 31st Division December 1917. Vol 22		
War Diary	Roclincourt	01/12/1917	06/12/1917
War Diary	St. Catherines	07/12/1917	09/12/1917
War Diary	Maroeuil	10/12/1917	31/12/1917
Heading	No. 93. F.A.		
War Diary	Maroeuil	01/01/1918	08/01/1918
War Diary	St Eloi	09/01/1918	18/01/1918
War Diary	Mt. St Eloi	19/01/1918	31/01/1918
Heading	No. 93. F.A.		
War Diary	Mt. St. Eloi	01/02/1918	28/02/1918
Heading	93rd Field Ambulance Mar. 1918		
War Diary	Hermin	01/03/1918	22/03/1918
War Diary	Blaireville	23/03/1918	27/03/1918
War Diary	Blaireville	24/03/1918	31/03/1918
Heading	93rd Field Ambulance Apr. 1918		
War Diary	Le Bac an Sud	01/04/1918	01/04/1918
War Diary	Sus St Leger	02/04/1918	02/04/1918
War Diary	Bajus	03/04/1918	10/04/1918
War Diary	Merris	11/04/1918	12/04/1918
War Diary	Strazeele	12/04/1918	12/04/1918
War Diary	Pradelles	13/04/1918	13/04/1918
War Diary	Lakreule	14/04/1918	19/04/1918
War Diary	Hazebrouck	14/04/1918	27/04/1918
War Diary	Lakreule	28/04/1918	30/04/1918
Heading	War Diary 93rd Field Ambulance May 1918		
War Diary	Lakreule	01/05/1918	01/05/1918
War Diary	Staple	02/05/1918	23/05/1918
War Diary	Lumbres	24/05/1918	31/05/1918
Heading	93rd. F. A. June 1918		
War Diary	Lumbres	01/06/1918	07/06/1918
War Diary	Racquinghem	08/06/1918	15/06/1918
War Diary	Wallon Cappel	15/06/1918	17/06/1918
War Diary	Racquinghem	18/06/1918	21/06/1918
War Diary	Les Cinq Rues	22/06/1918	24/06/1918
War Diary	Wallon Cappelle	25/06/1918	30/06/1918
Heading	July 1918 93rd. F.A.		
War Diary	Wallon Cappell	01/07/1918	31/07/1918
Heading	93rd. Fd Amb. Aug. 1918		
War Diary	Wallon Cappel	01/08/1918	24/08/1918
War Diary	Eblinghem	25/08/1918	31/08/1918
Heading	93rd Fd. Ambce. Sept. 1918		
War Diary	Caestre	01/09/1918	18/09/1918
War Diary	Borre	19/09/1918	30/09/1918

Heading	93rd F.A. Oct 1918		
War Diary	Borre	01/10/1918	09/10/1918
War Diary	Bailleul	10/10/1918	22/10/1918
War Diary	Armentieres	23/10/1918	24/10/1918
War Diary	Wambrechies	24/10/1918	24/10/1918
War Diary	Cuerne	25/10/1918	31/10/1918
Heading	No. 93 F.A. Nov 1918		
War Diary	Cuerne	01/11/1918	02/11/1918
War Diary	Lauwe	03/11/1918	05/11/1918
War Diary	Avelghem	06/11/1918	07/11/1918
War Diary	Swevelghem	08/11/1918	09/11/1918
War Diary	Avelghem	10/11/1918	10/11/1918
War Diary	Renaix	11/11/1918	14/11/1918
War Diary	Sweveghem	15/11/1918	15/11/1918
War Diary	Marcke	16/11/1918	24/11/1918
War Diary	Menin	25/11/1918	25/11/1918
War Diary	Vlamertinghe	26/11/1918	26/11/1918
War Diary	Staple	28/11/1918	28/11/1918
War Diary	St. Omer	29/11/1918	30/11/1918
Heading	No. 93. F.A. Dec 1918		
War Diary	St Omer	01/12/1918	31/12/1918
Heading	31 Div Box 2131 Jan 1919		
War Diary	St Omer	01/01/1919	29/01/1919
War Diary	Calais	30/01/1919	31/01/1919
Heading	No. 93 Field Ambulance Feb 1919		
War Diary	St Omer	01/02/1919	28/02/1919
Heading	93rd. F.A. Mar. 1919		
War Diary	St Omer	01/03/1919	31/03/1919
Heading	No. 93 F.a. Apr 1919		
War Diary	St Omer	01/04/1919	30/04/1919
Heading	No 93 Field Ambulance May 1919		
War Diary	St Omer	01/05/1919	19/05/1919
War Diary	Wizernes	15/07/1918	15/07/1918
War Diary	Dunkirk	19/05/1919	24/05/1919

95 Field Ambulance:

War Diary for March 1919 is missing.

31ST DIVISION
MEDICAL

93RD FLD AMBULANCE

MAR 1916-~~DEC 1918~~ 1919 MAY

3 Ind Div

Sailed from Alexandria, 1.3.16.
Reached Marseilles 8.3.16.

93 F Amb
Vol 1

March 1916
April 1916

31

Dec '18

Instructions regarding War Diaries and Intelligence Summaries are contained in F. S. Regs., Part II. and the Staff Manual respectively. Title Pages will be prepared in manuscript.

Army Form C. 2118

WAR DIARY
or
INTELLIGENCE SUMMARY
(Erase heading not required.) 93rd Field Ambulance

Place	Date	Hour	Summary of Events and Information	Remarks and references to Appendices
H.T. KNIGHT TEMPLAR	1/3/16.		Sailed from Alexandria today at 12 noon. The ship frightfully overcrowded. I placed Lieut Humphreys of the 93rd Field Ambulance in Medical charge of the ships hospital. Lieut Yorke 93rd Field Ambulance assisted me with the personel & superintended the sanitation on Board. B.C.	
H.T. KNIGHT TEMPLAR	2/3/16.		There were a few cases of seasickness but the general health of troops on Board was good. Nothing important to report. B.C.	

1875 Wt. W593/826 1,000,000 4/15 J.B.C. & A. A.D.S.S./Forms/C. 2118.

Instructions regarding War Diaries and Intelligence Summaries are contained in F. S. Regs., Part II. and the Staff Manual respectively. Title Pages will be prepared in manuscript.

WAR DIARY
or
INTELLIGENCE SUMMARY
(Erase heading not required.)

Army Form C. 2118

Place	Date	Hour	Summary of Events and Information	Remarks and references to Appendices
H.T. KNIGHT TEMPLAR	3/1/16.		There was Boat drill to day at 4 p.m. but owing to the overcrowding on Board there are not sufficient boats for all the troops, if the ship were actually in danger. BC	
H.T. KNIGHT TEMPLAR.	4/1/16.		Sighted MALTA this evening but did not put into port, we sailed about the outside of the harbour all night + then steered our course for MARSEILLES. BC.	
H.T. KNIGHT. TEMPLAR	5/3/16		We Sighted the Island of PANTELARIA, but kept well out to Sea. The health of the troop on board is extremely good, no serious cases have occured. BC	

1875 Wt. W593/826 1,000,000 4/15 I.B.C. & A. A.D.S.S./Forms/C. 2118.

Instructions regarding War Diaries and Intelligence Summaries are contained in F. S. Regs., Part II. and the Staff Manual respectively. Title Pages will be prepared in manuscript.

WAR DIARY
or
INTELLIGENCE SUMMARY

Army Form C. 2118

(Erase heading not required.) 93rd Field Ambulance

Place	Date	Hour	Summary of Events and Information	Remarks and references to Appendices
H.T. KNIGHT TEMPLAR	6/3/16.		Nothing important to record. B.C.	
H.T. KNIGHT TEMPLAR.	7/3/16.		We sighted the coast of France this evening there is nothing important to record, the health of the troops remaining extremely good in spite of the overcrowding B.C.	
H.T. KNIGHT TEMPLAR	8/3/16.		Reached MARSEILLES this morning & disembarked at 2pm. Owing, however, to a deficiency of rolling stock we were unable to entrain today & the troops slept the night on board. B.C.	
MARSEILLES	9/3/16.		Received orders today to entrain at 9.12 tomorrow morning. This unit bivouaced the night in a shed	

1875 Wt. W593/826 1,000,000 4/15 J.B.C. & A. A.D.S.S./Forms/C. 2118.

Instructions regarding War Diaries and Intelligence Summaries are contained in F. S. Regs., Part II. and the Staff Manual respectively. Title Pages will be prepared in manuscript.

WAR DIARY

or

INTELLIGENCE SUMMARY

(Erase heading not required.) 93rd Field Ambulance

Army Form C. 2118

Place	Date	Hour	Summary of Events and Information	Remarks and references to Appendices
			in the docks BC	
MARSEILLES.	10/3/16.		On arriving at the Station at 9.12 this morning it was found that there was not sufficient room for all the troops animals & baggage. I therefore sent Lieuts Yorke & Lieut Humphreys on with 205 Rank and file and followed by a later train at 4 pm with 11 rank & file, the horses and equipment. BC.	
	11/3/16.		Spent the day in the train. Destination unknown nothing important to record. BC	
	12/3/16.		Spent the greater part of the day in the train without any untoward incident and reached PONT DU REMY near Abbeville at 4 pm where we detrained, and marched to WANEL where we were alloted billets. BC	

1875 Wt. W593/826 1,000,000 4/15 J.B.C. & A. A.D.S.S./Forms/C. 2118.

Instructions regarding War Diaries and Intelligence Summaries are contained in F. S. Regs., Part II. and the Staff Manual respectively. Title Pages will be prepared in manuscript.

WAR DIARY
or
INTELLIGENCE SUMMARY

(Erase heading not required.) 93rd Field Ambulance

Army Form C. 2118

Place	Date	Hour	Summary of Events and Information	Remarks and references to Appendices
WANEL	13/3/16.		I went into HALLENCOURT to enquire about re equiping my unit with transport as in accordance with orders all had been left behind in Egypt. I was informed that the D.A.H.S at ABBEVILLE had all my transport ready + would deliver it to me on application to him. I interviewed him this afternoon and was informed that all my transport could be drawn tomorrow morning. B.C.	
WANEL	14/3/16.		Drew all my horse transport 3 horse Ambulances 6 G.S. Wagons 3 Limbers 3 Watercarts 1 Maltese Cart	

Army Form C. 2118

WAR DIARY
or
INTELLIGENCE SUMMARY

Instructions regarding War Diaries and Intelligence Summaries are contained in F. S. Regs., Part II. and the Staff Manual respectively. Title Pages will be prepared in manuscript.

(Erase heading not required.) 93rd Field Ambulance

Place	Date	Hour	Summary of Events and Information	Remarks and references to Appendices
			21 heavy draft.	
			25 Light draft.	
			6 Spare horses. B.C.	
WANEL	15/3/16.		Indented for all equipment necessary for bringing my unit up to establishment B.C.	
WANEL	16/3/16.		I instituted a daily route march for the men who seem to be getting out of condition. This is very useful as it also gives them a knowledge of the country. B.C.	
WANEL	17/3/16.		Nothing important to record. B.C.	
WANEL	18/3/16		Nothing important to record B.C.	
WANEL	19/3/16		Nothing important to record. B.C.	
WANEL	20/3/16.		Received information today that 6 officers & men could proceed on eight days leave	

1875 Wt. W593/826 1,000,000 4/15 J.B.C. & A. A.D.S.S./Forms/C. 2118.

Army Form C. 2118

Instructions regarding War Diaries and Intelligence Summaries are contained in F. S. Regs., Part II. and the Staff Manual respectively. Title Pages will be prepared in manuscript.

WAR DIARY
or
INTELLIGENCE SUMMARY
(Erase heading not required.) 93rd Field Ambulance

Place	Date	Hour	Summary of Events and Information	Remarks and references to Appendices
WANEL.	2/3/16.		Received tonight my motor transport 7 Motor Ambulances and 3 motor Cycles + 15 rank and file under a corporal. BC	
WANEL	22/3/16.		Received information today to prepare the unit to march to the Front line on the 26th inst. BC	
WANEL	23/3/16.		In accordance with instructions I sent the following Officers Capt R.G. CUMMING + Lieut FORBES to join the 109 Field Ambulances for instruction	
WANEL	24/3/16.		Nothing important to record. BC B.C.	

1875 Wt. W593/826 1,000,000 4/15 J.B.C. & A. A.D.S.S./Forms/C. 2118.

Instructions regarding War Diaries and Intelligence Summaries are contained in F. S. Regs., Part II. and the Staff Manual respectively. Title Pages will be prepared in manuscript.

WAR DIARY
or
INTELLIGENCE SUMMARY

(Erase heading not required.) 93rd Field Ambulance

Army Form C. 2118

Place	Date	Hour	Summary of Events and Information	Remarks and references to Appendices
WANEL	25/3/16	5pm	Received the following message from the A.D.M.S. 31st Division Your unit will move complete, on the morning of the 26th from billets at WANEL to billets at FLESSELS. under orders of the G.O.C 93rd Infantry Brigade. Orders for your move from WANEL to LONGPRES will be issued by the G.O.C. 93rd Infantry Brigade You will join column at LONGPRE reaching there at 8 am Route LONGPRE - CONDE - HANGEST. - BOURDON - POINT 77 - VIGNACOURT. to billets at FLESSELLES. Sick requiring evacuation on morning of 26th should be sent to No3 C.C.S ST. OUEN. If you are unable to obtain transport from NO1. M.A. CONVOY. ST OUEN you should use your own motor Ambulances. On completion of duty these should rejoin your unit at FLESSELLES. Signed G. W. Chase Major RAMC for A.D.M.S 31st Division D H Q 25/3/16	

1875 Wt. W593/826 1,000,000 4/15 J.B.C. & A. A.D.S.S./Forms/C. 2118.

Instructions regarding War Diaries and Intelligence Summaries are contained in F. S. Regs., Part II. and the Staff Manual respectively. Title Pages will be prepared in manuscript.

WAR DIARY
or
INTELLIGENCE SUMMARY
(Erase heading not required.) 93rd Field Ambulance

Army Form C. 2118

Place	Date	Hour	Summary of Events and Information	Remarks and references to Appendices
			In compliance with this order the unit prepared to march off next morning B.C.	
FLESSELLES	26/3/16	4pm	The unit marched off at 6·30 am this morning reaching LONGPRES at 8 a.m. where it joined the remainder of the 93rd Infantry Brigade. The weather was very inclement + told severely upon the men of the Brigade, who fell out in large numbers, several of these cases were relieved by the Field Ambulance. There were no cases for evacuation, But the men of all units appeared to suffer badly from Sore feet probably due to their marching on the hard roads ~~after~~ being accustomed to the soft sand of the Egyptian desert.	
		8pm	The following march table was received for the	

1875 Wt. W593/826 1,000,000 4/15 J.B.C. & A. A.D.S.S./Forms/C. 2118.

Instructions regarding War Diaries and Intelligence Summaries are contained in F. S. Regs., Part II. and the Staff Manual respectively. Title Pages will be prepared in manuscript.

WAR DIARY
or
INTELLIGENCE SUMMARY

(*Erase heading not required.*) 93rd Field Ambulance

Army Form C. 2118

Place	Date	Hour	Summary of Events and Information	Remarks and references to Appendices
			next day.	
			Moves on the 27th will take place in accordance with table below	

	FROM.	Hour of Start	Route.	Destination
H.Qrs. 93rd I.B. 16th W. Yorks 18th W. Yorks	VIGNACOURT.	8. am	HAVERNAS NAOURS. VERTGALAND FARM	BEAUVAL
223 F Coy RE. 93rd F. Amb. 1 Coy ASC	FLESSELLES	8.45 am	—	BEAUVAL
15th West Yorks	VIGNACOURT.	7.0 am	FLESSELLES	BEAUQESNE.
18th D L I	FLESSELLES	8.10 am.	Pt 130 North of. VILLERS BOCAGE TALMAS-LA VICOGNE	

The 223 Field Coy RE. 93rd Field Amb. 1 Coy A.S.C. join Column for BEAUVAL at NAOURS.

25/3/16

Signed C. T. Davey Capt
Staff Capt 93rd Inf Bgde

1875 Wt. W593/826 1,000,000 4/15 J.B.C. & A. A.D.S.S./Forms/C. 2118.

Instructions regarding War Diaries and Intelligence Summaries are contained in F. S. Regs., Part II. and the Staff Manual respectively. Title Pages will be prepared in manuscript.

WAR DIARY
or
INTELLIGENCE SUMMARY

(Erase heading not required.) 93rd Field Ambulance

Army Form C. 2118

Place	Date	Hour	Summary of Events and Information	Remarks and references to Appendices
BEAUVAL	27/3/16.		In accordance with the foregoing time table the 93rd Field Ambulance continued on the line of march. The men of the Brigade still suffered acutely from sore feet & 6 cases were evacuated to No 4 C.C.S at BEAUVAL	
		4pm	I received a message directing me to proceed through BEAUQUESNE, - MARIEUX. to our destination at VAUCHELLES. B.C.	
VAUCHELLES	28/3/16	12AM.	The unit arrived at VAUCHELLES & relieved the 2nd W RIDING TERRITORIAL FIELD Ambulance. All ranks very tired, but practically no men of my unit fell out during the march. The weather most of the time was extremely trying & told severely upon the men.	

1875 Wt. W593/826 1,000,000 4/15 J.B.C. & A. A.D.S.S./Forms/C. 2118.

Instructions regarding War Diaries and Intelligence Summaries are contained in F. S. Regs., Part II. and the Staff Manual respectively. Title Pages will be prepared in manuscript.

WAR DIARY
or
INTELLIGENCE SUMMARY
(Erase heading not required.) 93rd Field Ambulance

Army Form C. 2118

Place	Date	Hour	Summary of Events and Information	Remarks and references to Appendices
			the transport was very satisfactory as in spite of the hilly country there were no break downs on the journey. B.C.	
VAUCHELLES	29/3/16		The Ambulance at once opened a dressing station for the reception of sick. & the Motor Ambulances were busy all day collecting sick from all units and 52 admission were made in the first 24 hours. B.C.	
VAUCHELLES	30/3/16		Total number of sick to day 52 evacuated 11 to GEZAINCOURT. B.C.	
VAUCHELLES	31/3/16		Interviewed the ADMS today with a view to fixing up the Ambulance as a rest Camp. Total number of Patients in the hospital today at noon	

1875 Wt. W593/826 1,000,000 4/15 J.B.C. & A. A.D.S.S./Forms/C. 2118.

Army Form C. 2118

WAR DIARY
or
INTELLIGENCE SUMMARY
(Erase heading not required.) 93rd Field Ambulance

Instructions regarding War Diaries and Intelligence Summaries are contained in F. S. Regs., Part II. and the Staff Manual respectively. Title Pages will be prepared in manuscript.

Place	Date	Hour	Summary of Events and Information	Remarks and references to Appendices
			75, Evacuations Nil	
			B. Connell Lieut Col	
			Commanding 93rd Field Ambulance	
			31st Division.	

1875 Wt. W593/826 1,000,000 4/15 J.B.C. & A. A.D.S.S./Forms/C. 2118.

Instructions regarding War Diaries and Intelligence Summaries are contained in F. S. Regs., Part II. and the Staff Manual respectively. Title Pages will be prepared in manuscript.

WAR DIARY
or
INTELLIGENCE SUMMARY

(Erase heading not required.) 93rd Field Ambulance

Army Form C. 2118

Place	Date	Hour	Summary of Events and Information	Remarks and references to Appendices
WANEL.	13/3/16.		I went into Hallencourt to enquire about re-equiping my unit with transport as in accordance with orders all had been left behind in Egypt. I was informed that the D.A.H.T. at Abbeville had all my transport ready & would delivery it to me on application to him. I interviewed him this afternoon & was informed that it could all be drawn tomorrow morning. I accordingly arranged that this should be done. B.C.S.	
WANEL	14/3/16.		Drew all our Transport. 3 horse Ambulances. 6 G.S. Waggons. 3 Limbers 3 Water carts 1 Maltese Cart	

1875 Wt. W593/826 1,000,000 4/15 J.B.C. & A. A.D.S.S./Forms/C. 2118.

Instructions regarding War Diaries and Intelligence Summaries are contained in F. S. Regs., Part II. and the Staff Manual respectively. Title Pages will be prepared in manuscript.

Army Form C. 2118

WAR DIARY
or
INTELLIGENCE SUMMARY

(Erase heading not required.) 93rd Field Ambulance Vol 2

Place	Date	Hour	Summary of Events and Information	Remarks and references to Appendices
VAUCHELLES	1/4/16		Lieut John Bradbury Alexander reported himself for duty with this Ambulance and was taken on its strength. Nothing import occurred to day worth recording	
VAUCHELLES	2/4/16		"A" Section today took over charge of B.C. the dressing Station at VAUCHELLES. Lieut H E Yorke in Charge. B.C	
VAUCHELLES	3/4/16		Nothing important to record. B.C.	
VAUCHELLES	4/4/16		B & C. Sections were ordered to load their wagons & Check all deficiencies in order that these may be replaced. The A.P.M. 31st Division lectured the A.S.C attached	

Instructions regarding War Diaries and Intelligence Summaries are contained in F. S. Regs., Part II. and the Staff Manual respectively. Title Pages will be prepared in manuscript.

WAR DIARY
or
INTELLIGENCE SUMMARY

(Erase heading not required.) 93rd Field Ambulance

Army Form C. 2118

Place	Date	Hour	Summary of Events and Information	Remarks and references to Appendices
			to this unit on the rules of the road in the area occupied by the VIII Corps. B.C	
VAUCHELLES	5/4/16		Nothing important to record B.C.	

1875 Wt. W593/826 1,000,000 4/15 J.B.C. & A. A.D.S.S./Forms/C. 2118.

Instructions regarding War Diaries and Intelligence Summaries are contained in F. S. Regs., Part II. and the Staff Manual respectively. Title Pages will be prepared in manuscript.

WAR DIARY
or
INTELLIGENCE SUMMARY

(Erase heading not required.) 93rd Field Ambulance.

Army Form C. 2118

Place	Date	Hour	Summary of Events and Information	Remarks and references to Appendices
VAUCHELLES	6/4/16.		Received the following message today from A.D.M.S. 31st Division Information has been received that no 60200 Pte R. Loudon RAMC of the unit under your Command, a patient in hospital at ABBEVILLE is a suspected case of Relapsing Fever. All Sanitary precautions must be taken, and the kits of all contacts at once disinfected. ~~Those of~~ the remainder of the unit should then be done Signed A.M. Bewley Col A.D.M.S. 31st Division D.H.Q. 6/4/16	

Instructions regarding War Diaries and Intelligence Summaries are contained in F. S. Regs., Part II. and the Staff Manual respectively. Title Pages will be prepared in manuscript.

WAR DIARY
or
INTELLIGENCE SUMMARY
(Erase heading not required.)

Army Form C. 2118

Place	Date	Hour	Summary of Events and Information	Remarks and references to Appendices
			Steps were immediately taken to have this order carried out.	
VAUCHELLES	7/4/16	8.am	The following was sent me from A.D.M.S. 31st Division To A.D.M.S. 31st Division Reference D.M.S. wire No DM 168 dtd 5th aaa. Arrange with division to isolate 93rd Field Ambulance and all patients under its present care aaa. Disinfect all all Clothing & blankets to ensure complete destruction of lice. Ambulance should not receive patients until further orders aaa. Acknowledge. From D.D.M.S. 8th Corps.	

1875 Wt. W593/826 1,000,000 4/15 J.B.C. & A. A.D.S.S./Forms/C. 2118.

Instructions regarding War Diaries and Intelligence Summaries are contained in F. S. Regs., Part II. and the Staff Manual respectively. Title Pages will be prepared in manuscript.

WAR DIARY
or
INTELLIGENCE SUMMARY

(Erase heading not required.) 93rd Field Ambulance

Army Form C. 2118

Place	Date	Hour	Summary of Events and Information	Remarks and references to Appendices
			In reference to the above I received the following minute from A.D. M S 31st Division.	
			O.C. 93rd Field Ambulance	
			Attached copy of telegram is forwarded for necessary action. You must use the 2 disinfectors of Sanitary Section as well as the one you have.	
			Both other Field Ambulances have been instructed not to send sick to you	
			A. W. Bewley Col. A.D. M S 31st Division	
			D.H.Q 6/4/16 4/15 pm per Special Messenger	

1875 Wt. W593/826 1,000,000 4/15 J.B.C. & A. A.D.S.S./Forms/C. 2118.

Army Form C. 2118

Instructions regarding War Diaries and Intelligence Summaries are contained in F. S. Regs., Part II. and the Staff Manual respectively. Title Pages will be prepared in manuscript.

WAR DIARY
or
INTELLIGENCE SUMMARY
(Erase heading not required.) 93rd Field Ambulance.

Place	Date	Hour	Summary of Events and Information	Remarks and references to Appendices
VAUCHELLES	7/4/16	12 am	The following message was despatched to me. Furnish full particulars of case of Relapsing fever in your unit giving dates of admission arrival in France etc. Report progress of disinfection aaa Have asked for Steam disinfector aaa Reply by bearer Urgent aaa Signed ADMS 31st Division D. H. Q 11·25 am	

1875 Wt. W593/826 1,000,000 4/15 J.B.C. & A. A.D.S.S./Forms/C. 2118.

Army Form C. 2118

Instructions regarding War Diaries and Intelligence Summaries are contained in F. S. Regs., Part II. and the Staff Manual respectively. Title Pages will be prepared in manuscript.

WAR DIARY
or
INTELLIGENCE SUMMARY

(Erase heading not required.) 93rd Field Ambulance

Place	Date	Hour	Summary of Events and Information	Remarks and references to Appendices
	1pm.		The following Memorandum was sent me. ADMS 31st Division With reference to my telegram of todays date, No. C M 69. regarding the isolation of 93rd Field Ambulance on account of Relapsing Fever in that unit. It is notified that the period of isolation is 10 days provided that there are no fresh cases, which should be notified to this office immediately HQ VIII Corps. April 6th 1916. J. S. Dunne Capt DADMS for DDMS VIII Corps.	

1875 Wt. W593/826 1,000,000 4/15 J.B.C. & A. A.D.S.S./Forms/C. 2118.

Instructions regarding War Diaries and Intelligence Summaries are contained in F. S. Regs., Part II. and the Staff Manual respectively. Title Pages will be prepared in manuscript.

Army Form C. 2118

WAR DIARY
or
INTELLIGENCE SUMMARY
(Erase heading not required.) 93rd Field Ambulance

Place	Date	Hour	Summary of Events and Information	Remarks and references to Appendices
VAUCHELLES.	8/4/16.		In view of the outbreak of Relapsing fever, All precautions are being taken to prevent the spreading of this disease. Three disinfectors are working under competent management and all clothing & blankets are being treated with superheated steam. The men have been warned against associating with other units. B.C.	
VAUCHELLES.	9/4/16.		As this unit is now strictly isolated no patients are now admitted or discharged. The process of disinfection is progressing slowly but satisfactorily. There have been no further outbreaks of Relapsing Fever. B.C.	

1875 Wt. W593/826 1,000,000 4/15 J.B.C. & A. A.D.S.S./Forms/C. 2118.

Army Form C. 2118

WAR DIARY
or
INTELLIGENCE SUMMARY
(Erase heading not required.) 93rd Field Ambulance.

Instructions regarding War Diaries and Intelligence Summaries are contained in F. S. Regs., Part II. and the Staff Manual respectively. Title Pages will be prepared in manuscript.

Place	Date	Hour	Summary of Events and Information	Remarks and references to Appendices
VAUCHELLES	10/4/16.		All Blankets in this unit have been disinfected. and progress is being made with the mens kits. There have been no further outbreaks of Relapsing fever. B.C.	
VAUCHELLES	11/4/16		The A.D. M. S. 31st Division made an inspection this morning of all the disinfecting arrangements in progress. There have been no further outbreaks to record. I inspected the Surgical material of the Field Ambulance with a view to making the necessary indents in case the unit is suddenly called upon. B.C.	
VAUCHELLES.	12/4/16.		Nothing important to record except that there have been no further outbreaks of Relapsing Fever and the disinfection is progressing satisfactorily. B.C.	

1875 Wt. W593/826 1,000,000 4/15 J.B.C. & A. A.D.S.S./Forms/C. 2118.

Instructions regarding War Diaries and Intelligence Summaries are contained in F. S. Regs., Part II. and the Staff Manual respectively. Title Pages will be prepared in manuscript.

WAR DIARY
or
INTELLIGENCE SUMMARY

(Erase heading not required.) 93rd Field Ambulance.

Army Form C. 2118

Place	Date	Hour	Summary of Events and Information	Remarks and references to Appendices
VAUCHELLES.	13/4/16.		Nothing important to record.	
VAUCHELLES	14/4/16		Nothing important to record BC. BC	
VAUCHELLES	15/4/16.		The following is an extract from a letter addressed O.C. 93rd Field Ambulance from ADMS 21st Division marked Confidential. The Corps Commander considers that every available man from the unit under your Command should be employed on Digging, Repair and upkeep of Roads, Sanitary Work, Divisional Baths and Clothing disinfection, Working on dugouts for advanced dressing Stations or police duties.	
			Signed Alb. Bruely Col. ADMS. 21st Division	
			DHQ 14.4.16 }	
			BC.	

1875 Wt. W593/826 1,000,000 4/15 I.B.C. & A. A.D.S.S./Forms/C. 2118.

Instructions regarding War Diaries and Intelligence Summaries are contained in F. S. Regs., Part II. and the Staff Manual respectively. Title Pages will be prepared in manuscript.

WAR DIARY
or
INTELLIGENCE SUMMARY

(Erase heading not required.) 93rd Field Ambulance.

Army Form C. 2118

Place	Date	Hour	Summary of Events and Information	Remarks and references to Appendices
16/4/16.			Pte H. Sweetenham 16 West Yorks was evacuated this afternoon suffering from Enteric.	
			Lieut H. Hart R.A.M.C having reported himself for duty with this Ambulance was today taken on its strength and posted to B. Section.	
			I was notified today that Capt E. Dobson R.A.M.C was certified fit for home service only and was accordingly struck off the Strength of this unit.	
			B.C.	
17/4/16			This unit was released from quarantine and ordered to resume its duties as usual.	
			It has accordingly been opened up as a rest Camp.	
			B.C.	

1875 Wt. W593/826 1,000,000 4/15 J.B.C. & A. A.D.S.S./Forms/C. 2118.

Instructions regarding War Diaries and Intelligence Summaries are contained in F. S. Regs., Part II. and the Staff Manual respectively. Title Pages will be prepared in manuscript.

WAR DIARY
or
INTELLIGENCE SUMMARY

Army Form C. 2118

(Erase heading not required.) 93rd Field Ambulance.

Place	Date	Hour	Summary of Events and Information	Remarks and references to Appendices
VAUCHELLES.	18/4/16.		Nothing important to record. B.C.	
VAUCHELLES	19/4/16.		Divisional baths were opened by this unit to day. Officers of various units have been communicated with and arrangements have been made to bathe about 150 men daily. B.C.	
VAUCHELLES	20/4/16.		A sergeant and five men joined this ambulance to day as reinforcements. B.C.	
VAUCHELLES	21/4/16.		Nothing important to record. B.C.	

1875 Wt. W593/826 1,000,000 4/15 J.B.C. & A. A.D.S.S./Forms/C. 2118.

Instructions regarding War Diaries and Intelligence Summaries are contained in F. S. Regs., Part II. and the Staff Manual respectively. Title Pages will be prepared in manuscript.

WAR DIARY
or
INTELLIGENCE SUMMARY
(Erase heading not required.) 93rd Field Ambulance.

Army Form C. 2118

Place	Date	Hour	Summary of Events and Information	Remarks and references to Appendices
VAUCHELLES	22/4/16.		Nothing important to record. B.C.	
VAUCHELLES	23/4/16.		Nothing important to record. B.C.	
VAUCHELLES.	24/4/16.		No 60427. Pte J. Gilmour was sent in accordance with instructions to 4th Army Aircraft Park. for permanent duty and was accordingly struck off the strength of this unit. Two extra drivers A.S.C. M. Transport joined us today and were taken on the Strength. No M.S./3932 Pte W. Brosmand and M2/031474 Pte W H R Donovan. B.C.	
VAUCHELLES	25/4/16.		Nothing important to record. B.C.	
VAUCHELLES	26/4/16.		Nothing important to record. B.C.	

1875 Wt. W593/826 1,000,000 4/15 J.B.C. & A. A.D.S.S./Forms/C. 2118.

Army Form C. 2118

Instructions regarding War Diaries and Intelligence Summaries are contained in F. S. Regs., Part II. and the Staff Manual respectively. Title Pages will be prepared in manuscript.

WAR DIARY
or
INTELLIGENCE SUMMARY

(Erase heading not required.) 93rd Field Ambulance.

Place	Date	Hour	Summary of Events and Information	Remarks and references to Appendices
VAUCHELLES	27/4/16		In accordance with instructions from D D M S VIII Corps Lieut A.D Forbes 93rd Field Ambulance was detailed to report himself to the town Major and O.C Troops at SARTON as Sanitary Officer and also to render medical attention to such units as were not provided for. This as a temporary measure, this officer being still on our establishment. B.C	
VAUCHELLES	28/4/16		Nothing important to record. B.C	
VAUCHELLES	29/4/16		An inspection of all ranks was held this morning at 11·30am by the CO with a view to ascertaining if all gas appliances were complete. All men appear to be well supplied in compliance with orders. B.C	

Instructions regarding War Diaries and Intelligence Summaries are contained in F. S. Regs., Part II. and the Staff Manual respectively. Title Pages will be prepared in manuscript.

Army Form C. 2118

WAR DIARY
or
INTELLIGENCE SUMMARY

(Erase heading not required.) 93rd Field Ambulance

Place	Date	Hour	Summary of Events and Information	Remarks and references to Appendices
VAUCHELLES	30/4/16		The following was received today. O.C. 93rd Field Ambulance. Please send one Officer RAMC on 1st May for duty with 10th Batt East Yorkshire Regt at this Station. Lieut F. S. B. Fletcher RAMC will on relief be posted to your unit for duty. The Officer detailed should report at this Office at 11 am 1-5-16. Signed A. W. Bewley Col ADMS 31st Division Lieut H. W. Hart was detailed for the above duty B. Cornell Lieut Col Commanding 93rd Field Ambulance	

1875 Wt. W593/826 1,000,000 4/15 J.B.C. & A. A.D.S.S./Forms/C. 2118.

31st Div

May 1916.

No. 93 F. Amb.

Instructions regarding War Diaries and Intelligence Summaries are contained in F. S. Regs., Part II. and the Staff Manual respectively. Title Pages will be prepared in manuscript.

WAR DIARY
or
INTELLIGENCE SUMMARY
(Erase heading not required.) 93rd Field Ambulance.

Army Form C. 2118

Vol 3

Place	Date	Hour	Summary of Events and Information	Remarks and references to Appendices
VAUCHELLES	1/5/16		There is a gradual expansion of the rest Camp. The number now admitted is 212. B.C.	
VAUCHELLES	2/5/16		The number of patients in hospital today 190. B.C.	
VAUCHELLES	3/5/16		Number of patients in hospital today 199. B.C.	
VAUCHELLES	4/5/16.		Lieut F. S. B. Fletcher was detailed today to Relieve Capt Mitchell R.A.M.C. for tempory duty with VIII Corps troops. Number of rest cases in the Ambulance today 174. Patients 22. B.C.	
VAUCHELLES	5/5/16		Number of rest cases 180. Patients in Ambulance ~~17~~ 20. B.C.	

1875 Wt. W593/826 1,000,000 4/15 J.B.C. & A. A.D.S.S./Forms/C. 2118.

Instructions regarding War Diaries and Intelligence Summaries are contained in F. S. Regs., Part II. and the Staff Manual respectively. Title Pages will be prepared in manuscript.

WAR DIARY
or
INTELLIGENCE SUMMARY

(Erase heading not required.) 93rd Field Ambulance

Army Form C. 2118

Place	Date	Hour	Summary of Events and Information	Remarks and references to Appendices
VAUCHELLES	6/5/16		Rest Cases 180. Patients 17 B.C	
VAUCHELLES	7/5/16.		Rest Cases 175. Patients 15 B.C.	
VAUCHELLES	8/5/16.		Rest Cases 166. Patients 19 B.C.	
VAUCHELLES	9/5/16.		Rest Cases 168. Patients 21. B.C.	
VAUCHELLES	10/5/16		Rest Camp 180. Patients 21. B.C	
VAUCHELLES	11/5/16		Rest Camp 181 Patients 17 B.C	

1875 Wt. W593/826 1,000,000 4/15 J.B.C. & A. A.D.S.S./Forms/C. 2118.

Instructions regarding War Diaries and Intelligence Summaries are contained in F. S. Regs., Part II. and the Staff Manual respectively. Title Pages will be prepared in manuscript.

WAR DIARY
or
INTELLIGENCE SUMMARY

(*Erase heading not required.*) 93rd Field Ambulance

Army Form C. 2118

Place	Date	Hour	Summary of Events and Information	Remarks and references to Appendices
VAUCHELLES	12/5/16		Rest Camp 184 Patients 19. B.C. 097630 Pte R. Jessop 31st Divisional Ammunition Sub park (workshops) BEAUSQUENE was evacuated to Highland C.C.S. with Cerebro-Spinal Meningitis. B.C.	
VAUCHELLES	13/5/16		Rest Camp 182 Patients 23 B.C.	
VAUCHELLES	14/5/16.		Rest Camp 175 Patients 20. Lieut S.S. B. Fletcher returned to this unit after a tour of temporary duty with 8th Corps Troops.	
VAUCHELLES	15/5/16		Rest Cases 177 Patients 23. B.C.	
VAUCHELLES.	16/5/16		Received instructions today from the A.D.M.S. 31st Division that as the Cinema Palace at SARTON was not vacant	

1875 Wt. W593/826 1,000,000 4/15 J.B.C. & A. A.D.S.S./Forms/C. 2118.

Instructions regarding War Diaries and Intelligence Summaries are contained in F. S. Regs., Part II. and the Staff Manual respectively. Title Pages will be prepared in manuscript.

WAR DIARY
or
INTELLIGENCE SUMMARY
(Erase heading not required.) 93rd Field Ambulance

Army Form C. 2118

Place	Date	Hour	Summary of Events and Information	Remarks and references to Appendices
			Ideas was to send a party of my personnel to occupy it. I instructed Capt R. S. Cumming C Section to detail a party of 25 men to do so this afternoon. B.C	
VAUCHELLES	17/5/16		In Compliance with instructions I detailed Capt R.S. Cumming with "C" Section to Proceed to SARTON & open up a Dressing Station at the Cinema Palace today.	
			Total numbers in Rest Camp today 178	
			Patients 22	
			B.C	
VAUCHELLES	18/5/16		Numbers in rest Camp 197	
			Hospital 24. B.C	
VAUCHELLES	19/5/16		Numbers in rest Camp 195.	
			Hospital 25 B.C	

Instructions regarding War Diaries and Intelligence Summaries are contained in F. S. Regs., Part II. and the Staff Manual respectively. Title Pages will be prepared in manuscript.

WAR DIARY
or
INTELLIGENCE SUMMARY
(Erase heading not required.) 93rd Field Ambulance

Army Form C. 2118

Place	Date	Hour	Summary of Events and Information	Remarks and references to Appendices
VAUCHELLES	20/5/16.		Numbers in Rest Camp 192 Hospital 25 B.C.	
VAUCHELLES	21/5/16		Capt A.D. Forbes left for England on 8 days leave. Numbers in rest Camp. 197 In Hospital 22 B.C.	
VAUCHELLES	22/5/16.		In Rest Camp 184 In Hospital 23 B.C.	
VAUCHELLES	23/5/16		Numbers in rest Camp 182. In hospital 24 B.C.	
VAUCHELLES	24/5/16.		Numbers in Rest Camp 190. In hospital 26 B.C.	
VAUCHELLES	25/5/16.		Numbers in Rest Camp 194. In hospital 27. B.C.	

1875 Wt. W593/826 1,000,000 4/15 J.B.C. & A. A.D.S.S./Forms/C. 2118.

Instructions regarding War Diaries and Intelligence Summaries are contained in F. S. Regs., Part II. and the Staff Manual respectively. Title Pages will be prepared in manuscript.

WAR DIARY
or
INTELLIGENCE SUMMARY

(Erase heading not required.) 93rd Field Ambulance

Army Form C. 2118

Place	Date	Hour	Summary of Events and Information	Remarks and references to Appendices
VAUCHELLES	26/5/16.		Numbers in Rest Camp 190. In hospital 29 B.C.	
VAUCHELLES	27/5/16.		Numbers in Rest Camp 190 In Hospital 30 B.C.	
VAUCHELLES	28/5/16.		Lieut C.E. Morgan in compliance with instructions left the Ambulance to attend a five days Course at the Anti-gas School at Noyelles. Numbers in Rest Camp 192. In Hospital 33 B.C.	
VAUCHELLES	29/5/16.		Numbers in Rest Camp 224 In hospital 33 Capt A.D. Forbes returned to duty from 8 days leave in England. Received the following order marked Secret. B.C.	

1875 Wt. W593/826 1,000,000 4/15 J.B.C. & A. A.D.S.S./Forms/C. 2118.

Army Form C. 2118.

Instructions regarding War Diaries and Intelligence Summaries are contained in F. S. Regs., Part II. and the Staff Manual respectively. Title Pages will be prepared in manuscript.

WAR DIARY
or
INTELLIGENCE SUMMARY
(Erase heading not required.)

93rd Field Ambulance

Place	Date	Hour	Summary of Events and Information	Remarks and references to Appendices
			The O.C. 93rd Field Ambulance. In accordance with VIII Corps No Q S 15/5/ forwarded under D.D. M S VIII Corps No M 21/16 dated 27/5/16. one Officer and twenty five men will in the event of active operations be required for duty at No 29 Casualty Clearing Station at GEZAINCOURT. for duty as stretcher bearers. The officer will probably have to be supplied from the Officers hospital GEZAINCOURT. and the twenty five men from your Rest Station. Please arrange to post up on a Slate or Blackboard in your Station, a Roster or daily State. showing how it is proposed to dispose of the patients in the	

2449 Wt. W14957/M90 750,000 1/16 J.B.C. & A. Forms/C.2118/12.

Instructions regarding War Diaries and Intelligence Summaries are contained in F. S. Regs., Part II. and the Staff Manual respectively. Title Pages will be prepared in manuscript.

WAR DIARY
or
INTELLIGENCE SUMMARY
(Erase heading not required.) 93rd Field Ambulance

Army Form C. 2118.

Place	Date	Hour	Summary of Events and Information	Remarks and references to Appendices
			rest Station, on the date in question should active operations commence. Patients should be divided into three categories 1) Those too ill to do any duty, who should at once be evacuated to a Casualty Clearing Station, on the commencement of operations. 2) Those for light duty. Of these 25 men should be detailed at the Casualty Clearing Station, as directed above 3) Those who are sufficiently recovered to return to the trenches or who are suffering from some minor ailment (such as scabies) which does not incapacitate them from fighting. These cases should all return to their unit at once. In this way the Rest Station can be closed down at a	

Instructions regarding War Diaries and Intelligence Summaries are contained in F. S. Regs., Part II. and the Staff Manual respectively. Title Pages will be prepared in manuscript.

WAR DIARY
or
INTELLIGENCE SUMMARY
(Erase heading not required.)

Army Form C. 2118.

Place	Date	Hour	Summary of Events and Information	Remarks and references to Appendices
			few hours notice and the personnel be free to act as Reserve Field Ambulance. Please acknowledge receipt.	
			R.W. Bewley Col. A.D.M.S. 31st Division	
			No S49. 28/5/16.	
			B.C.	
VAUCHELLES	30/5/16.		Patients in Rest Camp 221 In Hospital 41	
			B.C.	
VAUCHELLES	31/5/16.		Patients in Rest Camp 203 In Hospital 45	
			B. Cornell Lieut Col Commanding 93rd Ambulance	

2449 Wt. W14957/M90 750,000 1/16 J.B.C. & A. Forms/C.2118/12.

June 1916.

5

No. 93 F.A.

Instructions regarding War Diaries and Intelligence Summaries are contained in F. S. Regs., Part II. and the Staff Manual respectively. Title Pages will be prepared in manuscript.

WAR DIARY
or
INTELLIGENCE SUMMARY

(Erase heading not required.) 93rd Field Ambulance

Army Form C. 2118.

Vol 4

June

Place	Date	Hour	Summary of Events and Information	Remarks and references to Appendices
VAUCHELLES LES AUTHIE.	1/6/16		Number of patients in Rest Camp. 177. In Hospital 35 B.C	
VAUCHELLES LES AUTHIE.	2/6/16		Number of Patients in Rest Camp 177. In hospital 33. The DDMS VIII Corps made an surprise inspection of the rest Camp at 4 p.m. The time was most unfortunate as the men were at tea at the time and the dropping of crumbs & other small particles of food on the ground gave rise to a considerable amount of unfavourable criticism. The only remedy I can suggest is that these cases should have proper dining tents which at present I am unable to provide as I have not the materials for carrying out this improvement. B.C	
VAUCHELLES LES AUTHIE.	3/6/16		Number of Rest Cases 190 Sick 30 B.C	
VAUCHELLES LES AUTHIE.	4/6/16		Number of Rest Cases 187. Sick 28. Lieut J. L. Humphreys in accordance with ~~instructions~~ was detailed today to report to the O.C. 12th York & Lancs for temporary duty. B.C	

2449 Wt. W14957/M90 750,000 1/16 J.B.C. & A. Forms/C.2118/12.

Instructions regarding War Diaries and Intelligence Summaries are contained in F. S. Regs., Part II. and the Staff Manual respectively. Title Pages will be prepared in manuscript.

WAR DIARY
or
INTELLIGENCE SUMMARY
(Erase heading not required.)

Army Form C. 2118.

93rd Field Ambulance.

Place	Date	Hour	Summary of Events and Information	Remarks and references to Appendices
VAUCHELLES LES AUTHIE	5/6/16		Rest Cases 199 Sick 24 B.C.	
VAUCHELLES LES AUTHIE	6/6/16		Rest Cases 188. Sick 24 Received the following marked M 1021. dated 5/6/16 from A.D.M.S. 31st Division. The Corps Commander directs that 20 or 25 men who are fit for light duty are to be sent to Corps Headquarters from the Rest Station. Please select these men and be ready to send them when orders are received. They should be inspected daily and will sleep at the rest Station being rationed by you and treated as patients, they will be marched to and from Corps Headquarters under Command of an N.C.O. D.H.Q. 5/6/16. A W Bewley Col. A.D.M.S. 31st Division	

2449 Wt. W14957/M90 750,000 1/16 J.B.C. & A. Forms/C.2118/12.

Army Form C. 2118.

Instructions regarding War Diaries and Intelligence Summaries are contained in F. S. Regs., Part II. and the Staff Manual respectively. Title Pages will be prepared in manuscript.

WAR DIARY
or
INTELLIGENCE SUMMARY

(Erase heading not required.) 93rd Field Ambulance.

Place	Date	Hour	Summary of Events and Information	Remarks and references to Appendices
VAUCHELLES LES AUTHIE.	7/6/16		Numbers in Rest Camp. 169 Numbers in Hospital 25 B.C.	
VAUCHELLES LES. AUTHIE.	8/6/16		Received the following wire numbered M573. dated 8/6/16. Following wire received from D.D.M.S. VIII Corps. begins Detail a Senior Officer 93rd Field Ambulance to assume duties of town Major SARTON. ends Comply and Report name to this Office Medical 31st Division time 10.20 am Signed G. [illegible] Major. Captain R.S. Cumming was detailed for this duty Numbers in Rest Camp. 161. Number in Hospital 20. B.C.	
VAUCHELLES LES. AUTHIE.	9/6/16.		Received the following message marked urgent. Orders have been received for your unit to move to SARTON. I have asked for a motor lorry to assist the move. You should send some	

2449 Wt. W14957/M90 750,000 1/16 J.B.C. & A. Forms/C.2118/12.

Instructions regarding War Diaries and Intelligence Summaries are contained in F. S. Regs., Part II. and the Staff Manual respectively. Title Pages will be prepared in manuscript.

WAR DIARY
or
INTELLIGENCE SUMMARY

(Erase heading not required.) 93rd Field Ambulance

Army Form C. 2118.

Place	Date	Hour	Summary of Events and Information	Remarks and references to Appendices
			of your Stores today by your own transport. They could be stored in the estaminet or Cinema. Please let me know if you will be able to accommodate your sick in the Cinema & tents. – If more tents are required you should indent for them through this office. Also let me know if you require more horsed transport. The field N. E. of the Cinema can be used.	
			D.H.Q. 9-6-16 } A W Beveley Col. A.D.M.S. 31st Division	
			Number in Rest Camp. 162 In Hospital 21. B.C.	

Army Form C. 2118.

WAR DIARY
or
INTELLIGENCE SUMMARY
(Erase heading not required.) 93rd Field Ambulance

Instructions regarding War Diaries and Intelligence Summaries are contained in F. S. Regs., Part II. and the Staff Manual respectively. Title Pages will be prepared in manuscript.

Place	Date	Hour	Summary of Events and Information	Remarks and references to Appendices
VAUCHELLES LES AUTHIE.	10/6/16.		In accordance with the previous days orders I made preparation to ~~move~~ to SARTON. All heavy stores were accordingly despatched to SARTON. I proceeded there in the afternoon and in company with the Town Major selected billets for my men.	
			Number in Rest. 162.	
			In Hospital 19.	
			Received the following message from the ADMS 4th Division "The divisional headquarters are taking over this Ambulance as a temporary measure. Capt Owen the bearer of this will take over any stores belonging to the 11th F.A.	
			Signed W. M. O'Callaghan Col. ADMS"	

Army Form C. 2118.

Instructions regarding War Diaries and Intelligence Summaries are contained in F. S. Regs., Part II. and the Staff Manual respectively. Title Pages will be prepared in manuscript.

WAR DIARY
or
INTELLIGENCE SUMMARY

(Erase heading not required.) 93rd Field Ambulance

Place	Date	Hour	Summary of Events and Information	Remarks and references to Appendices
VAUCHELLES LES AUTHIE.	11/6/16.		The Ambulance today proceeded to SARTON to occupy the Cinema Theatre, the Cafe De La Place, and the Curé's presbytery. The Cinema was converted into a large dressing station accommodating about 50 cases. The Cafe De La Place was utilised as an inspection room & in an emergency could accommodate about 20 cases. The Curé's Presbytery was converted into Offices, Medical Stores, operating theatre, & two officers Wards. The men were billeted in Sections in the town Lieut Yorke relieved Capt Cumming of Medical Charge "C" Section going into reserve. A Paddock adjoining the Cinema was converted into a Rest Camp. Capt F.W. Stone was granted 14 days leave of absence to proceed to England on Private Affairs B.C.	

Army Form C. 2118.

Instructions regarding War Diaries and Intelligence Summaries are contained in F. S. Regs., Part II. and the Staff Manual respectively. Title Pages will be prepared in manuscript.

WAR DIARY
or
INTELLIGENCE SUMMARY

(Erase heading not required.) 93rd Field Ambulance

Place	Date	Hour	Summary of Events and Information	Remarks and references to Appendices
SARTON.	12/6/16.		The whole of the day was devoted to getting the Ambulance into working order. I have ~~two~~ officers doing Staff duty. Capt R.S. Cumming Town Major SARTON. Lieut D. Forbes. Sanitary Officer.	
SARTON	13/6/16.		Total numbers in Rest Camp today 144. B.C. In Hospital 12	
SARTON	14/6/16		B.C. Numbers in Rest Camp 157. In Hospital 12	
SARTON.	15/6/16		B.C. Numbers in Rest Camp 172 In Hospital 11	
SARTON	16/6/16.		B.C. Numbers in Rest Camp 139 In Hospital 7 B.C.	

Instructions regarding War Diaries and Intelligence Summaries are contained in F. S. Regs., Part II. and the Staff Manual respectively. Title Pages will be prepared in manuscript.

WAR DIARY
or
INTELLIGENCE SUMMARY

(*Erase heading not required.*) 93rd Field Ambulance

Army Form C. 2118.

Place	Date	Hour	Summary of Events and Information	Remarks and references to Appendices
17/6/16. SARTON	17/6/16		Numbers in Rest Camp 116 Sick 8 B.C.	
SARTON	18/6/16		Rest Camp 85 Sick 7 B.C.	
SARTON	19/6/16		Rest Camp 66 Sick 9 B.C.	
SARTON.	20/6/16		Rest Camp 65 Sick 12 B.C.	
SARTON	21/6/16.		Rest Camp 85 Sick 12 B.C.	
SARTON	22/6/16		Received the following message from A.D.M.S. 31st Division	

2449 Wt. W14957/M90 750,000 1/16 J.B.C. & A. Forms/C.2118/12.

Army Form C. 2118.

Instructions regarding War Diaries and Intelligence Summaries are contained in F. S. Regs., Part II. and the Staff Manual respectively. Title Pages will be prepared in manuscript.

WAR DIARY
or
INTELLIGENCE SUMMARY

(Erase heading not required.) 93rd Field Ambulance.

Place	Date	Hour	Summary of Events and Information	Remarks and references to Appendices
			In accordance with orders from D.D.M.S. VIII Corps please hold the undermentioned personel in readiness to move to No 4 Casualty Clearing Station BEAUVAL on the night Y/Z. one officer RAMC Two N.C.Os RAMC Thirteen other Ranks RAMC. Please let me have a nominal roll of those selected for this duty Signed A.W. Bewley Col ADMS 31st Division Names were submitted in accordance with the above. Received the following RAMC Operation Order No 1 31st Division Copy No 1. by ADMS 31st Division	

2449 Wt. W14957/M90 750,000 1/16 J.B.C. & A. Forms/C.2118/12.

Instructions regarding War Diaries and Intelligence Summaries are contained in F. S. Regs., Part II. and the Staff Manual respectively. Title Pages will be prepared in manuscript.

WAR DIARY
or
INTELLIGENCE SUMMARY

(Erase heading not required.) 93rd Field Ambulance

Army Form C. 2118.

Place	Date	Hour	Summary of Events and Information	Remarks and references to Appendices
			Reference map - Sheet 57D 1:40000.	
			I. Personel of Field Ambulances will be distributed as follows when active operations commence.	
			Tent Subdivision - 93rd Field Ambulance	
			"A" Tent Subdivision will remain at SARTON. B and C will pack up equipment and be prepared to move at short notice.	
			94th Field Ambulance. One at main dressing station BUS, one at advanced dressing station Colincamps and one at advanced dressing station EUSTON.	
			95 Field Ambulance Two at main dressing station Bus or in Camp Warnimont Wood.	
			Bearer Subdivision.	
			93rd Field Ambulance to be in reserve at Colincamps or	

2449 Wt. W14957/M90 750,000 1/16 J.B.C. & A. Forms/C.2118/12.

Army Form C. 2118.

Instructions regarding War Diaries and Intelligence Summaries are contained in F. S. Regs., Part II. and the Staff Manual respectively. Title Pages will be prepared in manuscript.

WAR DIARY
or
INTELLIGENCE SUMMARY
(Erase heading not required.) 93rd Field Ambulance

Place	Date	Hour	Summary of Events and Information	Remarks and references to Appendices
			night Y Z. 94th Field Ambulance will move wounded from left sector of attack (which will be carried out by 94th Infantry Brigade) to the Advanced Dressing Station at EUSTON. 95th Field Ambulance will remove wounded from the right sector of the attack - in accordance with plan already issued. This attack will be carried out by 93rd Infantry Brigade. Each bearer subdivision will be in charge of a senior NCO and the three bearer subdivisions of each Ambulance will be under the direction of 2 officers. If possible the full number of bearers (ie 6 per squad) should not be sent - as many men as possible being kept in reserve. Details of positions and reliefs are to be arranged by the Commanding Officers Concerned. Officers Commanding Field Ambulances will arrange early with	

2449 Wt. W14957/M90 750,000 1/16 J.B.C. & A. Forms/C.2118/12.

Army Form C. 2118.

Instructions regarding War Diaries and Intelligence Summaries are contained in F. S. Regs., Part II. and the Staff Manual respectively. Title Pages will be prepared in manuscript.

WAR DIARY
or
INTELLIGENCE SUMMARY

(Erase heading not required.) 93rd Field Ambulance

Place	Date	Hour	Summary of Events and Information	Remarks and references to Appendices
			the town Major Colincamps for the accommodation of the bearer subdivision assigned to ~~that~~ station. (Billet ho 50 next to the advanced dressing station has been set aside for this purpose.)	
			Rations will be dumped at the main dressing station at BUS daily and taken up at night to the advanced dressing stations and bearers.	
			A Reserve of rations for ~~patients~~ should be kept in Colincamps and EUSTON by 94th Field Ambulance.	
			Officer Commanding 93rd Field Ambulance will arrange with Officer commanding 94th Field Ambulance to ration the reserve bearers of his unit at Colincamps.	
			Reserve stretchers will be kept at EUSTON and Colincamps as under	
			94th F. Ambulance 30 EUSTON and 10 at COLINCAMPS.	
			95th F. Ambulance 20 EUSTON and 10 at COLINCAMPS.	

2449 Wt. W14957/M90 750,000 1/16 J.B.C. & A. Forms/C.2118/12.

Army Form C. 2118.

WAR DIARY
or
INTELLIGENCE SUMMARY
(Erase heading not required.) 93rd Field Ambulance

Instructions regarding War Diaries and Intelligence Summaries are contained in F. S. Regs., Part II. and the Staff Manual respectively. Title Pages will be prepared in manuscript.

Place	Date	Hour	Summary of Events and Information	Remarks and references to Appendices
			Trench stretchers will be kept at EUSTON and employed in carrying wounded from the front line. Transport. The Motor Transport from Advanced dressing Station will be under the direction of the Officer Commanding 94th Field Ambulance who will responsible for its distribution. Four Sideley Deasy cars and one Ford will be supplied by 94th and 95th Field Ambulances. One orderly man to each car Lightly wounded will be evacuated to Acheux by (1) Reserve Motor Ambulances (2) Horse Ambulances (3) Fitted G. S wagons of 94 & 95th Field Ambulances. Signed Alle Beesley Col ADMS 31st Division	

2449 Wt. W14957/M90 750,000 1/16 J.B.C. & A. Forms/C.2118/12.

Instructions regarding War Diaries and Intelligence Summaries are contained in F. S. Regs., Part II. and the Staff Manual respectively. Title Pages will be prepared in manuscript.

WAR DIARY
or
INTELLIGENCE SUMMARY

Army Form C. 2118.

(Erase heading not required.) 93rd Field Ambulance

Place	Date	Hour	Summary of Events and Information	Remarks and references to Appendices
SARTON	23/6/16.		Capt A.W. Forbes. rejoined this unit after performing his duties as Sanitary Officer.	
			Received the following Operation Orders. SECRET. Copy Nos	
			Operation Order Nos VIII Corps	
			By Col J.J. Pessard D.D.M.S VIII Corps	
			D.D.M.S No M21/44. 22 June 1916 VIII Corps. June 22nd 1916.	
			Reference Map 57 D 1/40,000	
			I Evacuation	
			Nos 0 Motor Ambulance Convoy will evacuate cases to 4 C.C.S BEAUVAL & 35 C.C.S DOULLENS only.	
			All other lying down cases will be evacuated by light Railway to 29 C.C.S GEZAINCOURT. Sitting up cases will be evacuated	

2449 Wt. W14957/M90 750,000 1/16 J.B.C. & A. Forms/C.2118/12.

Instructions regarding War Diaries and Intelligence Summaries are contained in F. S. Regs., Part II. and the Staff Manual respectively. Title Pages will be prepared in manuscript.

WAR DIARY
or
INTELLIGENCE SUMMARY
(Erase heading not required.)

Army Form C. 2118.

Place	Date	Hour	Summary of Events and Information	Remarks and references to Appendices
			by light Railway or Motor Ambulance Convoy to 29 C.C.S only. VIII Corps Medical operation order No 7. dated 17/6/16 paragraph 1. Evacuation should be amended accordingly II Entraining Medical Officer Acheux Light Railway Capt J. C. G. Thompson RAMC (TF) 89th Field Ambulance is appointed for this duty. He will keep in close touch with the R.T.O. Acheux He will coordinate the entraining of sitting up cases of X Corps at Clairfaye and from VIII Corps collecting station at Acheux. to meet the circumstances of the moment. The whole of the lying down [illegible] accomodation on the train will be at the disposal of VIII Corps Should it be necessary to stop the train at LOUVENCOURT he will inform the R.T.O. Acheux who will make the	

2449 Wt. W14957/M90 750,000 1/16 J.B.C. & A. Forms/C.2118/12.

Instructions regarding War Diaries and Intelligence Summaries are contained in F. S. Regs., Part II. and the Staff Manual respectively. Title Pages will be prepared in manuscript.

WAR DIARY
or
INTELLIGENCE SUMMARY

(Erase heading not required.)

Army Form C. 2118.

Place	Date	Hour	Summary of Events and Information	Remarks and references to Appendices
			necessary arrangements.	
			The entraining Medical Officer will take steps to see that the blankets and stretchers which accompany wounded on the train are exchanged for the same number at the time of loading.	
			3. Special Cases.	
			The Officer Commanding 1/2 South Midland Field Ambulance will notify ADMS X Division direct should the accommodation become full.	
			4. Additional Personnel for C C S.	
			The Parties detailed in Stations Operation Order No. 1 of 17/6/16 para 3 are to proceed to C C S.s and act as stated therein.	

Army Form C. 2118.

WAR DIARY
or
INTELLIGENCE SUMMARY
(Erase heading not required.)

Instructions regarding War Diaries and Intelligence Summaries are contained in F. S. Regs., Part II. and the Staff Manual respectively. Title Pages will be prepared in manuscript.

Place	Date	Hour	Summary of Events and Information	Remarks and references to Appendices
			5 Sick.	
			Each AD MS. will arrange to keep open the divisional Rest Station for the reception of sick from his division only.	
			All cases now in Field Ambulances will be evacuated to C.C.S by the end of the week except.	
			(a) Men who will be fit for duty in 48 hours.	
			(b) Those who can be employed on light duty in the division as temporarily unfit	
			All sick to be admitted direct to divisional Rest Stations, they are not to be shown as transferred from other Field Ambulances.	
			Main dressing Station admission and discharge books should be kept entirely for wounded and the divisional	

2449 Wt. W14957/M90 750,000 1/16 J.B.C. & A. Forms/C.2118/12.

Instructions regarding War Diaries and Intelligence Summaries are contained in F. S. Regs., Part II. and the Staff Manual respectively. Title Pages will be prepared in manuscript.

Army Form C. 2118.

WAR DIARY
or
INTELLIGENCE SUMMARY

(Erase heading not required.) 93rd Field Ambulance

Place	Date	Hour	Summary of Events and Information	Remarks and references to Appendices
			Rest Station for sick.	
			Sick are to be sent to Divisional Rest Station in Divisional Ambulance wagons.	
			6 Arms	
			Attention is directed to D.D.M.S. VIII Corps No 21/29 dtd 12/6/16 regarding the handing over of all arms from advanced dressing stations to the nearest battle post.	
			7 Acknowledge.	
			Signed S. Boyle Smith Major for D.D.M.S. VIII Corps	
			H.Q. VIII Corps 22 June 1916	

2449 Wt. W14957/M90 750,000 1/16 J.B.C. & A. Forms/C.2118/12.

Army Form C. 2118.

WAR DIARY
or
INTELLIGENCE SUMMARY
(Erase heading not required.)

Instructions regarding War Diaries and Intelligence Summaries are contained in F. S. Regs., Part II. and the Staff Manual respectively. Title Pages will be prepared in manuscript.

Place	Date	Hour	Summary of Events and Information	Remarks and references to Appendices
			In accordance with Instructions 25 men temporarily unfit men from the Rest Camp were sent to 29th C.C.S. to act as stretcher bearers.	
			Received the following message from D.A.A. & Q.M.G. 31st Division	
			Until the day before the bombardment commences the first line transport of units may be used, but when the bombardment starts all first line vehicles will be packed with their authorised ready to move at a moments notice. S.A.A., Grenades tools etc should therefore be ready for instant loading	
			Signed Cecil Wilson Major D.A.A. & Q.M.G. 31st Division	
			D.H.Q. 2nd June 1916	

2449 Wt. W14957/M90 750,000 1/16 J.B.C. & A. Forms/C.2118/12.

Instructions regarding War Diaries and Intelligence Summaries are contained in F. S. Regs., Part II. and the Staff Manual respectively. Title Pages will be prepared in manuscript.

WAR DIARY
or
INTELLIGENCE SUMMARY

(Erase heading not required.) 93rd Field Ambulance

Army Form C. 2118.

Place	Date	Hour	Summary of Events and Information	Remarks and references to Appendices
SARTON.	24/6/16		Received the following orders marked SECRET. Rame Operation Order No 2 31st Division Copy No1. by ADMS 31st Division Reference map 57 Dne 1-20,000 Tent Subdivisions 93rd Field Ambulance. Two reserve subdivisions at SARTON will be packed and ready to move at short notice. 94th Field Ambulance. ~~Three bearer~~ "C" subdivision to move to Advance dressing Station at EUSTON "B" to advance dressing Station at COLINCAMPS. on V Day under orders O.C. 94th Field Ambulance 95th Field Ambulance Two subdivisions to move to Main dressing Station at BUS as soon as possible (the camp is now vacated). Bearer Subdivisions.	

Instructions regarding War Diaries and Intelligence Summaries are contained in F. S. Regs., Part II. and the Staff Manual respectively. Title Pages will be prepared in manuscript.

WAR DIARY
or
INTELLIGENCE SUMMARY

(Erase heading not required.) 93rd Field Ambulance

Army Form C. 2118.

Place	Date	Hour	Summary of Events and Information	Remarks and references to Appendices
			93rd Field Ambulance. 3 bearer subdivisions (less 12 bearers) with 2 bearer officers will move to BUS en route for COLINCAMPS on Y day.	
			94 Field Ambulance working with 94th Infantry Brigade and one company KOYLI.	
			Route 94. Infantry Bgde} Mearnmont Wood. X Road J 20 c 22. – through BUS Wood to road junction J 20 d 52 – X roads J 26 b 90. track junction J 27 b. 6.1. – follow track to J 28 a. 7.6. thence across country to Mill J 30 b 7.6. thence assembly trenches via Central Northern + Wagram Avenues.	
			Head of Column to pass SAILLY AU BOIS – MAILLY ROAD at 10 pm.	
			All units to be in position 1-30 am on Z day.	
			O.C. 94th Field Ambulance will arrange for his bearer subdivisions to be in the positions assigned by 1.30 am on Z day.	

2449 Wt. W14957/M90 750,000 1/16 J.B.C. & A. Forms/C.2118/12.

Instructions regarding War Diaries and Intelligence Summaries are contained in F. S. Regs., Part II. and the Staff Manual respectively. Title Pages will be prepared in manuscript.

WAR DIARY
or
INTELLIGENCE SUMMARY

(Erase heading not required.) 93rd Field Ambulance

Army Form C. 2118.

Place	Date	Hour	Summary of Events and Information	Remarks and references to Appendices
			95 Field Ambulance working with 93rd Infantry Brigade and one company KOYLI. Route of 93rd Infantry Brigade } BUS X Roads J.26.b 9.0 along track to Cemetery J27 d. COURCELLES.– COLINCAMPS (marching N of village) thence to assembly trenches via Railway and SOUTHERN avenues. O.C. 95th Field Ambulance will arrange for his bearer subdivisions to be in position assigned to them by 1.30 am on Z day. Strict orders will be issued that. (a) Perfect silence must be maintained on the road and in the trenches. (b) No smoking or lights will be permitted after leaving billets (c) Ranks must be well closed up on the march Signed Alb. Bewley Col. A.D.M.S. 31st Division	

2449 Wt. W14957/M90 750,000 1/16 J.B.C. & A. Forms/C.2118/12.

Instructions regarding War Diaries and Intelligence Summaries are contained in F. S. Regs., Part II. and the Staff Manual respectively. Title Pages will be prepared in manuscript.

WAR DIARY
or
INTELLIGENCE SUMMARY

(Erase heading not required.) 93rd Field Ambulance.

Army Form C. 2118.

Place	Date	Hour	Summary of Events and Information	Remarks and references to Appendices
SARTON	25/6/16.		In compliance with instructions 70 men Temporary Unfit were sent to the A.A. & Q.M.G. 31st Division from the Rest Camp for light duty.	
			One N.C.O. + 9 men Temporary unfit were sent from the Rest Camp for light duty to 35 C.C.S. DOULLENS.	
			The Rest Camp was now closed, and opened only for the Divisional Sick during active operations.	
			Capt. F. W. Stone returned to duty from leave in England.	
SARTON	26/6/16.		Received the following. Memorandum Marked Secret. 31D/S/143/15. Through A.D.M.S. 31st Division	
			In future operations all officers will be dressed as nearly	

2449 Wt. W14957/M90 750,000 1/16 J.B.C. & A. Forms/C.2118/12.

Instructions regarding War Diaries and Intelligence Summaries are contained in F. S. Regs., Part II. and the Staff Manual respectively. Title Pages will be prepared in manuscript.

WAR DIARY
or
INTELLIGENCE SUMMARY

(Erase heading not required.) 93rd Field Ambulance

Army Form C. 2118.

Place	Date	Hour	Summary of Events and Information	Remarks and references to Appendices
			as possible like their men. Putties will always be worn if necessary over riding pants. As soon as possible badges of rank will be worn on the shoulder strap instead of on the sleeve.	
			Signed J. Amesly Lt Col. A.A. & Q.M.G 31st Division	
			D.H.Q 25/6/16.	
			The following was also received 31D/S/143/22	
			SECRET.	
			All Vermorel sprayers will be left stored in trenches by Brigades who will arrange to send for them if required	

Army Form C. 2118.

Instructions regarding War Diaries and Intelligence Summaries are contained in F. S. Regs., Part II. and the Staff Manual respectively. Title Pages will be prepared in manuscript.

WAR DIARY
or
INTELLIGENCE SUMMARY

(Erase heading not required.) 93rd Field Ambulance.

Place	Date	Hour	Summary of Events and Information	Remarks and references to Appendices
SARTON			There is a reserve supply in charge of the Divisional Gas Officer, intimation should at once be sent to Divisional Headquarters if more are required by Brigades. Box Respirators will be retained in possession at all times and never left behind. Helmets will be worn by all troops in any case where there is any doubt, by way of precaution. This applies especially to unknown tear shells. Troops wearing gas helmets should not run or shout or do anything to cause the use of an unusual amount of air for breathing purposes. Attention of officers is particularly called to this matter D.H.Q. Signed J. Ormesby Lt Col. 25/6/16 AA + QMG. 31st Division	

2449 Wt. W14957/M90 750,000 1/16 J.B.C. & A. Forms/C.2118/12.

Instructions regarding War Diaries and Intelligence Summaries are contained in F. S. Regs., Part II. and the Staff Manual respectively. Title Pages will be prepared in manuscript.

WAR DIARY
or
INTELLIGENCE SUMMARY

Army Form C. 2118.

(Erase heading not required.) 93rd Field Ambulance

Place	Date	Hour	Summary of Events and Information	Remarks and references to Appendices
SARTON.	26/6/16.		The following marked SECRET. was Received.	
			M 3193.	
			O.C. 93rd Field Ambulance	
			In accordance with my No 376 dtd 19-6-16. Please arrange to send Two officers Two N.C.Os and 13 other ranks to No 4 Casualty Clearing Station on the night Y Z. The extra officer cannot now be supplied from another unit	
			Signed A.W. Bewley. Col.	
			26/6/16. A.D.M.S. 31st Division	
			Captain F.W. Stone has been selected as the extra Officer Lieut F.W. Fletcher having been already detailed for this duty. B.C.	

2449 Wt. W14957/M90 750,000 1/16 J.B.C. & A. Forms/C.2118/12.

Instructions regarding War Diaries and Intelligence Summaries are contained in F. S. Regs., Part II. and the Staff Manual respectively. Title Pages will be prepared in manuscript.

WAR DIARY
or
INTELLIGENCE SUMMARY

(*Erase heading not required.*) 93rd Field Ambulance

Army Form C. 2118.

Place	Date	Hour	Summary of Events and Information	Remarks and references to Appendices
SARTON	27/6/16		Nothing important to record. B.C	
SARTON	28/6/16		In compliance with previous instructions at 1 pm. Three bearer subsections under Capt J. N. Humphreys & Lieut Maryon were sent to BUS. to be held in readiness to proceed to the trenches when required At 5 pm. 13 men 2 N.C.O.s and Capt F.W. Stone, & Lieut L.S.B Fletcher proceeded to No 44 C.C.S BEAUVAL. Thirty men temporary unfit were sent for light duty to 95th Field Ambulance. At 7.30 the 3 bearer subsections with two Officers returned from BUS. with the following message marked SECRET. O.C 93rd Field Ambulance Zero hour has been postponed, I am therefore ordering your	

2449 Wt. W14957/M90 750,000 1/16 J.B.C. & A. Forms/C.2118/12.

Army Form C. 2118.

Instructions regarding War Diaries and Intelligence Summaries are contained in F. S. Regs., Part II. and the Staff Manual respectively. Title Pages will be prepared in manuscript.

WAR DIARY
or
INTELLIGENCE SUMMARY
(Erase heading not required.) 93rd Field Ambulance.

Place	Date	Hour	Summary of Events and Information	Remarks and references to Appendices
			bearers to return to SARTON – They should be prepared to start at short notice. The Wagons and horses can remain with 94th Field Ambulance transport	
			Signed G. W. Clare. Major for A.D. M.S. 31st Division	
			D.H.Q 28/6/16	
SARTON	29/6/16		Sent 32 men temporarily unfit B.C. to the Town Major BUS for light duty in compliance with instructions.	
			Received the following message.	
			O.C. 93rd Field Ambulance M/705 dtd 29/6/15.	
			In accordance with order of D. M. S. you will reopen as Divisional Rest Station.	
			The Daily State Army Form W 3185 should be rendered to this Office in accordance with NO M/705 dated 19/4/16, namely, a	

2449 Wt. W14957/M90 750,000 1/16 J.B.C. & A. Forms/C.2118/12.

Army Form C. 2118.

WAR DIARY
or
INTELLIGENCE SUMMARY

(Erase heading not required.) 93rd Field Ambulance

Instructions regarding War Diaries and Intelligence Summaries are contained in F. S. Regs., Part II. and the Staff Manual respectively. Title Pages will be prepared in manuscript.

Place	Date	Hour	Summary of Events and Information	Remarks and references to Appendices
			a Separate form being used for rest patients.	
			A. W. Bewley	
			Col. A.D.M.S. 31st Division	
			D H Q 29/6/16	
			B.C	
SARTON.	30/6/16	3pm	Received the following message marked Urgent & SECRET.	
			M 3007.	
			O.C 93rd Field Ambulance	
			ZERO will be at 7.30 am tomorrow July 1st 1916	
			Your bearers should be moved up forthwith	
			Signed G. W. Ware Major	
			D H Q 30/6/16	

2449 Wt. W14957/M90 750,000 1/16 J.B.C. & A. Forms/C.2118/12.

Instructions regarding War Diaries and Intelligence Summaries are contained in F. S. Regs., Part II. and the Staff Manual respectively. Title Pages will be prepared in manuscript.

WAR DIARY
or
INTELLIGENCE SUMMARY

(Erase heading not required.) 93rd Field Ambulance

Army Form C. 2118.

Place	Date	Hour	Summary of Events and Information	Remarks and references to Appendices
			In Compliance with this order Capt J. J. Humphrey & Lieut Meryon with 110 Rank + file were ordered to proceed to BUS-LES-ARTOIS immediately B.C.	

2449 Wt. W14957/M90 750,000 1/16 J.B.C. & A. Forms/C.2118/12.

94

Confidential 31st Division Vol VIII

War Diary of 93rd Field Amb:

July 1916

S

1st July to 31st July. 1916.

Instructions regarding War Diaries and Intelligence Summaries are contained in F. S. Regs., Part II. and the Staff Manual respectively. Title Pages will be prepared in manuscript.

VOL VII

WAR DIARY
or
INTELLIGENCE SUMMARY
(Erase heading not required.) 93rd Field Ambulance

Army Form C. 2118.

Place	Date	Hour	Summary of Events and Information	Remarks and references to Appendices
SARTON	1/7/16	7.30 A.M.	Heavy firing was heard throughout the night and early this morning. Reports to hand confirm the news that the 31st Division have captured the village of SERRE. B.C	
SARTON	2/7/16		Received the following operation order DDMS SECRET. No M21/44 Copy 3 RAMC Operation Order No 6 By Col. Gerrard DDMS VIII Corps Reference Map Sheet 62D 1/40000 July 1st 1916 I Evacuation of Indians. An Indian Field Ambulance has been formed at VECQUEMONT to which	

Instructions regarding War Diaries and Intelligence Summaries are contained in F. S. Regs., Part II. and the Staff Manual respectively. Title Pages will be prepared in manuscript.

WAR DIARY
or
~~INTELLIGENCE SUMMARY~~

(Erase heading not required.) 93rd Field Ambulance

Army Form C. 2118.

Place	Date	Hour	Summary of Events and Information	Remarks and references to Appendices
			Indians admitted to Corps medical units should be evacuated. DMS. 4th Army No 19/59 dtd 29/6/16 Signed S. Boylan Smith Major DADMS VIII Corps Forwarded O.C. 93rd Field Ambulance Forwarded. please acknowledge receipt Alb Bewley Col ADMS 31st Division DHQ 1/7/16	

2449 Wt. W14957/M90 750,000 1/16 J.B.C. & A. Forms/C.2118/12.

Instructions regarding War Diaries and Intelligence Summaries are contained in F. S. Regs., Part II. and the Staff Manual respectively. Title Pages will be prepared in manuscript.

WAR DIARY

~~or~~

~~INTELLIGENCE SUMMARY~~

(Erase heading not required.) 93rd Field Ambulance.

Army Form C. 2118.

Place	Date	Hour	Summary of Events and Information	Remarks and references to Appendices
		7pm	Received the following Wire. G.P. 23. 2/7/16. Message from Corps Commander Begins: Well done my Comrades of the 31st Division AAA Your discipline and determination were magnificent and it was bad luck alone ~~that~~ has temporarily robbed you of Success Signed Aylmer Hunter Weston. From 31st Division Signed G. Pierson. B.C.	
~~July 3rd~~ SARTON	3/7/16.		Received information ~~that~~ that 94th Bgde were compelled to evacuate the village of SERRE taken the previous day. B.C.	

Army Form C. 2118.

Instructions regarding War Diaries and Intelligence Summaries are contained in F. S. Regs., Part II. and the Staff Manual respectively. Title Pages will be prepared in manuscript.

WAR DIARY
or
~~INTELLIGENCE SUMMARY~~

(Erase heading not required.) 93rd Field Ambulance

Place	Date	Hour	Summary of Events and Information	Remarks and references to Appendices
SARTON	4/7/16		Capt J. L. Humphreys & Lieut Meryon with 3 bearer subdivisions returned after duty in the firing line reporting five Casualties. Received the following message M 3226. O.C. 93rd Field Ambulance Please note that your unit less one section will be required to march to the Reserve Area with the 93rd Infantry Brigade on 6th July. The Regulation equipment of the sections will be taken and the Surplus left in charge of the Personnel remaining behind. Particulars will be notified later Sd A.W. Bewley. Col. D.H.Q. 4/7/16 A.D.M.S. 31st Division	

2449 Wt. W14957/M90 750,000 1/16 J.B.C. & A. Forms/C.2118/12.

Instructions regarding War Diaries and Intelligence Summaries are contained in F. S. Regs., Part II. and the Staff Manual respectively. Title Pages will be prepared in manuscript.

WAR DIARY
or
INTELLIGENCE SUMMARY

Army Form C. 2118.

(Erase heading not required.) 93rd Field Ambulance.

Place	Date	Hour	Summary of Events and Information	Remarks and references to Appendices
SARTON	5/7/16	9 AM	Received the following wire E. Co. 73 dtd 4/7/16. Lt and QM. A. Allen RAMC reported arrival today and left for duty with you. From ADMS Havre. Received the following SECRET. No 4. Ref map 57 D 1/40000 OC 93rd Field Ambulance Your Field Ambulance - less one section. will move on the morning of the 6th as follows.	

Instructions regarding War Diaries and Intelligence Summaries are contained in F. S. Regs., Part II. and the Staff Manual respectively. Title Pages will be prepared in manuscript.

Army Form C. 2118.

WAR DIARY
or
INTELLIGENCE SUMMARY

(Erase heading not required.) 93rd Field Ambulance.

Place	Date	Hour	Summary of Events and Information	Remarks and references to Appendices
			(A) Troops will march as one Column under Orders of the G.O.C. 93rd Infantry Brigade. (B). Columns to be clear of the Western entrance LOUVENCOURT by 9 a.m. Route SARTON. TERRAMESNIL. to destination billets at BEAUVAL. The section of your Field Ambulance remaining at SARTON will march to the new Area under Arrangements made by the A D M S. of the Division D.H.Q 5/7/16 Sd G. W. Ware Major. P.T.O.	

2449 Wt. W14957/M90 750,000 1/16 J.B.C. & A. Forms/C.2118/12.

Instructions regarding War Diaries and Intelligence Summaries are contained in F. S. Regs., Part II. and the Staff Manual respectively. Title Pages will be prepared in manuscript.

WAR DIARY
or
INTELLIGENCE SUMMARY

(*Erase heading not required.*) 93rd Field Ambulance.

Army Form C. 2118.

Place	Date	Hour	Summary of Events and Information	Remarks and references to Appendices
			Your Horsed Ambulances should arrange to collect sick on the line of march.	
			GW	
		2pm	Received the following	
			O.C.	
			93rd Field Ambulance	
			Main body should join the Column at SARTON. Two Motor Ambulances should be sufficient to join the Column at LOUVENCOURT. with one M.O.	
			Headquarters 93rd Infantry Brigade are at LOUVENCOURT today. You should consult G.O.C. re billets etc in the new area.	
			DHQ 5/7/16. S G. W. Clare Major	
			BC	

2449 Wt. W14957/M90 750,000 1/16 J.B.C. & A. Forms/C.2118/12.

Army Form C. 2118.

Instructions regarding War Diaries and Intelligence Summaries are contained in F. S. Regs., Part II. and the Staff Manual respectively. Title Pages will be prepared in manuscript.

WAR DIARY
or
INTELLIGENCE ~~SUMMARY~~

(Erase heading not required.) 93rd Field Ambulance

Place	Date	Hour	Summary of Events and Information	Remarks and references to Appendices
SARTON	6/7/16		Received the following message O.C. 93rd Field Ambulance Main body should join the Column at SARTON Two motor Ambulances should be sufficient to join the Column at LOUVENCOURT with one M.O. Headquarters 93 Infantry Brigade are at LOUVENCOURT today, You should consult G.O.C. re Billets in new area. Sd G. W. Ware Major D.H.Q 5/7/16 At 10 A.M. The Ambulance less one section joined the Brigade. There was a halt at TERRASMENIL for half	

2449 Wt. W14957/M90 750,000 1/16 J.B.C. & A. Forms/C.2118/12.

Army Form C. 2118.

Instructions regarding War Diaries and Intelligence Summaries are contained in F. S. Regs., Part II. and the Staff Manual respectively. Title Pages will be prepared in manuscript.

WAR DIARY
or
INTELLIGENCE SUMMARY

(Erase heading not required.) 93rd Field Ambulance

Place	Date	Hour	Summary of Events and Information	Remarks and references to Appendices
			an hour. Troops were marching well and few men fell out The march was continued to BEAUVAL which was reached at 12.30 pm. The unit billeted in the RUE DE CANDAS.	
BEAUVAL	7/7/16		The march was resumed at 7 am this morning. The Brigade marched through CANDAS to FIENVILLERS. The 93rd F.A. billeted in CANDAS	
CANDAS	7/7/16	4 pm	Received instructions from the A.D. M.S. 31st Division to return to SARTON to assist A Section to close the Dressing Station. I returned to SARTON with all the Motor Ambulances and evacuated 190 cases to 29 C.C.S. GEZAINCOURT A Dump of all Surplus Stores was formed and left in charge of 2 men The unit then proceeded to CANDAS and reached there at 12 midnight B.C.	

Army Form C. 2118.

WAR DIARY
or
INTELLIGENCE SUMMARY

(Erase heading not required.) 93rd Field Ambulance

Instructions regarding War Diaries and Intelligence Summaries are contained in F. S. Regs., Part II. and the Staff Manual respectively. Title Pages will be prepared in manuscript.

Place	Date	Hour	Summary of Events and Information	Remarks and references to Appendices
CANDAS	8/7/16	6AM	Received the following message marked urgent. 93rd Infantry Brigade Order No 23 — Copy No 8 — 8-7-16 Reference MAP LENS. SHEET 11. 1:100000 I. The Brigade will move to 1st Army area by Rail. Entrainment will commence 8th July and be carried out in accordance with the attached table. 2. All units will arrive at entraining Station 3 hours before the time laid down for the departure of the train. Officers Commanding units will be responsible that their units arrive at the entraining Station at the required time. 3. The Sections of the 93rd Brigade Machine Gun Coy and Light Trench Mortar Battery will march with the unit with which they travel except the Machine Gun Section travelling in No 15 train which will march with the 15th Yorks Regt	

Army Form C. 2118.

WAR DIARY
or
~~INTELLIGENCE SUMMARY~~

(*Erase heading not required.*)

92nd Field Ambulance

Instructions regarding War Diaries and Intelligence Summaries are contained in F. S. Regs., Part II. and the Staff Manual respectively. Title Pages will be prepared in manuscript.

Place	Date	Hour	Summary of Events and Information	Remarks and references to Appendices
			4. Officers Commanding units will ensure the route to the entraining Station is thoroughly reconnoitred	
			5. Vehicles will be placed in trucks fully loaded	
			6. Officers Commanding Units will detail parties before arrival at the Station for loading baggage vehicles and animals	
			7. 1 Officer and 1 N.C.O per unit will take over the train and allot accomodation. The officer will be in possession of all details of personel & transport showing 4 wheeled vehicles and 2 wheeled. Carriages and trucks will be marked in chalk showing number of men and company allotted.	

Instructions regarding War Diaries and Intelligence Summaries are contained in F. S. Regs., Part II. and the Staff Manual respectively. Title Pages will be prepared in manuscript.

WAR DIARY

or

~~INTELLIGENCE SUMMARY~~

(Erase heading not required.) 93rd Field Ambulance

Army Form C. 2118.

Place	Date	Hour	Summary of Events and Information	Remarks and references to Appendices
			8. Billeting parties as below will report to Brigade H.Q at Contwille Station at 2pm July 8th and proceed by first train.	
			Officers . N.C.O.s	
			15 West York Regt. 1 . 3	
			16 do 1 . 3	
			18 do 1 - 3	
			18 Durham L.I. 1 - 3	
			Bde M G Coy. 1 - 1	
			211 Coy RE 1 - 1	
			93rd Field Ambulance 1 - 1	
			Machine Gun Coy will arrange billets for light trench Mortar Batt.	
			9. Brigade H.Q will close at FIENVILLERS July 8th 9.30AM	

2449 Wt. W14957/M90 750,000 1/16 J.B.C. & A. Forms/C.2118/12.

Instructions regarding War Diaries and Intelligence Summaries are contained in F. S. Regs., Part II. and the Staff Manual respectively. Title Pages will be prepared in manuscript.

WAR DIARY
or
INTELLIGENCE SUMMARY
(Erase heading not required.) 93rd Field Ambulance

Army Form C. 2118.

Place	Date	Hour	Summary of Events and Information	Remarks and references to Appendices
			Acknowledge.	
			Signed A H Howard Major	
			Brigade Major 93rd Infantry Bde	
			Capt A. D. Forbes was appointed billeting officer.	
			Lieut & QrMr A Allen was appointed Officer i/c of train	
CANDAS	9/7/16		The 93rd Field Ambulance entrained at Conteville B.C. at 10.52 am after a four hours journey it detrained at BURGETTE and marched to Billets at BUSNES.	
			The Motor Ambulances proceeded by road under Capt Yorke route DOULLENS.- ST POL - BETHUNE. - BURGETTE. - BUSNES	
BUSNES	10/7/16		Orders were received that the Ambulance would not open out to receive patients. The men were accordingly rested.	

2449 Wt. W14957/M90 750,000 1/16 J.B.C. & A. Forms/C.2118/12.

Instructions regarding War Diaries and Intelligence Summaries are contained in F. S. Regs., Part II. and the Staff Manual respectively. Title Pages will be prepared in manuscript.

WAR DIARY
or
~~INTELLIGENCE SUMMARY~~

(Erase heading not required.) 93rd Field Ambulance

Army Form C. 2118.

Place	Date	Hour	Summary of Events and Information	Remarks and references to Appendices
BUSNES.	11/7/16		Lieut J. B. Alexander was placed as a temporary measure in Medical Charge 211 Coy RE. Capt J. G. Humphreys was appointed Sanitary Officer BUSNES and placed in charge of baths.	
BUSNES	12/7/16		Men were rested only minor fatigues being carried out. The D. D. M. S. XI Corps visited the unit today. BC	
BUSNES	13/7/16		The Corps Commander XI Corps summoned all officers of the unit to meet him at 93rd Infantry Brigade Headquarters at 9.45 this morning. BC	
BUSNES	14/7/16		Received the following orders. OC 93rd Field Ambulance Ref map Sheet 36A 1/40000	M 3266 [illegible]

2449 Wt. W14957/M90 750,000 1/16 J.B.C. & A. Forms/C.2118/12.

Army Form C. 2118.

Instructions regarding War Diaries and Intelligence Summaries are contained in F. S. Regs., Part II. and the Staff Manual respectively. Title Pages will be prepared in manuscript.

WAR DIARY
or
INTELLIGENCE SUMMARY

(Erase heading not required.) 93rd Field Ambulance

Place	Date	Hour	Summary of Events and Information	Remarks and references to Appendices
			O.C. 93rd Field Ambulance will send 2 officers, 2 N.C.Os and 8 men by motor Ambulance from BUSNES to ZELOBES (R27.C05) on evening of 14th inst to take over from a field Ambulance of the 61st Division.	
			The A.D.S at GREEN BARN will also be taken over.	
			The remainder of the 93rd Field Ambulance will proceed by road to ZELOBES on the 15th inst and will establish itself in the dressing station there, orders for march will be issued later.	
			2 Officers will be detailed for temporary duty from the 94th Field Ambulance, to join at ZELOBES on evening of the 15th inst.	
			The Officer in charge of the Divisional Supply Column	

2449 Wt. W14957/M90 750,000 1/16 J.B.C. & A. Forms/C.2118/12.

Instructions regarding War Diaries and Intelligence Summaries are contained in F. S. Regs., Part II. and the Staff Manual respectively. Title Pages will be prepared in manuscript.

WAR DIARY
or
INTELLIGENCE SUMMARY

(Erase heading not required.) 93rd Field Ambulance

Army Form C. 2118.

Place	Date	Hour	Summary of Events and Information	Remarks and references to Appendices
			should be withdrawn as soon as possible.	
			HQ 14/7/16 Sd A.W. Bewley Col ADMS 31st Division	
			Capt AD Forbes and Capt J.N. Humphreys were accordingly immediately dispatched with 2 NCOs + 8 men to take over the Dressing Station at ZELOBES and the Advanced dressing station at GREENBARN.	
			Lieut CE MERYON was recalled from Divisional Supply Column. BL	
BUSNES	15/7/16.		In compliance with orders the Ambulance marched off from BUSNES to ZELOBES at 1pm. Route. ROBECQ - RIEZ VINAGE - CORNER MALO - ZELOBES	

Instructions regarding War Diaries and Intelligence Summaries are contained in F. S. Regs., Part II. and the Staff Manual respectively. Title Pages will be prepared in manuscript.

WAR DIARY
or
INTELLIGENCE SUMMARY

(Erase heading not required.) 93rd Field Ambulance

Army Form C. 2118.

Place	Date	Hour	Summary of Events and Information	Remarks and references to Appendices
			Upon arrival A section under ~~Capt~~ Capt Yorke immediately took over the dressing Station at ZELOBES whilst Capt A.D. Forbes and Capt J.V. Humphreys proceeded to GREENBARN and took over the Advanced dressing Station from 2/3 South Midland Field Ambulance. B.C	
ZELOBES	16/6/16		Men rested after the march here, only minor fatigues being carried out. B.C	
ZELOBES	17/6/16		The whole area occupied by the Field Ambulance is in an insanitary condition and will need a great deal of attention.	
			The buildings will accommodate about 100 wounded.	
			The Advanced Dressing Station is about 4 miles from	

2449 Wt. W14957/M90 750,000 1/16 J.B.C. & A. Forms/C.2118/12.

Instructions regarding War Diaries and Intelligence Summaries are contained in F. S. Regs., Part II. and the Staff Manual respectively. Title Pages will be prepared in manuscript.

WAR DIARY
or
INTELLIGENCE SUMMARY
(Erase heading not required.) 93rd Field Ambulance

Army Form C. 2118.

Place	Date	Hour	Summary of Events and Information	Remarks and references to Appendices
			the main dressing Station and will accommodate about 30 cases. B.C	
ZELOBES	18/7/16		The unit today is distributed as follows.	
			B Section on duty at A.D.S. Green Barn under Capt A.W. FORBES. assisted by Lieut C.E. Merryon and Lieut A.W. [illegible]	
			"A" Section on duty at Headquarters dressing Station B.C	
ZELOBES	19/7/16		Lieut J. B Alexander and Lieut F J C. Blackmore were detailed to day for temporary duty with 61st Division B.C	
ZELOBES	20/7/16		Capt F.W. Stone and F S B Fletcher returned to Duty from No 4 C.C.S at BEAUVAL.	

2449 Wt. W14957/M90 750,000 1/16 J.B.C. & A. Forms/C.2118/12.

Instructions regarding War Diaries and Intelligence Summaries are contained in F. S. Regs., Part II. and the Staff Manual respectively. Title Pages will be prepared in manuscript.

WAR DIARY
or
INTELLIGENCE SUMMARY

(*Erase heading not required.*) 93rd Field Ambulance

Army Form C. 2118.

Place	Date	Hour	Summary of Events and Information	Remarks and references to Appendices
ZELOBES	20/7/16.		The 2 N.C.Os and 13 men sent with ~~them~~ are still detained B.C.	
ZELOBES	21/7/16		Capt R. S. Cumming rejoined this unit after relinquishing the appointment of Town Major SARTON. 1 N.C.O and 3 men also rejoined from this station B.C Lieut Frew + Blackmore were detailed to rejoin their unit the 94th Field Ambulance today.	
ZELOBES	22/7/16		With a view changing over duties B.C. A Section today handed over the Main Dressing Station to C. Section. B section has been warned to return to headquarters on the 24th inst and A section to take over from B. B.C	

2449 Wt. W14957/M90 750,000 1/16 J.B.C. & A. Forms/C.2118/12.

Army Form C. 2118.

Instructions regarding War Diaries and Intelligence Summaries are contained in F. S. Regs., Part II. and the Staff Manual respectively. Title Pages will be prepared in manuscript.

WAR DIARY
or
~~INTELLIGENCE~~ SUMMARY

(Erase heading not required.) 93rd Field Ambulance

Place	Date	Hour	Summary of Events and Information	Remarks and references to Appendices
ZELOBES	23/7/16.		Nothing important to record B.C.	
ZELOBES	24/7/16.		Nothing important to record B.C	
ZELOBES	25/7/16.		A Section under Capt H.E. P. Yorke and Capt J. N. Humphreys proceeded to GREEN BARN. and relieved B Section under Capt A.B. Forbes. Bathing Rooms at PONT DU HEM handed over to day to 61st Division B.C	
ZELOBES	26/7/16.		Capt F.W. Stone was evacuated today to No 2 CCS B.C.	

2449 Wt. W14957/M90 750,000 1/16 J.B.C. & A. Forms/C.2118/12.

Instructions regarding War Diaries and Intelligence Summaries are contained in F. S. Regs., Part II. and the Staff Manual respectively. Title Pages will be prepared in manuscript.

WAR DIARY
or
INTELLIGENCE SUMMARY
(Erase heading not required.) 93rd Field Ambulance

Army Form C. 2118.

Place	Date	Hour	Summary of Events and Information	Remarks and references to Appendices
ZELOBES	26/7/16		The Divisional Commander made an inspection of the Ambulance today and expressed himself satisfied B.C	
ZELOBES	28/7/16		Baths at Croix BARBE were taken over today from 95th Field Ambulance 2 Sergts and 12 men returned from No 4 C.C.S. BEAUVAL B.C	
ZELOBES	29/7/16		Nothing important to record B.C	
ZELOBES	30/7/16		Nothing important to record B.C.	

2449 Wt. W14957/M90 750,000 1/16 J.B.C. & A. Forms/C.2118/12.

Army Form C. 2118.

Instructions regarding War Diaries and Intelligence Summaries are contained in F. S. Regs., Part II. and the Staff Manual respectively. Title Pages will be prepared in manuscript.

WAR DIARY
or
INTELLIGENCE SUMMARY
(Erase heading not required.) 93rd Field Ambulance

Place	Date	Hour	Summary of Events and Information	Remarks and references to Appendices
ZELOBES	31/7/16		B section under Captain R.S. CUMMING assisted by Lieut. T.B. Alexander and Lieut F.S.B. Fletcher proceeded to GREEN BARN ~~tonight~~ to relieve A Section.	
			A. section rejoins Headquarters	
			B. Section takes over charge of Main Dressing Station	
			B.C.	
			B Connell O.C. 93rd Field Ambulance	

2449 Wt. W14957/M90 750,000 1/16 J.B.C. & A. Forms/C.2118/12.

Confidential   31st Div.   Vol VIII

August 1916

War Diary

of

93rd Fd Ambulance

Aug 1916.

Army Form C. 2118.

Instructions regarding War Diaries and Intelligence Summaries are contained in F. S. Regs., Part II. and the Staff Manual respectively. Title Pages will be prepared in manuscript.

WAR DIARY
or
~~INTELLIGENCE SUMMARY~~

(Erase heading not required.) 93rd Field Ambulance.

Place	Date	Hour	Summary of Events and Information	Remarks and references to Appendices
ZELOBES	1/8/16		The unit is mostly employed on sanitating the area of its main dressing station. The whole appears to be in a very much neglected condition and will require a great amount of steady work before it can be put into a really satisfactory condition. The drains and ditches around the dressing station and billets are in a particularly dirty condition. BC	
ZELOBES	2/8/16		The transport wagons were thoroughly overhauled today, wagons are all being repainted and repaired where necessary. The horses of the unit are in particularly good condition at present. A permanent water supply has been obtained by sinking a well in the horse lines. This was very much needed with	

2449 Wt. W14957/M90 750,000 1/16 J.B.C. & A. Forms/C.2118/12.

Army Form C. 2118.

WAR DIARY
or
~~INTELLIGENCE~~ SUMMARY
(Erase heading not required.) 93rd Field Ambulance

Instructions regarding War Diaries and Intelligence Summaries are contained in F. S. Regs., Part II. and the Staff Manual respectively. Title Pages will be prepared in manuscript.

Place	Date	Hour	Summary of Events and Information	Remarks and references to Appendices
			only other available supply was from the dikes and ditches around the transport lines. This supply was extremely foul. B.C.	
ZELOBES	2/8/16.	3pm	Received ~~instructions~~ to detail an officer from my unit to report for temporary duty with 11th East Yorkshire Regt in relief of Lieut Irvine RAMC. Capt J. L. Humphreys was detailed for this duty. ~~[illegible]~~ B C	
ZELOBES	3/8/16		Nothing important to record. B.C.	
ZELOBES	4/8/16		The duties allotted to this unit were as follows "A" Section on fatigue	

2449 Wt. W14957/M90 750,000 1/16 J.B.C. & A. Forms/C.2118/12.

Instructions regarding War Diaries and Intelligence Summaries are contained in F. S. Regs., Part II. and the Staff Manual respectively. Title Pages will be prepared in manuscript.

WAR DIARY
or
~~INTELLIGENCE~~ SUMMARY

(Erase heading not required.) 93rd Field Ambulance

Place	Date	Hour	Summary of Events and Information	Remarks and references to Appendices
			B. section on duty at Main Dressing Station	
			C. section on duty at Advanced Dressing Station at Green Barn.	
			This appears to be an equal distribution of labour	
			The above, change duties weekly so this arrangement appears to work satisfactorily to all parties	
			B.C.	
ZELOBES	5/8/16.		The D.D.M.S. XI Corps inspected this unit today	
			B.C.	
ZELOBES	6/8/16.		Fatigues are still busy sanitating the area occupied by this unit.	
			They have also taken in hand the general repairs to their billets	
			B.C.	

Instructions regarding War Diaries and Intelligence Summaries are contained in F. S. Regs., Part II. and the Staff Manual respectively. Title Pages will be prepared in manuscript.

WAR DIARY
or
INTELLIGENCE SUMMARY

(Erase heading not required.) 93rd Field Ambulance

Army Form C. 2118.

Place	Date	Hour	Summary of Events and Information	Remarks and references to Appendices
ZELOBES	7/8/16		Sections change over duties today A. Section takes over main dressing Station at ZELOBES B Section proceeds to Advanced Dressing Station at Green Barn. C. Section returns to Headquarters for general fatigues B.C.	
ZELOBES	8/8/16		Nothing important to record B.C.	
ZELOBES	9/8/16		In Compliance with instructions Lieut J. B. Alexander took over medical charge of the 12th KOYLI during the temporary absence of Capt E. Forbes RAMC on leave to England. B.C.	

2449 Wt. W14957/M90 750,000 1/16 J.B.C. & A. Forms/C.2118/12.

Army Form C. 2118.

Instructions regarding War Diaries and Intelligence Summaries are contained in F. S. Regs., Part II. and the Staff Manual respectively. Title Pages will be prepared in manuscript.

WAR DIARY
or
~~INTELLIGENCE~~ SUMMARY
(Erase heading not required.) 93rd Field Ambulance

Place	Date	Hour	Summary of Events and Information	Remarks and references to Appendices
ZELOBES	10/8/16		Nothing important to record. B.C	
ZELOBES	11/8/16.		Various improvements have been taken in hand at the advanced Dressing Station, several dugouts for the reception of wounded have been strengthened and rendered more or less shell proof. The walls have been sandbagged up and the whole building is in a much safer condition than it was a week or two ago. B.C	
ZELOBES	12/8/16		Nothing important to record. B.C	
ZELOBES	13/8/16		Capt J. L. Humphreys returned to this unit today after a period of temporary duty with the 11th East Yorkshire Regt. Fatigue parties of this unit are all busy improving horse lines, roads around this area, sanitation and the general improvement	

2449 Wt. W14957/M90 750,000 1/16 J.B.C. & A. Forms/C.2118/12.

Instructions regarding War Diaries and Intelligence Summaries are contained in F. S. Regs., Part II. and the Staff Manual respectively. Title Pages will be prepared in manuscript.

WAR DIARY
or
~~INTELLIGENCE SUMMARY~~
(Erase heading not required.) 93rd Field Ambulance

Army Form C. 2118.

Place	Date	Hour	Summary of Events and Information	Remarks and references to Appendices
			of billets	
ZELOBES	14/8/16		Reliefs took place today as follows	
			A Section to A.D.S. & Green barn	
			B Section to return to Headquarters	
			C. Section on duty at main dressing Station	
			Captain J. M. Pooley reported [illegible] for duty from No 7 General Hospital and was taken on the strength of this unit.	
			B C	
ZELOBES	15/8/16		Nothing important to record	
			B C	

2449 Wt. W14957/M90 750,000 1/16 J.B.C. & A. Forms/C.2118/12.

Army Form C. 2118.

WAR DIARY
or
INTELLIGENCE SUMMARY

(*Erase heading not required.*) 93rd Field Ambulance

Instructions regarding War Diaries and Intelligence Summaries are contained in F. S. Regs., Part II. and the Staff Manual respectively. Title Pages will be prepared in manuscript.

Place	Date	Hour	Summary of Events and Information	Remarks and references to Appendices
ZELOBES	16/8/16.		Received the following marked Secret.	
			Copy No 1.	
			Rame Orders No 3. 31st Division	
			by A.D. M. S 31st Division	
			16 August 1916.	
			Reference Map 36A. SE $\frac{1}{20000}$	
			I. Officer Commanding 93rd Field Ambulance will handover the advanced dressing Station at Green Barn (M.27 d 5.2) and the regimental aid posts at M 19 9.5 Hole (M 35 C 5 6) and Stirling Castle (S4 d 4 10.) at 7pm on the 18th inst.	
			These posts will be taken over by the 3rd Field Ambulance	

2449 Wt. W14957/M90 750,000 1/16 J.B.C. & A. Forms/C.2118/12.

Instructions regarding War Diaries and Intelligence Summaries are contained in F. S. Regs., Part II. and the Staff Manual respectively. Title Pages will be prepared in manuscript.

WAR DIARY
or
INTELLIGENCE SUMMARY
(Erase heading not required.) 93rd Field Ambulance

Army Form C. 2118.

Place	Date	Hour	Summary of Events and Information	Remarks and references to Appendices
			61st Division	
			Completion of Relief to be reported to head quarters	
			(S) A.W. Bewley Col AMS ADMS 31st Division	
ZELOBES	17/8/16		Nothing important to record BC	
ZELOBES	18/8/16		I made an inspection of all transport and horses today and found everything in a very satisfactory condition. In view of an extra section arriving today from Green Barn and the shortness of accommodation here. The tents of the unit have been pitched for this emergency.	

2449 Wt. W14957/M90 750,000 1/16 J.B.C. & A. Forms/C.2118/12.

Army Form C. 2118.

Instructions regarding War Diaries and Intelligence Summaries are contained in F. S. Regs., Part II. and the Staff Manual respectively. Title Pages will be prepared in manuscript.

WAR DIARY
or
INTELLIGENCE SUMMARY
(Erase heading not required.) 2/3rd Field Ambulance

Place	Date	Hour	Summary of Events and Information	Remarks and references to Appendices
ZELOBES	18/8/16	7 pm	Capt H.L.P. Yorke in Command of A Section reported his arrival with his Section at headquarters after handing over the Advanced Dressing Station at Green Barn	
			B C	
ZELOBES	19/8/16		Nothing important to record	
			B C	
ZELOBES	20/8/16		Great improvements have been made in the horse lines. In view of the approach of winter, steps have been taken to have the horse lines thoroughly stoned, as the fields in the winter become veritable quagmires, and unless precautions of this nature are taken now, the animals suffer a great deal in consequence.	
			B C	

2449 Wt. W14957/M90 750,000 1/16 J.B.C. & A. Forms/C.2118/12.

Instructions regarding War Diaries and Intelligence Summaries are contained in F. S. Regs., Part II. and the Staff Manual respectively. Title Pages will be prepared in manuscript.

WAR DIARY
or
~~INTELLIGENCE~~ SUMMARY

(Erase heading not required.) 93rd Field Ambulance

Army Form C. 2118.

Place	Date	Hour	Summary of Events and Information	Remarks and references to Appendices
ZELOBES	21/8/16		Received the following message. M/1335/2 dtd 20/8/16 Lieut Fletcher should proceed to England forthwith. Please notify me of date on which he is proceeding and a warrant will be sent to you (Sd) G. W. Ware. Major for Col ADMS 31st Division B.C	
ZELOBES	22/8/16		Lieut F S B Fletcher having taken his departure for England on the Expiry of his contract, was struck off the strength of this unit. B.C	

Instructions regarding War Diaries and Intelligence Summaries are contained in F. S. Regs., Part II. and the Staff Manual respectively. Title pages will be prepared in manuscript.

WAR DIARY
or
~~INTELLIGENCE SUMMARY.~~

(*Erase heading not required.*) 93rd Field Ambulance.

Army Form C. 2118.

Hour, Date, Place	Summary of Events and Information	Remarks and references to Appendices
5pm. 23/8/16 ZELOBES.	Received the following message. S142. M3378 OC 93rd Field Ambulance. Please detail Capt H.E.P. Yorke to assume temporary Medical Charge of the 18 Batt West Yorkshire Regt during the absence of their Medical Officer on 14 days leave. He should proceed to Le Touret Thursday the 24 inst and take over Medical Charge of the Regiment next day. At Le TOURET. he should get into touch with the Quartermaster of the 18th West Yorkshire Regt who will arrange for his transport to Battalion H.Q. LE TOURET. X 16 b. Reference Map BETHUNE 1/40000 Signed [illegible] Major for ADMS 31st Division	

D HQ 23/8/16

Instructions regarding War Diaries and Intelligence Summaries are contained in F. S. Regs., Part II. and the Staff Manual respectively. Title pages will be prepared in manuscript.

Army Form C. 2118.

WAR DIARY
or
INTELLIGENCE SUMMARY.

(Erase heading not required.) 93rd Field Ambulance.

Hour, Date, Place	Summary of Events and Information	Remarks and references to Appendices
	Capt H.E.P. Yorke was accordingly detailed ~~M3378~~ to comply with this order	
	B.C.	
10 A.M. 23/8/16 ZELOBES.	Received the following order M/3380.	
	O.C. 93rd Field Ambulance.	
	Reference my M/3378 of 22/8/16	
	Capt H.E.P. Yorke should proceed to relieve the MO i/c 18th West Yorkshire Regt today Wednesday 23rd	
	He should report at LE TOURET this evening	
	(Sd) G.W. Ware Major	
	for Col	
	L.H.Q. 23/8/16 ADMS 31st Division	

Instructions regarding War Diaries and Intelligence Summaries are contained in F. S. Regs., Part II. and the Staff Manual respectively. Title pages will be prepared in manuscript.

WAR DIARY
or
~~INTELLIGENCE~~ SUMMARY.
(*Erase heading not required.*)

93rd Field Ambulance

Army Form C. 2118.

Hour, Date, Place	Summary of Events and Information	Remarks and references to Appendices
4pm 23/8/16 ZELOBES	In Compliance with the foregoing Capt. H. E. P. Yorke proceeded on temporary duty with 18th West Yorkshire Regt. BC	
24/8/16 ZELOBES	Nothing important to record.	
25/8/16 ZELOBES	Sent the following message to A.D. M.S. 31st Division In view of the possibility of this unit wintering in its present area, extra accommodation in the Shape of huts will be necessary. At present the total covered accommodation will only provide for 100 men 20 of whom are in a canvas hut. At least 2 huts will be necessary for the accommodation	

(73989) W4141—463. 400,000. 9/14. H.&J.Ltd. Forms/C. 2118/10.

Instructions regarding War Diaries and Intelligence Summaries are contained in F. S. Regs., Part II. and the Staff Manual respectively. Title pages will be prepared in manuscript.

WAR DIARY

or

~~INTELLIGENCE~~ SUMMARY.

(*Erase heading not required.*) 93rd Field Ambulance

Army Form C. 2118.

Hour, Date, Place	Summary of Events and Information	Remarks and references to Appendices
	of 35 men of the A.S.C Transport and 4 huts for the remainder of the Ambulance, if they are not employed at Advanced Dressing Stations. At present the emergency is met by putting about 100 men under canvas, which of course will be impossible in the winter.	
	25/8/16 B Connell Lieut Col OC 93rd Field Ambulance	
	Under instructions from the ADMS 31st Division 2 N.C.Os and 18 men were detailed to work under the CRE in constructing and improving dugouts	

(73989) W4141—463. 400,000. 9/14. H.&J.Ltd. Forms/C. 2118/10.

Instructions regarding War Diaries and Intelligence Summaries are contained in F. S. Regs., Part II. and the Staff Manual respectively. Title pages will be prepared in manuscript.

WAR DIARY
or
~~INTELLIGENCE SUMMARY.~~

(*Erase heading not required.*) 93rd Field Ambulance

Army Form C. 2118.

Hour, Date, Place	Summary of Events and Information	Remarks and references to Appendices
	at St Georges Post.	
5pm. 25/8/16. ZELOBES	Received the following marked Secret. M 394. OC 94th Field Ambulance Please arrange with OC Field Ambulance 61st Division at present holding the Advanced Dressing Station at GREEN BARN - to take over from him on the 26th inst and report to this Office when transfer is Completed. (Sd) Abb Bewley. Col ADMS 31st Division	

S 145.
25/8/16

Instructions regarding War Diaries and Intelligence Summaries are contained in F. S. Regs., Part II. and the Staff Manual respectively. Title pages will be prepared in manuscript.

Army Form C. 2118.

WAR DIARY
or
~~INTELLIGENCE~~ SUMMARY.

(*Erase heading not required.*) 93rd Field Ambulance

Hour, Date, Place	Summary of Events and Information	Remarks and references to Appendices
	In view of this message I wrote to the ADMS pointing out the impracticability of sending 20 men to do fatigues at [illegible] GEORGES Post as this belongs to the 95th Field Ambulance who should be able to provide its own fatigues. The absence of 20 men from headquarters will leave a great deal of desireable work undone. B C	
10 AM. 26/8/16 ZELOBES	In compliance with instructions Capt J S Pooley was detailed today to take over medical and Sanitary Charge of the Wagon lines B & C	

(73989) W4141—463. 400,000. 9/14. H.&J.Ltd. Forms/C. 2118/10.

Instructions regarding War Diaries and Intelligence Summaries are contained in F. S. Regs., Part II. and the Staff Manual respectively. Title pages will be prepared in manuscript.

WAR DIARY
or
~~INTELLIGENCE~~ SUMMARY.

(*Erase heading not required.*) 93rd Field Ambulance

Army Form C. 2118.

Hour, Date, Place	Summary of Events and Information	Remarks and references to Appendices
	Batteries 169 Bgde R.F.A.	
5pm. 26/8/16 ZELOBES.	Capt A.L. Forbes proceeded to GREEN BARN to take over the Advanced Dressing Station from the 2/3 Field Ambulance 61st Division. B.C	
27/8/16 ZELOBES.	Lieut J. B. ALEXANDER handed over the medical charge of the 12th KOYLI. to Capt E Forbes RAMC returned to duty from 14 days leave in England. B.C	
28/8/16 ZELOBES.	The A.D.S at GREEN BARN being in want of better protection, the section posted there have been employed sandbagging the walls and dugouts	

Instructions regarding War Diaries and Intelligence Summaries are contained in F. S. Regs., Part II. and the Staff Manual respectively. Title pages will be prepared in manuscript.

WAR DIARY
or
INTELLIGENCE SUMMARY.
(Erase heading not required.) 93rd Field Ambulance

Army Form C. 2118.

Hour, Date, Place	Summary of Events and Information	Remarks and references to Appendices
	The interior of some of these dugouts is extremely dark as a means of improving this condition the walls are being whitewashed.	
	B.C.	
29/8/16 ZELOBES	Nothing important to record	
	B.C.	
30/8/16 ZELOBES.	There has been a heavy downpour of rain during the last 24 hours as a result the roof of the men's billets are leaking badly, this has only shown itself now, that there has been a break in the fine weather. I have applied to the CRE 31st Division to attend to this matter in view of the unit wintering in its present area.	
	The men are billeted at present in two barns which	

(73989) W4141—463. 400,000. 9/14. H.&J.Ltd. Forms/C. 2118/10.

Instructions regarding War Diaries and Intelligence Summaries are contained in F. S. Regs., Part II. and the Staff Manual respectively. Title pages will be prepared in manuscript.

WAR DIARY
or
INTELLIGENCE SUMMARY.
(*Erase heading not required.*) 93rd Field Ambulance

Army Form C. 2118.

Hour, Date, Place	Summary of Events and Information	Remarks and references to Appendices
	are otherwise in good condition. Rethatching the roof or spreading a tarpaulin covering over the damaged portion ought to deal with the difficulty quite effectually.	
	B.C.	
31/8/16 ZELOBES.	Nothing important to record.	
	B. Connell Lieut Col O.C. 93rd Field Ambulance	

(73989) W4141—463. 400,000. 9/14. H.&J.Ltd. Forms/C. 2118/10.

140/1436

Confidential

Vol 9

Sept. 1916

War Diary

93rd Field Ambulance 31st Division

September 1916.

Army Form C. 2118.

Instructions regarding War Diaries and Intelligence Summaries are contained in F. S. Regs., Part II. and the Staff Manual respectively. Title Pages will be prepared in manuscript.

WAR DIARY

~~or~~

~~INTELLIGENCE SUMMARY~~

(*Erase heading not required.*) 93rd Field Ambulance

Place	Date	Hour	Summary of Events and Information	Remarks and references to Appendices
ZELOBES	1/9/16		The Unit is distributed as follows. A Section is employed at the Main dressing Station B. Section at the Advanced dressing Station at GREEN BARN. C Section in Reserve. The fatigues are well employed on Sanitation, constructing horse standings in the horse lines in view of the approach of Winter ~~and~~ the Section at the Advanced Dressing Station is busy constructing new dugouts under the supervision of the one of the Field Companys Royal Engineers. B.C.	

Army Form C. 2118.

Instructions regarding War Diaries and Intelligence Summaries are contained in F. S. Regs., Part II. and the Staff Manual respectively. Title Pages will be prepared in manuscript.

WAR DIARY
or
~~INTELLIGENCE SUMMARY~~

(Erase heading not required.) 93rd Field Ambulance

Place	Date	Hour	Summary of Events and Information	Remarks and references to Appendices
ZELOBES	2/9/16		Having reported to the CRE that the roofs of some of my billets leaked badly, it has been proposed that the Royal Engineers will supply me with Straw if I have any men in my unit who are familiar with thatching. I have found some men who are expert thatchers and the work is now progressing most satisfactorily, when the work is completed it will enable me to billet the whole of my unit in ZELOBES if the contingency should ever ~~arise~~ arise. B.C.	

2449 Wt. W14957/M90 750,000 1/16 J.B.C. & A. Forms/C.2118/12.

Instructions regarding War Diaries and Intelligence Summaries are contained in F. S. Regs., Part II. and the Staff Manual respectively. Title Pages will be prepared in manuscript.

WAR DIARY

~~or~~

~~INTELLIGENCE~~ SUMMARY

(Erase heading not required.) 93rd Field Ambulance

Army Form C. 2118.

Place	Date	Hour	Summary of Events and Information	Remarks and references to Appendices
ZELOBES.	3/9/16		The detachment posted to MOGGS HOLE has been withdrawn to EBENEZER FARM. This step has been taken at the request of the Regimental M.O. 2/7 Worcester Regt posted at EBENEZER FARM, as his regimental Stretcher bearers bring their cases down through MOGGS HOLE to EBENEZER FARM and the detachment at the former post is unnecessary. B C	

Instructions regarding War Diaries and Intelligence Summaries are contained in F. S. Regs., Part II. and the Staff Manual respectively. Title Pages will be prepared in manuscript.

WAR DIARY
or
~~INTELLIGENCE~~ SUMMARY

(Erase heading not required.)

93rd Field Ambulance

Army Form C. 2118.

Place	Date	Hour	Summary of Events and Information	Remarks and references to Appendices
ZELOBES.	4/9/16.		Owing to a Change in the Front line trenches, the detachments posted to the Regimental Aid Posts have again been changed. There is now a Regimental Medical Officer at each of the following. EBENEZER FARM. – MOGG'S HOLE. – STIRLING CASTLE. and two stretcher bearers have been posted to each of the above for the conveyance of wounded to the A.D.S. Lieut H.P. AUBREY reported himself for duty with this unit this afternoon B Connell	

2449 Wt. W14957/M90 750,000 1/16 J.B.C. & A. Forms/C.2118/12.

Army Form C. 2118.

WAR DIARY

~~or~~

~~INTELLIGENCE~~ SUMMARY

(Erase heading not required.) 93rd Field Ambulance

Instructions regarding War Diaries and Intelligence Summaries are contained in F. S. Regs., Part II. and the Staff Manual respectively. Title Pages will be prepared in manuscript.

Place	Date	Hour	Summary of Events and Information	Remarks and references to Appendices
ZELOBES	5/9/16		Lieut H.P. AUBREY is posted to B. Section.	
			The D M S. first Army inspected this unit this morning everything appeared satisfactory.	
ZELOBES	6/9/16		Received the following message at 10 A M this morning	
			O.C. 93rd Field Ambulance M 3445.	
			Please attend at 2 30 pm tomorrow 6th inst for a conference	
			(Sgd) C. W. Vane Major Ram for A.D.M.S 31st Div	
			DHB 5/9/16.	

2449 Wt. W14957/M90 750,000 1/16 J.B.C. & A. Forms/C.2118/12.

Instructions regarding War Diaries and Intelligence Summaries are contained in F. S. Regs., Part II. and the Staff Manual respectively. Title Pages will be prepared in manuscript.

WAR DIARY
~~or~~
~~INTELLIGENCE SUMMARY~~

(Erase heading not required.) 93rd Field Ambulance

Army Form C. 2118.

Place	Date	Hour	Summary of Events and Information	Remarks and references to Appendices
x			In compliance with the above I attended the conference and was informed that the division would probably attack the German trenches on the 10th inst. and preparation should be made for this contingency. The 92 + 94 Infantry Brigade were intended to make the attack the 93rd Infantry Brigade being in Reserve. B Connell	
ZELOBES	7/9/16		In view of this impending attack, I thoroughly overhauled all my equipment to be prepared for all emergencies. Indented 700 extra rations to feed the wounded as they arrived. and also laid in an extra stock of surgical dressings ~~meat~~ B.C.	

Instructions regarding War Diaries and Intelligence Summaries are contained in F. S. Regs., Part II. and the Staff Manual respectively. Title Pages will be prepared in manuscript.

WAR DIARY

or

~~INTELLIGENCE~~ SUMMARY

(Erase heading not required.) 93rd Field Ambulance

Army Form C. 2118.

Place	Date	Hour	Summary of Events and Information	Remarks and references to Appendices
ZELOBES	8/9/16		Received the following M3464. O.C. 93rd Field Ambulance. Captain H.E.P. YORKE has been posted as Medical Officer to the 13th Battalion E. Yorks Regiment from 9.9.16 and should be struck off the strength of your unit from ~~that~~ date (Signed) G. W. Ware Major for Col. ADMS 31st Division D.H.Q. 8/9/16.	

2449 Wt. W14957/M90 750,000 1/16 J.B.C. & A. Forms/C.2118/12.

Army Form C. 2118.

WAR DIARY

or

~~INTELLIGENCE~~ SUMMARY

(Erase heading not required.) 93rd Field Ambulance

Instructions regarding War Diaries and Intelligence Summaries are contained in F. S. Regs., Part II. and the Staff Manual respectively. Title Pages will be prepared in manuscript.

Place	Date	Hour	Summary of Events and Information	Remarks and references to Appendices
ZELOBES	9/9/16.		In Compliance with the above Capt H E YORKE was struck off the strength of this unit. B.C.	
ZELOBES	10/9/16		In view of the approach of Winter I have arranged with the C.R.E to have the floors of all billets boarded. This is a most necessary Sanitary measure as it will ensure the men sleeping off the damp ground. B.C.	
ZELOBES	11/9/16		Nothing important to record B.C.	

2449 Wt. W14957/M90 750,000 1/16 J.B.C. & A. Forms/C.2118/12.

Army Form C. 2118.

Instructions regarding War Diaries and Intelligence Summaries are contained in F. S. Regs., Part II. and the Staff Manual respectively. Title Pages will be prepared in manuscript.

WAR DIARY
or
~~INTELLIGENCE~~ SUMMARY

(*Erase heading not required.*) 93rd Field Ambulance.

Place	Date	Hour	Summary of Events and Information	Remarks and references to Appendices
ZELOBES.	13/9/16		Sent the following message to the O.C. B. Section 93rd Field Ambulance. You will be relieved from the A.D.S. tomorrow the 13th inst at 5 p.m. by C. Section. You will hand over the 19 Spare Stretchers with slings to the O.C. C. Section and take a receipt. B.C.	

2449 Wt. W14957/M90 750,000 1/16 J.B.C. & A. Forms/C.2118/12.

Instructions regarding War Diaries and Intelligence Summaries are contained in F. S. Regs., Part II. and the Staff Manual respectively. Title Pages will be prepared in manuscript.

WAR DIARY

or

~~INTELLIGENCE~~ SUMMARY

(*Erase heading not required.*) 93rd Field Ambulance.

Army Form C. 2118.

Place	Date	Hour	Summary of Events and Information	Remarks and references to Appendices
ZELOBES.	13/9/16		C. Section relieved B Section at the A.D.S. GREEN BARN today.	
ZELOBES	14/9/16.		BC D. D. M. S. XI Corps inspected this unit today and expressed himself satisfied	
ZELOBES	15/9/16.		BC Fatigues are employed on Sanitation and draining the dykes and ditches in the area of this unit. In many cases the water has become stagnant and gives rise to the most offensive smells owing	

Army Form C. 2118.

Instructions regarding War Diaries and Intelligence Summaries are contained in F. S. Regs., Part II. and the Staff Manual respectively. Title Pages will be prepared in manuscript.

WAR DIARY
or
~~INTELLIGENCE~~ SUMMARY

(Erase heading not required.) 93rd Field Ambulance

Place	Date	Hour	Summary of Events and Information	Remarks and references to Appendices
			to the troops throwing refuse and other insanitary material into them as an easy means of disposal.	
ZELOBES	16/9/16		The following is an extract of Secret B.C. orders received today.	
			Secret. Copy No 1.	
			31st Division.	
			R.A.M.C. Operation Order No 24.	
			by.	
			Col A.C. Bewley A.M.S., A.D.M.S. 31st Division	
			Reference Combined Sheet BETHUNE 1/40000.	

2449 Wt. W14957/M90 750,000 1/16 J.B.C. & A. Forms/C.2118/12.

Army Form C. 2118.

WAR DIARY
or
INTELLIGENCE SUMMARY
(Erase heading not required.) 93rd Field Ambulance.

Instructions regarding War Diaries and Intelligence Summaries are contained in F. S. Regs., Part II. and the Staff Manual respectively. Title Pages will be prepared in manuscript.

Place	Date	Hour	Summary of Events and Information	Remarks and references to Appendices
			31st Division will relieve 30th Division taking over the FESTUBERT and GIVENCHY Section.	
			Relief to be completed by 6 am on the 20th inst.	
			(1). The 93rd Field Ambulance will	
			(a) Hand over the Advanced Dressing Station at GREEN BARN (M27. d 5.2.) to a Field Ambulance 61st Division at 6 pm. 16 inst.	
			(b) Hand over the main Dressing Station at LE LOBES (M 27 c 0 5). to the 95th Field Ambulance on the morning of the 17th inst	

2449 Wt. W14957/M90 750,000 1/16 J.B.C. & A. Forms/C.2118/12.

Army Form C. 2118.

WAR DIARY
or
~~INTELLIGENCE SUMMARY~~

(Erase heading not required.) 93rd Field Ambulance

Instructions regarding War Diaries and Intelligence Summaries are contained in F. S. Regs., Part II. and the Staff Manual respectively. Title Pages will be prepared in manuscript.

Place	Date	Hour	Summary of Events and Information	Remarks and references to Appendices
			(c). Take over the main dressing Station at the ECOLE MATERNELLE, BETHUNE. (E.5. c.4.8.) and the Advanced Dressing Station at LONE FARM. (F.7. d.2.3.) on the 17th inst.	
			(d). Take over the dressing Station at ANNEZIN (E.9. b.2.6.) from the 97 F. Ambulance by 6pm 16 inst.	
			Signed A.W. Bowley, Col. A.D.M.S. 31st Division	
			15/9/16.	

2449 Wt. W14957/M90 750,000 1/16 J.B.C. & A. Forms/C.2118/12.

Army Form C. 2118.

WAR DIARY
or
INTELLIGENCE SUMMARY
(Erase heading not required.)

93rd Field Ambulance

Instructions regarding War Diaries and Intelligence Summaries are contained in F. S. Regs., Part II. and the Staff Manual respectively. Title Pages will be prepared in manuscript.

Place	Date	Hour	Summary of Events and Information	Remarks and references to Appendices
ZELOBES	16/9/16	6 pm	Received the following message No 775. 16/9/16 All reliefs ordered in Operation Order No 4 will be accelerated by 24 hours where possible. Medical 31st Division	
		6 pm	Sent the following message: O.C. B Section 93rd Field Ambulance. You will hand over the A.D.S. GREEN BARN to the 2/3 South Midland Field Ambulance to day at 7 pm and rejoin your unit at H.Q. at ZELOBES. Bring all equipment and Stores belonging to this unit with you. 16/9/16 B Connell Lieut Col O.C. 93rd Field Ambulance	

Army Form C. 2118.

WAR DIARY
or
~~INTELLIGENCE~~ SUMMARY

(Erase heading not required.) 93rd Field Ambulance

Instructions regarding War Diaries and Intelligence Summaries are contained in F. S. Regs., Part II. and the Staff Manual respectively. Title Pages will be prepared in manuscript.

Place	Date	Hour	Summary of Events and Information	Remarks and references to Appendices
ZELOBES	16/9/16	9 pm	Lieut J. B. Alexander, in compliance with instructions was ordered to report at 9 am on the 17th inst at the Town Sanitary Office BETHUNE to take over the duties of Sanitary Officer BETHUNE	
ZELOBES	16/9/16	10 pm	Received the following. A.D.M.S. 30/Division M.448/9. dated 15/9/16 I have arranged with the Town Major BETHUNE to take over the Cinema Hall at W 28 d 8 8 as additional accommodation to the Ecole Maternelle. I would recommend that this arrangement be maintained while the	

Army Form C. 2118.

Instructions regarding War Diaries and Intelligence Summaries are contained in F. S. Regs., Part II. and the Staff Manual respectively. Title Pages will be prepared in manuscript.

WAR DIARY
or
~~INTELLIGENCE SUMMARY~~

(Erase heading not required.)

93rd Field Ambulance

Place	Date	Hour	Summary of Events and Information	Remarks and references to Appendices
			Mairie of BETHUNE is in occupation of part of the Ecole Maternelle.	
			(Sgd) J. A. Alexander Col	
			Sept 15th 1916. ADMS 30th Division	
			2.	
			O.C. 93rd Field Ambulance — ADMS 31st Division M/1464. 16/9/16	
			The Cinema Hall mentioned above should be retained by your unit	
			(Sgd) Alb. Bewley Col ADMS 31st Division	
			DHQ 16/9/16	

2449 Wt. W14957/M90 750,000 1/16 J.B.C. & A. Forms/C.2118/12.

Instructions regarding War Diaries and Intelligence Summaries are contained in F. S. Regs., Part II. and the Staff Manual respectively. Title Pages will be prepared in manuscript.

WAR DIARY
or
~~INTELLIGENCE SUMMARY~~

(Erase heading not required.) 93rd Field Ambulance

Army Form C. 2118.

Place	Date	Hour	Summary of Events and Information	Remarks and references to Appendices
ZELOBES	16/9/16	10pm	I detailed Capt A.D. Forbes with 20 N.C.Os & men to proceed to ANNEZIN to take over the dressing station there from the O.C. 97th Field Ambulance. I did this after interviewing the O.C. 97th Field Ambulance who expressed a wish to be relieved immediately as he was awaiting orders to entrain at short notice. B.C.	

2449 Wt. W14957/M90 750,000 1/16 J.B.C. & A. Forms/C.2118/12.

Instructions regarding War Diaries and Intelligence Summaries are contained in F. S. Regs., Part II. and the Staff Manual respectively. Title Pages will be prepared in manuscript.

WAR DIARY
or
~~INTELLIGENCE SUMMARY~~
(Erase heading not required.) 93rd Field Ambulance.

Army Form C. 2118.

Place	Date	Hour	Summary of Events and Information	Remarks and references to Appendices
ZELOBES	17/9/16	8.30 AM	Received the following message marked urgent. M 3497 In accordance with instructions from D.D.M.S. XI Corps please detail Captain A.D. Forbes to report to A.D.M.S. 30th Division for duty on the 17th inst. An officer from the 94th Field Ambulance will report to you at 10 am on the 17th inst. Please arrange to convey both these officers to H.Q. 30th Division at BETHUNE to report to A.D.M.S. 30th Division before noon. (Signd) A.W. Bewley Col. A.D.M.S. 31st Division D.H.Q. 16/9/16	

Instructions regarding War Diaries and Intelligence Summaries are contained in F. S. Regs., Part II. and the Staff Manual respectively. Title Pages will be prepared in manuscript.

WAR DIARY
or
~~INTELLIGENCE SUMMARY~~

(Erase heading not required.)

93rd Field Ambulance

Army Form C. 2118.

Place	Date	Hour	Summary of Events and Information	Remarks and references to Appendices
			In Compliance with this order Capt A.D. Forbes was instructed to report to the A.D.M.S. 30th Division And was struck off the strength of this unit.	
ZELOBES		8.30 AM.	I handed over the main dressing Station at ZELOBES to the O.C. 95th Field Ambulance	
		10 AM.	The Ambulance fell in and marched to BETHUNE. on arrival there the men were billeted in the Cinema palace pending the departure of the ~~[illegible]~~ 96th Field Ambulance. As it had received instruction not entrain until the 19th inst.	
			I took over the main dressing Station at the	

2449 Wt. W14957/M90 750,000 1/16 J.B.C. & A. Forms/C.2118/12.

Army Form C. 2118.

WAR DIARY
or
INTELLIGENCE SUMMARY
(Erase heading not required.) 93rd Field Ambulance

Instructions regarding War Diaries and Intelligence Summaries are contained in F. S. Regs., Part II. and the Staff Manual respectively. Title Pages will be prepared in manuscript.

Place	Date	Hour	Summary of Events and Information	Remarks and references to Appendices
			ECOLE MATERNELLE in the Rue Pasteur, the Cinema Palace and the Advanced dressing Station at LONE FARM (F 7. d 23) Combined Map BETHUNE. B. Section proceeded to ANNEZIN and took over the dressing Station from the 97th Field Ambulance. B. C.	
BETHUNE	18/9/16		In compliance with orders I took over the 30th Divisional baths at LE QUESNOY and GONNEHEM. The baths at LE QUESNOY are in a very dirty condition and will require a good many fatigues to put the place in order. The daily average number bathed here is about 300. There is sufficient change of underclothing for 300. The baths at GONNEHEM are very good	

2449 Wt. W14957/M90 750,000 1/16 J.B.C. & A. Forms/C.2118/12.

Instructions regarding War Diaries and Intelligence Summaries are contained in F. S. Regs., Part II. and the Staff Manual respectively. Title Pages will be prepared in manuscript.

WAR DIARY
or
~~INTELLIGENCE~~ SUMMARY
(Erase heading not required.) 93rd Field Ambulance

Army Form C. 2118.

Place	Date	Hour	Summary of Events and Information	Remarks and references to Appendices
			The duties of this Ambulance are now distributed as follows	
			I A Section at H.Q. Rue Pasteur Bethune	
			II B. Section at ANNEZIN under Capt Pooley	
			III Capt R. S. CUMMING with half of C Section at the A.D. S LONE FARM The remainder of C Section posted to H.Q.	
			B.C.	
BETHUNE	19/9/16		The Unit is busy settling down in its new Quarters	
			The billets for men are excellent.	
			The accommodation for the patients is equally good	

2449 Wt. W14957/M90 750,000 1/16 J.B.C. & A. Forms/C.2118/12.

Instructions regarding War Diaries and Intelligence Summaries are contained in F. S. Regs., Part II. and the Staff Manual respectively. Title Pages will be prepared in manuscript.

WAR DIARY
or
~~INTELLIGENCE~~ SUMMARY

(Erase heading not required.) 93rd Field Ambulance

Army Form C. 2118.

Place	Date	Hour	Summary of Events and Information	Remarks and references to Appendices
			The School at BETHUNE could accommodate about 100 patients the Cinema palace would accommodate about another 100.	
			The Dressing Station at ANNEZIN will accommodate about 120 cases.	
			The A.D.S. at LONE FARM could hold about 40 cases	
			Arrangements have been made in case BETHUNE is heavily shelled and the Main dressing Station becomes untenable. All patients + personnel can be transferred to ANNEZIN.	
			B. C.	

2449 Wt. W14957/M90 750,000 1/16 J.B.C. & A. Forms/C.2118/12.

Instructions regarding War Diaries and Intelligence Summaries are contained in F. S. Regs., Part II. and the Staff Manual respectively. Title Pages will be prepared in manuscript.

WAR DIARY
or
~~INTELLIGENCE SUMMARY~~

(*Erase heading not required.*) 93rd Field Ambulance

Army Form C. 2118.

Place	Date	Hour	Summary of Events and Information	Remarks and references to Appendices
BETHUNE	19/9/16	1pm	Capt S. MILLING reported for duty with this Ambulance today and was taken on its strength. BC	
BETHUNE	20/9/16		Nothing important to record. BC	
BETHUNE	21/9/16		Received the following message M3308. O.C. 93rd Field Ambulance In the event of an outbreak of Cholera a site has been chosen at K 2 d 84. map BETHUNE (combined Sheet 1-40000) - west of ANNEZIN	

2449 Wt. W14957/M90 750,000 1/16 J.B.C. & A. Forms/C.2118/12.

Instructions regarding War Diaries and Intelligence Summaries are contained in F. S. Regs., Part II. and the Staff Manual respectively. Title Pages will be prepared in manuscript.

WAR DIARY

or

~~INTELLIGENCE SUMMARY~~

(Erase heading not required.)

93rd Field Ambulance

Army Form C. 2118.

Place	Date	Hour	Summary of Events and Information	Remarks and references to Appendices
			An officer and the personnel of one tent subdivision from your unit will administer this camp. A copy of each of the following is forwarded for the information of the Officer detailed (1) Cholera notes by Rogers (2). Hypertonic + Permanganate treatment by Rogers (3) Anti Cholera Vaccine Please let me know the name of the Officer detailed (Signed) A.W. Beveley ADMS 31st Division DHQ 20/9/16	

2449 Wt. W14957/M90 750,000 1/16 J.B.C. & A. Forms/C.2118/12.

Army Form C. 2118.

WAR DIARY
or
INTELLIGENCE SUMMARY

(Erase heading not required.) 93rd Field Ambulance

Instructions regarding War Diaries and Intelligence Summaries are contained in F. S. Regs., Part II. and the Staff Manual respectively. Title Pages will be prepared in manuscript.

Place	Date	Hour	Summary of Events and Information	Remarks and references to Appendices
			In compliance with this order Capt R S CUMMINS was detailed to take on these duties in this emergency. B.C.	
BETHUNE	22/9/16		The men are all employed on fatigues in their respective dressing stations. all hands are now fully employed as the area occupied requires very careful sanitation B.C.	
BETHUNE	23/9/16		In accordance with orders I handed over the baths at GONNEHEM to the O.C. Westmoreland and Cumberland Yeomanry and withdrew the detachment of these to Headquarters. B.C.	

2449 Wt. W14957/M90 750,000 1/16 J.B.C. & A. Forms/C.2118/12.

Army Form C. 2118.

Instructions regarding War Diaries and Intelligence Summaries are contained in F. S. Regs., Part II. and the Staff Manual respectively. Title Pages will be prepared in manuscript.

WAR DIARY
or
INTELLIGENCE SUMMARY

(Erase heading not required.) 93rd Field Ambulance

Place	Date	Hour	Summary of Events and Information	Remarks and references to Appendices
BETHUNE	24/9/16		LIEUT H P. AUBREY was transferred to the Dressing Station at ANNEZIN in relief of Lieut C.E. MERYON who was transferred to the A.D.S at LONE FARM. B.C	
BETHUNE	25/9/16		Nothing important to record B.C	
BETHUNE	26/9/16		Inspected the A.D.S at LONE FARM, several improvements are necessary in connection with the general safety of this post. Several Sandbags have rotted away and require renewing. I have applied to the CRE 31st Division to detail an engineer	

2449 Wt. W14957/M90 750,000 1/16 J.B.C. & A. Forms/C.2118/12.

Instructions regarding War Diaries and Intelligence Summaries are contained in F. S. Regs., Part II. and the Staff Manual respectively. Title Pages will be prepared in manuscript.

WAR DIARY

or

~~INTELLIGENCE~~ SUMMARY

(Erase heading not required.) 93rd Field Ambulance

Army Form C. 2118.

Place	Date	Hour	Summary of Events and Information	Remarks and references to Appendices
			officer ~~to~~ to inspect the place and carry out necessary improvements	
			B.C	
BETHUNE	27/9/16		Nothing important to record	
			B.C	
BETHUNE	28/9/16		The horse lines are very inferior to the those allotted to this unit at ZELOBES and several fatigues will be necessary before they are in good condition. Arrangements are being carried out with a view ~~to~~ to having them covered in for the winter.	
			B.C	

2449 Wt. W14957/M90 750,000 1/16 J.B.C. & A. Forms/C.2118/12.

Instructions regarding War Diaries and Intelligence Summaries are contained in F. S. Regs., Part II. and the Staff Manual respectively. Title Pages will be prepared in manuscript.

WAR DIARY
or
INTELLIGENCE SUMMARY

(Erase heading not required.) 93rd Field Ambulance

Army Form C. 2118.

Place	Date	Hour	Summary of Events and Information	Remarks and references to Appendices
BETHUNE	29/9/16		Received the following message marked Secret	
			S 171.	
			O.C. 93rd Field Ambulance	
			(1). The 31st Division will be relieved by the 5th Division in the Line at an early date.	
			(2). The 31st Division will be transferred to the fourth Army.	
			(3). Preparations for the move and for making the men fit are to take precedence of all other work.	
			(4). Care must be taken that no reports shall get	

Instructions regarding War Diaries and Intelligence Summaries are contained in F. S. Regs., Part II. and the Staff Manual respectively. Title pages will be prepared in manuscript.

WAR DIARY
or
INTELLIGENCE SUMMARY.

(*Erase heading not required.*) 93rd Field Ambulance

Army Form C. 2118.

Hour, Date, Place	Summary of Events and Information	Remarks and references to Appendices
	abroad which may indicate to the enemy the proposed move.	
	(5). Acknowledge.	
	(Signed) AHBobby ADMS	
	29/9/16 Col. 31st Divn.	
BETHUNE. 30/9/16	Nothing important to record today. In view of the order warning the division to be prepared to move at an early date. The unit has been busy preparing for this emergency	
	B Connell Lieut Col	
	O.C. 93rd Field Ambulance	

(73989) W4141—463. 400,000. 9/14. H.&J.Ltd. Forms/C. 2118/10.

140/1817

Oct. 1916

5

Confidential

Volume X

War Diary.

9 3rd Field Ambulance 31st Division

October 1916

Instructions regarding War Diaries and Intelligence Summaries are contained in F. S. Regs., Part II. and the Staff Manual respectively. Title pages will be prepared in manuscript.

WAR DIARY
or
~~INTELLIGENCE~~ SUMMARY.
(Erase heading not required.) 93rd Field Ambulance.

Army Form C. 2118.

Hour, Date, Place	Summary of Events and Information	Remarks and references to Appendices
Oct 1st 1916 BETHUNE.	I inspected the A.D. S at LONE FARM. and found everything satisfactory. Certain improvements in protecting the Building from Shell fire are now well in hand. B.C.	
Oct 2nd 1916. BETHUNE.	Inspected the Dressing Station at ANNEZIN. and found everything Satisfactory ~~Without the exception of patients requiring dental treatment~~, all Cases from here are ~~transferred~~ to the main dressing Station at BETHUNE. B.C	

Instructions regarding War Diaries and Intelligence Summaries are contained in F. S. Regs., Part II. and the Staff Manual respectively. Title pages will be prepared in manuscript.

WAR DIARY

or

~~INTELLIGENCE SUMMARY.~~

(*Erase heading not required.*) 93rd Field Ambulance.

Army Form C. 2118.

Hour, Date, Place	Summary of Events and Information	Remarks and references to Appendices
Oct 3rd 1916 BETHUNE.	I received orders today, to hand over the main dressing station at BETHUNE to a Field Ambulance of the 5th Division tomorrow and proceed to ANNEZIN. The following telegram was received. O.C. Secret. 93rd Field Ambulance The following moves will take place on 4.10.16. O.C. 93rd Field Ambulance will hand over to a field Ambulance of the	

(73989) W4141—463. 400,000. 9/14. H.&J.Ltd. Forms/C. 2118/10.

3

Instructions regarding War Diaries and Intelligence Summaries are contained in F. S. Regs., Part II. and the Staff Manual respectively. Title pages will be prepared in manuscript.

WAR DIARY
or
~~INTELLIGENCE SUMMARY.~~

(*Erase heading not required.*) 93rd Field Ambulance

Army Form C. 2118.

Hour, Date, Place	Summary of Events and Information	Remarks and references to Appendices
	5th Division and will move from BETHUNE to ANNEZIN. O.C. 94th Field Ambulance will hand over to a Field Ambulance of the 5th Division and will move with the RAMC personel of the Field Ambulance from MESPLAUX to White House. The A.S.C personnel and transport will remain at the present Main Dressing Station O.C. 95th Field Ambulance will	

(73989) W4141—463. 400,000. 9/14. H.&J.Ltd. Forms/C. 2118/10.

4

Instructions regarding War Diaries and Intelligence Summaries are contained in F. S. Regs., Part II. and the Staff Manual respectively. Title pages will be prepared in manuscript.

WAR DIARY
or
~~INTELLIGENCE SUMMARY~~.
(*Erase heading not required.*) 93rd Field Ambulance

Army Form C. 2118.

Hour, Date, Place	Summary of Events and Information	Remarks and references to Appendices
	hand over to a Field Ambulance of the 5th Division and will move from VIELLE CHAPELLE to ZELOBES. Details of reliefs to be arranged between O.C.s concerned.	
	G. W. Ware. Major for Col ADMS 31st Division	
D.H.Q 9/10/16		
S. 174.		

(73989) W4141—463. 400,000. 9/14. H.&J.Ltd. Forms/C. 2118/10.

5

Army Form C. 2118.

WAR DIARY

or

~~INTELLIGENCE~~ SUMMARY.

(*Erase heading not required.*) 93rd Field Ambulance

Instructions regarding War Diaries and Intelligence Summaries are contained in F. S. Regs., Part II. and the Staff Manual respectively. Title pages will be prepared in manuscript.

Hour, Date, Place	Summary of Events and Information	Remarks and references to Appendices
	The O.C. 14th Field Ambulance 5th Division inspected the Dressing Station at the Rue PASTUER. the Cinema Hall at the A.D.S LONE FARM with a view to taking over tomorrow B.C.	
4/10/16. BETHUNE.	The Ambulance proceeded today to ANNEZIN and reached there 2pm. The Dressing Station at BETHUNE with Motor Ambulances & Motor Cycles & Personnel A.S.C M.T. were handed over to the 14th Field Ambulance. B.C.	

(73989) W4141—463. 400,000. 9/14. H.&J.Ltd. Forms/C. 2118/10.

6

Instructions regarding War Diaries and Intelligence Summaries are contained in F. S. Regs., Part II. and the Staff Manual respectively. Title pages will be prepared in manuscript.

WAR DIARY
or
~~INTELLIGENCE SUMMARY.~~

(*Erase heading not required.*) 93rd Field Ambulance

Army Form C. 2118.

Hour, Date, Place	Summary of Events and Information	Remarks and references to Appendices
ANNEZIN 5/10/16	Received the following. Secret. Extract from 31st Division Order 58 dtd 4/10/16. Ref. First Army 1/40000 Administrative Map. I. In Continuation of Division Order 57 dated Oct 1st x x x x x Field Ambulance will move to Billeting Areas near Entraining Stations at MERVILLE, LILLERS and BERGUETTE. A revised table is attached Sd W. B. Spender LtCol General Staff 31st Division	

(73989) W4141—463. 400,000. 9/14. H.&J.Ltd. Forms/C. 2118/10.

Instructions regarding War Diaries and Intelligence Summaries are contained in F. S. Regs., Part II. and the Staff Manual respectively. Title pages will be prepared in manuscript.

WAR DIARY

or

~~INTELLIGENCE SUMMARY.~~

(*Erase heading not required.*) 93rd Field Ambulance

Army Form C. 2118.

Hour, Date, Place	Summary of Events and Information	Remarks and references to Appendices
	S177.	
	True Copy	
	A.W. Bewley	
	Col ADMS 31st Division	
	D.H.Q	
	4/10/16	
	Extract from march table issued with 31st Division Order No 38	

Unit	From	move on 5th to
93rd Field Ambulance	ANNEZIN	BUSNES area.

(73989) W4141—463. 400,000. 9/14. H.&J.Ltd. Forms/C. 2118/10.

Instructions regarding War Diaries and Intelligence Summaries are contained in F. S. Regs., Part II. and the Staff Manual respectively. Title pages will be prepared in manuscript.

WAR DIARY
or
~~INTELLIGENCE SUMMARY~~.
(*Erase heading not required.*)

Army Form C. 2118.

Hour, Date, Place	Summary of Events and Information	Remarks and references to Appendices
	In compliance with this order this unit marched off from ANNEZIN at 3pm and Billeted in BUSNES at 6 pm. The Dressing Station at ANNEZIN was handed over to the 14th Field Ambulance before departure. B.C.	
BUSNES 6/10/16.	Received the following.	
	ADMS.	
	Secret. S179.	
	O.C. 93rd Field Ambulance	
	The following extracts from 31st Division order No 59 dated 6th October 1916 are	

Army Form C. 2118.

Instructions regarding War Diaries and Intelligence Summaries are contained in F. S. Regs., Part II. and the Staff Manual respectively. Title pages will be prepared in manuscript.

WAR DIARY
or
~~INTELLIGENCE SUMMARY~~.

(*Erase heading not required.*) 93rd Field Ambulance

Hour, Date, Place	Summary of Events and Information	Remarks and references to Appendices
	forwarded for your information	
	1. The 31st Division on transfer to the XIII Corps Reserve Army will move by Rail in accordance with attached table	
	2. x x x x	
	3. The following units are transferred to the Division	
	Motor Ambulance Cars 55th Division (now in Reserve Army Area).	
	4. 5. 6 x x x x x x	
	7. Units will entrain with their	

(73989) W4141—463. 400,000. 9/14. H.&J.Ltd. Forms/C. 2118/10.

10

Instructions regarding War Diaries and Intelligence Summaries are contained in F. S. Regs., Part II. and the Staff Manual respectively. Title pages will be prepared in manuscript.

WAR DIARY
or
INTELLIGENCE ~~SUMMARY~~.

(*Erase heading not required.*) 93rd Field Ambulance

Army Form C. 2118.

Hour, Date, Place	Summary of Events and Information	Remarks and references to Appendices
	Supply & Baggage wagons (train transport) current days rations on Supply wagons 8. All units other than Infantry will be at the Station 3 hours before departure of the trains. 9. Entraining states showing men horses vehicles (G.S. 4 wheeled, limbered, 2 wheeled) will be handed in to R.T.O 3 hours before departure of train. 10. Breast and head ropes must be provided by unit. Railway provides Lashings for vehicles 11. × × × × × × ×	

11

Army Form C. 2118.

WAR DIARY
or
~~INTELLIGENCE SUMMARY.~~

Instructions regarding War Diaries and Intelligence Summaries are contained in F. S. Regs., Part II. and the Staff Manual respectively. Title pages will be prepared in manuscript.

(*Erase heading not required.*) 93rd Field Ambulance

Hour, Date, Place	Summary of Events and Information	Remarks and references to Appendices
	12 Unless otherwise ordered units will proceed to entraining stations and from detraining stations to final billets by quickest routes.	
	13 x x x x x.	
	14 Divisional Headquarters will close at LOCON at 7 A.M. on the 8th Oct and will open at MARIEUX at 10 A.M. on that day.	
	G. W. Ware Major for Col ADMS 31st Division	
DHQ 6/10/16.		

(73989) W4141—463. 400,000. 9/14. H.&J.Ltd. Forms/C. 2118/10.

Instructions regarding War Diaries and Intelligence Summaries are contained in F. S. Regs., Part II. and the Staff Manual respectively. Title pages will be prepared in manuscript.

WAR DIARY
or
~~INTELLIGENCE SUMMARY~~.
(Erase heading not required.)

Army Form C. 2118.

Hour, Date, Place	Summary of Events and Information	Remarks and references to Appendices
	Secret S179.	
	O.C. 93rd Field Ambulance	
	The following particulars of entrainment of your unit are forwarded for information. I presume detailed orders will be issued to you by G.O.C. 93rd Infantry Brigade	

Train No	Serial No.	Time of departure	Entraining Station	detraining Station
H.T. 4	91.	2.57. am on 9/10/16.	LILLERS	DOULLENS.

Journey from LILLERS to DOULLENS
3 hours 43 minutes
New Billeting area THIEVRES.

DHQ
8/10/16

G. W. Ware for Col ADMS
31st Division

Bl

(73989) W4141—463. 400,000. 9/14. H.&J.Ltd. Forms/C. 2118/10.

13

Army Form C. 2118.

Instructions regarding War Diaries and Intelligence Summaries are contained in F.S. Regs., Part II. and the Staff Manual respectively. Title pages will be prepared in manuscript.

WAR DIARY
or
~~INTELLIGENCE~~ SUMMARY.
(Erase heading not required.) 93rd Field Ambulance

Hour, Date, Place	Summary of Events and Information	Remarks and references to Appendices
BUSNES ~~6/10/16~~ 6/10/16	Received the following Brigade Orders. Brigade Orders by Brigadier General B.D. Ingles. Commanding 93rd Infantry Brigade Oct 5th 1916 589. <u>Command</u>. The following units come under the Command of the G.O.C 93rd Infantry Brigade on the evening of the 5th inst 93rd Field Ambulance 210 F. Coy RE 590. <u>Conference</u>. There will be a conference of Commanding Officers at Brigade Headquarters at 5pm the 6th inst.	

(73989) W4141—463. 400,000. 9/14. H.&J.Ltd. Forms/C. 2118/10.

14

Instructions regarding War Diaries and Intelligence Summaries are contained in F. S. Regs., Part II. and the Staff Manual respectively. Title pages will be prepared in manuscript.

WAR DIARY
or
~~INTELLIGENCE~~ SUMMARY.

(*Erase heading not required.*) 93rd Field Ambulance

Army Form C. 2118.

Hour, Date, Place	Summary of Events and Information	Remarks and references to Appendices
	591. Estaminets No N.C.O. or man is to enter an Estaminet except between the hours of 12 noon to pm and 6 pm to 8 pm. 592. Gas Lecture There will be a gas lecture by the Divisional Gas Officer in BUSNES tomorrow the 6th inst at 4 pm. The following will attend. 1 Officer 4 N.C.O.s from each battalion 1 Officer 1 N.C.O. from 93 Machine Gun Coy. 1 Officer 1 N.C.O. from 93 Light Trench Mortar Coy 1 Officer 1 N.C.O. from 210 Field Coy R.E. An orderly will outside Brigade H.Q	

(73989) W4141—463. 400,000. 9/14. H.&J.Ltd. Forms/C. 2118/10.

15

Instructions regarding War Diaries and Intelligence Summaries are contained in F. S. Regs., Part II. and the Staff Manual respectively. Title pages will be prepared in manuscript.

WAR DIARY
or
~~INTELLIGENCE SUMMARY~~.
(*Erase heading not required.*) 93rd Field Ambulance

.Army Form C. 2118.

Hour, Date, Place	Summary of Events and Information	Remarks and references to Appendices
	at 3·45 pm as guide	
	Signed W H Roper Lt.	
	BC A/Staff Officer 93rd Inf Bgde	
BUSNES 7/10/16.	This unit rested.	
	BC	
BUSNES. 8/10/16.	The unit marched off at 10·30 pm and proceed to LILLERS to entrain. in compliance with orders. BC	
LILLERS. 9/10/16.	The unit entrained for DOULLENS at 2·57.	
	BC	

16

Army Form C. 2118.

WAR DIARY
or
~~INTELLIGENCE SUMMARY~~.
(Erase heading not required.) 93rd Field Ambulance

Instructions regarding War Diaries and Intelligence Summaries are contained in F. S. Regs., Part II. and the Staff Manual respectively. Title pages will be prepared in manuscript.

Hour, Date, Place	Summary of Events and Information	Remarks and references to Appendices
	Reached DOULLENS at 7 A.M.	
	at 7·30 A.M. LIEUT. J.B. ALEXANDER who proceeded in advance as billeting officer reported that the Ambulance was to billet in AMPLIERS.	
	Reached AMPLIERS and billeted there at 10·30 A.M.	
	B.C.	
AMPLIERS. 10/10/16.	Received the following message	
	Secret. M 3555.	
	O.C. 93rd Field Ambulance	
	Under instructions from DDMS XIII Corps the tent Division of your Field Ambulance	

17

Instructions regarding War Diaries and Intelligence Summaries are contained in F. S. Regs., Part II. and the Staff Manual respectively. Title pages will be prepared in manuscript.

WAR DIARY

or

~~INTELLIGENCE SUMMARY.~~

(*Erase heading not required.*) 93rd Field Ambulance

Army Form C. 2118.

Hour, Date, Place	Summary of Events and Information	Remarks and references to Appendices
	will proceed to LOUVENCOURT. in relief of 1/3 Highland Field Ambulance You will form a Corps Rest Station and be prepared to take in sick from all divisions of the Corps. The Bearer Division of your Field Ambulance will remain with and be rationed and billeted by 93rd Brigade The Tent division should proceed to LOUVENCOURT. on 10/10/16.	
	A. W. Ware Major for Col ADMS 31st Division	
	DHQ 9/10/16.	

Instructions regarding War Diaries and Intelligence Summaries are contained in F. S. Regs., Part II. and the Staff Manual respectively. Title pages will be prepared in manuscript.

WAR DIARY
or
~~INTELLIGENCE~~ SUMMARY.

(*Erase heading not required.*) 93rd Field Ambulance.

Army Form C. 2118.

Hour, Date, Place	Summary of Events and Information	Remarks and references to Appendices
	In compliance with this order the bearer division remained with the 93rd Infantry Bgde and the tent Division proceeded to LOUVENCOURT. and took over the XIII Corps Rest Station and the Officers Rest Station at the Chateau.	
	B.C.	
LOUVENCOURT. 11/10/16	Received the following message	
	Secret. S 159. 11/10/16.	
	O.C. 93rd Field Ambulance	
	Extracts from Medical Arrangements Reserve Army.	
	1. Casualty Clearing Stations of the Reserve Army	

(73989) W4141—463. 400,000. 9/14. H.&J.Ltd. Forms/C. 2118/10.

11

Instructions regarding War Diaries and Intelligence Summaries are contained in F. S. Regs., Part II. and the Staff Manual respectively. Title pages will be prepared in manuscript.

WAR DIARY
or
~~INTELLIGENCE SUMMARY.~~

(*Erase heading not required.*) 93rd Field Ambulance

Army Form C. 2118.

Hour, Date, Place	Summary of Events and Information	Remarks and references to Appendices
	are located as follows.	
	No 3. C.C.S PUCHEVILLERS	
	No 44 C.C.S ditto.	
	No 29 C.C.S. GEZAINCOURT.	
	2/1st Midland Cas. Clearing Station RECMENIL FARM.	
	(Self inflicted and infectious Cases only).	
	Officers Hospital (29 CCS) GEZAINCOURT	
	Operating Centres	
	Special Hospital WARLOY	
	Special Hospital AUTHIE.	
	MOTOR AMBULANCE CONVOYS are located	

(73989) W4141—463. 400,000. 9/14. H.&J.Ltd. Forms/C. 2118/10.

Instructions regarding War Diaries and Intelligence Summaries are contained in F. S. Regs., Part II. and the Staff Manual respectively. Title pages will be prepared in manuscript.

WAR DIARY
or
~~INTELLIGENCE~~ SUMMARY.

(*Erase heading not required.*) 93rd Field Ambulance

Army Form C. 2118.

Hour, Date, Place	Summary of Events and Information	Remarks and references to Appendices
	and attached to Corps as follows	
	No 31 M.A.C COUIN	
	attached XIII Corps.	
	2. EVACUATION of Wounded.	
	The following arrangements will come into force at a date and time to be notified later.	
	Lying down Cases	
	II & XIII Corps by Motor Ambulance Convoy to C.C.S at PUCHEVILLERS.	
	Sitting Cases	
	V and XIII Corps to V Corps Collecting Station ACHEUX.	
	Disposal of sick and Wounded Officers.	

(73989) W4141—463. 400,000. 9/14. H.&J.Ltd. Forms/C. 2118/10.

Instructions regarding War Diaries and Intelligence Summaries are contained in F. S. Regs., Part II. and the Staff Manual respectively. Title pages will be prepared in manuscript.

WAR DIARY
or
~~INTELLIGENCE SUMMARY.~~
(*Erase heading not required.*) 93rd Field Ambulance

Army Form C. 2118.

Hour, Date, Place	Summary of Events and Information	Remarks and references to Appendices
	will be evacuated to CCS allowed to the Corps and to the officers Hospital GEZAINCOURT. If they are considered fit to stand the journey.	
	G W. Ware Major for Col ADMS 31st Division	
D.H.Q 11/10/16	BC	
LOUVENCOURT 12/10/16	The Ambulance was employed today settling down to the ordinary routine.	
	BC.	

Instructions regarding War Diaries and Intelligence Summaries are contained in F. S. Regs., Part II. and the Staff Manual respectively. Title pages will be prepared in manuscript.

WAR DIARY
or
~~INTELLIGENCE SUMMARY.~~
(Erase heading not required.) 93rd Field Ambulance

Army Form C. 2118.

Hour, Date, Place	Summary of Events and Information	Remarks and references to Appendices
LOUVENCOURT. 13/10/16	Received the following message. O.C. 93rd Field Ambulance 90 bearers will remain with the Brigade the remainder should be retained for duty with your unit. The bearers with the Brigade are available at present for duty with your unit and can come in daily if you require their services. G. W. Ware for Col ADMS 31st Div D.H.Q 13/10/16 This welcome addition to my personal was very acceptable as the tent division was very short and scarcely able to compete with the work B.C.	

(73989) W4141—463. 400,000. 9/14. H.&J.Ltd. Forms/C. 2118/10.

Army Form C. 2118.

WAR DIARY

or

~~INTELLIGENCE~~ SUMMARY.

(*Erase heading not required.*) 93rd Field Ambulance

Instructions regarding War Diaries and Intelligence Summaries are contained in F. S. Regs., Part II. and the Staff Manual respectively. Title pages will be prepared in manuscript.

Hour, Date, Place	Summary of Events and Information	Remarks and references to Appendices
LOUVENCOURT 14/10/16.	The unit was working hard to put the Rest Camp in order. Several Sanitary requirements were taken in hand and some of the huts repaired. B.C.	
LOUVENCOURT 15/10/16.	Nothing important to record B.C.	

(73989) W4141—463. 400,000. 9/14. H.&J.Ltd. Forms/C. 2118/10.

Instructions regarding War Diaries and Intelligence Summaries are contained in F. S. Regs., Part II. and the Staff Manual respectively. Title pages will be prepared in manuscript.

WAR DIARY
or
INTELLIGENCE ~~SUMMARY.~~

Army Form C. 2118.

(*Erase heading not required.*) 93rd Field Ambulance

Hour, Date, Place	Summary of Events and Information	Remarks and references to Appendices
LOUVENCOURT. 16/10/16.	Received the following orders. Secret 31st Division Copy No 1. RAMC operation Order No 5. By Col AM Bewley ADMS 31st Div Reference Map 57 D. 1/40000 The 94th Field Ambulance (complete) will take over the Main Dressing Station at COUIN (J. 1). Move to be completed by noon 17 inst. The 95th Field Ambulance will send. 1) One tent division to COIGNEAUX (J. 9a) Move to be completed by noon the 17 inst A Holding party will be sent to COIGNEUX.	

(73989) W4141—463. 400,000. 9/14. H.&J.Ltd. Forms/C. 2118/10.

Instructions regarding War Diaries and Intelligence Summaries are contained in F. S. Regs., Part II. and the Staff Manual respectively. Title pages will be prepared in manuscript.

WAR DIARY

or

~~INTELLIGENCE SUMMARY.~~

(*Erase heading not required.*) 93rd Field Ambulance

Army Form C. 2118.

Hour, Date, Place	Summary of Events and Information	Remarks and references to Appendices
	(Strength 1 officer and 7 other ranks) by 4pm the 16th inst.	
	2) One bearer subdivision will take over the advanced dressing Station at HEBUTERNE (K15 b 62) move to be completed by 4pm 16th inst.	
	3) One bearer subdivision will take over the advanced dressing station at COLINCAMPS (K25. c06) move to be completed by noon the 17th inst.	
	4) The 94th Field Ambulance will remain at the Corps Rest Station at LOUVENCOURT. One tent subdivision being sent to VAUCHELLES	

Instructions regarding War Diaries and Intelligence Summaries are contained in F. S. Regs., Part II. and the Staff Manual respectively. Title pages will be prepared in manuscript.

WAR DIARY

or

~~INTELLIGENCE SUMMARY.~~

(*Erase heading not required.*) 93rd Field Ambulance

Army Form C. 2118.

Hour, Date, Place	Summary of Events and Information	Remarks and references to Appendices
	as a temporary measure pending the evacuation or transfer of the sick already there. When the Corps Rest Station at VAUCHELLES has been closed a holding party of 1 NCO and 6 men will remain there 2) 23 other ranks will be sent to the Special operating centre at the CHATEAU AUTHIE by 4 pm the 16th inst 3) A holding party of 1 NCO and 6 men will be sent to the BOIS LALEAU (I 9 and 10) by 4 pm 16 inst. Completion of reliefs to be sent to this Office D.H.Q. 16/10/16 A.W. Bewley Col ADMS 31st Division	

(73989) W4141—463. 400,000. 9/14. H.&J.Ltd. Forms/C. 2118/10.

Instructions regarding War Diaries and Intelligence Summaries are contained in F. S. Regs., Part II. and the Staff Manual respectively. Title pages will be prepared in manuscript.

WAR DIARY

or

~~INTELLIGENCE SUMMARY.~~

(*Erase heading not required.*) 93rd Field Ambulance

Army Form C. 2118.

Hour, Date, Place	Summary of Events and Information	Remarks and references to Appendices
	In compliance with this order	
	Capt S. MILLING with one tent subdivision	
	was sent to VAUCHELLES	
	One N.C.O and 6 men were sent to the BOIS	
	LALEAU	
	The party of 2 3 men were not sent to AUTHIE	
	as a later order cancelled this move	
	B.C.	
LOUVENCOURT 17/10/16.	Received the following orders.	
	Secret. 31st Division Copy No1	
	R.A.M.C Operation Order No6.	
	By Col A.W. Bewley ADMS 31st Division	
	1). The Corps Rest Stations at LOUVENCOURT	

(73989) W4141—463. 400,000. 9/14. H.&J.Ltd. Forms/C. 2118/10.

Instructions regarding War Diaries and Intelligence Summaries are contained in F. S. Regs., Part II. and the Staff Manual respectively. Title pages will be prepared in manuscript.

WAR DIARY
or
~~INTELLIGENCE SUMMARY~~.
(Erase heading not required.) 93rd Field Ambulance

Army Form C. 2118.

Hour, Date, Place	Summary of Events and Information	Remarks and references to Appendices
	and VAUCHELLES will be handed over to No 7 Field Ambulance 3rd Division by 2pm the 18th inst	
	(2) Suitable cases for retention in the Rest Station should be transferred to the main dressing Station at COUIN and the remainder evacuated to the CCS OC. 93rd Field Ambulance will notify OC. 31st MAC direct as to the number of cases requiring transfer.	
	(3) The OC. 93rd Field Ambulance will hand over ~~to the~~ relieving unit all Stores and Equipment surplus to Mobilisation Equipment and obtain receipts.	

(73989) W4141—463. 400,000. 9/14. H.&J.Ltd. Forms/C. 2118/10.

Army Form C. 2118.

WAR DIARY
or
~~INTELLIGENCE SUMMARY.~~

(Erase heading not required.) 93rd Field Ambulance

Instructions regarding War Diaries and Intelligence Summaries are contained in F. S. Regs., Part II. and the Staff Manual respectively. Title pages will be prepared in manuscript.

Hour, Date, Place	Summary of Events and Information	Remarks and references to Appendices
	4) The 93rd Field Ambulance will on relief proceed to the huts at BOIS LALEU north of AUTHIE. and remain there closed.	
	5) The 94th Field Ambulance at COUIN will act as Rest Station for the Corps.	
	6). The 95th Field Ambulance at COIGNEUX will open as the main dressing Station	
	7). The 95th Field Ambulance will hand over the Advanced Dressing Station at COLINCAMPS to a Field Ambulance of 3rd Division by 2pm the 18th inst.	
	On relief the personnel now at COLINCAMPS	

Army Form C. 2118.

Instructions regarding War Diaries and Intelligence Summaries are contained in F. S. Regs., Part II. and the Staff Manual respectively. Title pages will be prepared in manuscript.

WAR DIARY
or
~~INTELLIGENCE SUMMARY.~~

(*Erase heading not required.*) 93rd Field Ambulance

Hour, Date, Place	Summary of Events and Information	Remarks and references to Appendices
	and BUS will rejoin their units at COIGNEUX.	
	8) The holding party of the 95th Field Ambulance at WARNIMONT Wood will remain there till further orders	
	9) The Clayton disinfector at LOUVENCOURT will be brought to the Rest Station at COUIN	
	Please report completion of action. Acknowledge.	
	G. W. Ware Major	
	D.H.Q 17/10/16 for Col A.D.M.S 31st Division	

(73989) W4141—463. 400,000. 9/14. H.&J.Ltd. Forms/C. 2118/10.

Instructions regarding War Diaries and Intelligence Summaries are contained in F. S. Regs., Part II. and the Staff Manual respectively. Title pages will be prepared in manuscript.

WAR DIARY

or

~~INTELLIGENCE SUMMARY.~~

(*Erase heading not required.*) 93rd Field Ambulance

Army Form C. 2118.

Hour, Date, Place	Summary of Events and Information	Remarks and references to Appendices
LOVENCOURT. 17/10/16	In compliance with instructions LIEUT. J. B. ALEXANDER was detailed to day to take over the duties of Medical Officer Northumberland Hussars in exchange with Capt Joseph Rame B.C.	
LOUVENCOURT. 18/10/16	In complying with the previous days orders., the whole morning was spent evacuating and transferring the Sick from the Rest Stations at LOUVENCOURT and VAUCHELLES. At 2pm these Stations were handed over to the 7th Field Ambulance ~~And~~ at 2.30pm the unit moved off for	

(73989) W4141—463. 400,000. 9/14. H.&J.Ltd. Forms/C. 2118/10.

Army Form C. 2118.

Instructions regarding War Diaries and Intelligence Summaries are contained in F. S. Regs., Part II. and the Staff Manual respectively. Title pages will be prepared in manuscript.

WAR DIARY

or

~~INTELLIGENCE SUMMARY.~~

(Erase heading not required.) 93rd Field Ambulance

Hour, Date, Place	Summary of Events and Information	Remarks and references to Appendices
	the BOIS LALEAU and reached there at 4pm. B.C	
BOIS LALEAU. 19/10/16.	Received instructions today for the Bearer Division at THIEVRES to rejoin Headquarters I accordingly sent an Order to Capt R.S. CUMMING to rejoin me without delay. B.C.	

(73989) W4141—463. 400,000. 9/14. H.&J.Ltd. Forms/C. 2118/10.

Instructions regarding War Diaries and Intelligence Summaries are contained in F. S. Regs., Part II. and the Staff Manual respectively. Title pages will be prepared in manuscript.

WAR DIARY
or
~~INTELLIGENCE SUMMARY.~~

(*Erase heading not required.*) 93rd Field Ambulance

Army Form C. 2118.

Hour, Date, Place	Summary of Events and Information	Remarks and references to Appendices
BOIS LALEAU. 19/10/16.	Lieut H.P. AUBREY in compliance with orders left this unit today on temporary duty with the 42nd Heavy Artillery Group.	
	Capt J. S. Humphreys proceeded to join the 13th Batt. York and Lancashire Regt in Relief of Capt Keay R.A.M.C	
	B.C	
BOIS LALEAU. 20/10/16.	I made an inspection of the Camp in this wood and employed a large Sanitary party putting the place in order.	
	Received the following message M 3079.	
	O.C 93rd Field Ambulance	
	The necessary repairs to roads & huts in	

Instructions regarding War Diaries and Intelligence Summaries are contained in F. S. Regs., Part II. and the Staff Manual respectively. Title pages will be prepared in manuscript.

WAR DIARY
or
~~INTELLIGENCE~~ SUMMARY.

(*Erase heading not required.*) 93rd Field Ambulance

Army Form C. 2118.

Hour, Date, Place	Summary of Events and Information	Remarks and references to Appendices
	the camp now occupied by your unit should be taken in hand and carried out as soon as possible. It is probable that from 150 to 200 wounded may be sent to the Camp.	
	A W Bewley Col ADMS 31st Div	
	20/10/16. BL	
BOIS LALEAU. 21/10/16.	Nothing important to record BL	

(73989) W4141—463. 400,000. 9/14. H.&J.Ltd. Forms/C. 2118/10.

215

WAR DIARY
or
~~INTELLIGENCE SUMMARY.~~

Army Form C. 2118.

Instructions regarding War Diaries and Intelligence Summaries are contained in F. S. Regs., Part II. and the Staff Manual respectively. Title pages will be prepared in manuscript.

(Erase heading not required.) 93rd Field Ambulance

Hour, Date, Place	Summary of Events and Information	Remarks and references to Appendices
22/10/16. BOIS. LALEAU.	Nothing important to record. B.C	
23/10/16 BOIS LALEAU.	Received the following message M3593. O.C. 93rd Field Ambulance Please direct Capt MILLING to proceed for temporary duty with the 95th Field Ambulance at COIGNEUX. He should report on the morning of the 24th inst D.H.Q. 23/10/16 G.W. Clare Major to Col A.D.M.S. 31st Divn	B.C.

Instructions regarding War Diaries and Intelligence Summaries are contained in F. S. Regs., Part II. and the Staff Manual respectively. Title pages will be prepared in manuscript.

WAR DIARY
or
~~INTELLIGENCE SUMMARY.~~

(*Erase heading not required.*) 93rd Field Ambulance

Army Form C. 2118.

Hour, Date, Place	Summary of Events and Information	Remarks and references to Appendices
24/10/16. BOIS LALAE	Capt MILLING proceeded this morning to the 95th Field Ambulance on temporary duty.	
	Received the following orders	
	31st Division	
	Secret. Copy No 1	
	R.A.M.C. operation Order No 7.	
	By	
	Col A.W. Bewley. A.D.M.S. 31st Division	
	Reference Mapp 57 D. 1:40.000 and Map HEBUTERNE 57 D. N.E. 3 and 4 1:10.000	
	I. Intention	
	An attack is to be delivered during the course	

(73989) W4141—463. 400,000. 9/14. H.&J.Ltd. Forms/C. 2118/10.

Instructions regarding War Diaries and Intelligence Summaries are contained in F. S. Regs., Part II. and the Staff Manual respectively. Title pages will be prepared in manuscript.

WAR DIARY
or
INTELLIGENCE ~~SUMMARY.~~
(Erase heading not required.) 93rd Field Ambulance

Army Form C. 2118.

Hour, Date, Place	Summary of Events and Information	Remarks and references to Appendices
	of the next few days by the V Corps on our right to capture the line MIRAUMONT. BEAUREGRAND DOVECOT. and the North of SERRE in conjunction with an attack by the II Corps from the South across the valley of the ANCRE. The 3rd Division of the V Corps is the division on our right and its objectives are shown on the attached Sketch in Green Yellow + Blue which denote the advance of the different waves. II. Roll of the 31st Division The 31st Division will attack on the left	

Instructions regarding War Diaries and Intelligence Summaries are contained in F. S. Regs., Part II. and the Staff Manual respectively. Title pages will be prepared in manuscript.

WAR DIARY
or
~~INTELLIGENCE SUMMARY~~.
(*Erase heading not required.*) 93rd Field Ambulance

Army Form C. 2118.

Hour, Date, Place	Summary of Events and Information	Remarks and references to Appendices
	of the 3rd Division extending the left of the attack from John Copse inclusive up to about the point. K23 b 30 where the road from TOUVENT FARM. to LA LOUVIERRE FARM crosses our front trenches. The Role of the 51st Division is to seize the line shown in blue in the sketch and form a defensive flank.	
	3. Troops taking part	
	The attack will be made by 2 Battalion of the 92nd Infantry Bgde and in addition the Brigade will find the necessary carrying parties	
	Two section 211 Field Coy RE. will be	

Instructions regarding War Diaries and Intelligence Summaries are contained in F. S. Regs., Part II. and the Staff Manual respectively. Title pages will be prepared in manuscript.

WAR DIARY
or
~~INTELLIGENCE SUMMARY.~~

(Erase heading not required.) 93rd Field Ambulance

Army Form C. 2118.

Hour, Date, Place	Summary of Events and Information	Remarks and references to Appendices
	attached to assist in the construction of strong points.	
	2 Companies 12th KOYLI. (Pioneers) will undertake the Construction of communication trenches from our present lines to the enemies present front line.	
	(4) Communication Trenches	
	NAIRNE and JEAN BART. in Trenches and Home out trenches are available in our lines. NAIRNE and Home trench are entirely at the disposal of the 92nd Inf Bgde which will also have prior rights over the 93rd Inf Bgde on JEAN BART.	
	5. The Collection and evacuation of wounded	

(73989) W4141—463. 400,000. 9/14. H.&J.Ltd. Forms/C. 2118/10.

40

Army Form C. 2118.

WAR DIARY
or
~~INTELLIGENCE SUMMARY.~~
(*Erase heading not required.*) 93rd Field Ambulance

Instructions regarding War Diaries and Intelligence Summaries are contained in F. S. Regs., Part II. and the Staff Manual respectively. Title pages will be prepared in manuscript.

Hour, Date, Place	Summary of Events and Information	Remarks and references to Appendices
	from Regimental Aid Posts will be carried out by the 95th Field Ambulance. The Bearer division of the 93rd Field Ambulance will be in reserve at COIGNEUX and ~~that~~ of the 94th Field Ambulance will be at COUIN in readiness to move forward when required	
	One Officer and 38 other ranks with 18 stretchers will be at the collecting post in Papin trench (K21. c 97).	
	They will clear wounded from Regimental Aid Posts in or near Home Avenue to the Collecting Post in PAPIN TRENCH.	
	EVACUATION from this Collecting Post will	

41

Instructions regarding War Diaries and Intelligence Summaries are contained in F. S. Regs., Part II. and the Staff Manual respectively. Title pages will be prepared in manuscript.

WAR DIARY
or
~~INTELLIGENCE SUMMARY.~~

(*Erase heading not required.*) 93rd Field Ambulance

Army Form C. 2118.

Place	Date	Hour	Summary of Events and Information	Remarks and references to Appendices
			be carried out by the bearer Subdivision at the Advanced Dressing Station HEBUTERNE using PAPIN Trench or the tram line near HEBUTERNE – PARC A MOUTONS Road. In the event of heavy shelling on this Road evacuation will be done by means of Motor Ambulances which will be sent to point K20c23. returning to the main Dressing Station via COLINCAMPS and SAILLY AU BOIS.	
			b) At the Advanced Dressing Station HEBUTERNE one tent Subdivision and 2 Bearer Subdivisions 95th Field Ambulance	
			c). At Main Dressing Station COIGNEUX two tent subdivisions 95th Field Ambulance and Bearer Division 93rd Field Ambulance.	
			7.) <u>System of Reliefs</u>	
			Eight hours after ZERO the Bearers of the 95th Field Ambulance will be relieved by the Bearer Division 93rd Field Ambulance returning to the Main Dressing Station to rest.	
			After a further period of eight hours the bearer division 95th Field Ambulance will relieve that of the 93rd Field Ambulance	

Army Form C. 2118. 42

Instructions regarding War Diaries and Intelligence Summaries are contained in F. S. Regs., Part II. and the Staff Manual respectively. Title pages will be prepared in manuscript.

WAR DIARY
or
~~INTELLIGENCE SUMMARY.~~
(*Erase heading not required.*) 93rd Field Ambulance

Place	Date	Hour	Summary of Events and Information	Remarks and references to Appendices
			who will return to the Main Dressing Station. O's C Field Ambulances will arrange for hot meals and accommodation for the bearers when relieved.	
			8). Walking Wounded will proceed via marked route to the Cemetery South of SAILLY AU BOIS. from whence they will be taken to the Walking Wounded Collecting Station at J10 c 22 in Horsed Ambulance Wagons.	
			9). Disposal of Motor Ambulances.	
			18 Motor Ambulances will be distributed as follows.	
			5 Fords and 5 Heavy Motor Ambulances at COIGNEUX.	
			7 Heavy Motor Ambulances at COIN, and one Ford at Divisional Headquarters.	
			Detailed orders re distribution will be issued later.	
			10) Horse Ambulance Wagons of all three Field Ambulances will be sent to the Walking Wounded Collecting Station at J10 c 22 at an hour to be notified later.	

Instructions regarding War Diaries and Intelligence Summaries are contained in F. S. Regs., Part II. and the Staff Manual respectively. Title pages will be prepared in manuscript.

WAR DIARY
or
~~INTELLIGENCE~~ SUMMARY.
(Erase heading not required.) 93rd Field Ambulance

Army Form C. 2118.

4

Place	Date	Hour	Summary of Events and Information	Remarks and references to Appendices
			11). Orders contained in Medical arrangements XIII Corps Operations No 2. dated 9/10/16. re Sick, Gas Cases, Infectious diseases, Self Inflicted Wounds, Antitetanic Serum, German Wounded, Field Medical Cards and Returns will be carefully complied with.	
			12) Surplus Medical Stores & Equipment.	
			A reserve of blankets, stretchers, medical Comforts, dressings etc. is held at the Main Dressing Station COIGNEUX. Demands will be made in writing and the O.C. Main Dressing Station will send Supplies required to the Advanced Dressing Stations or Walking Wound Collecting Station by returning empty Ambulances.	
			Acknowledge.	
			A.W. Bewley Col. A.D.M.S. 31st Division	
			D.H.Q. 23rd Oct 1916.	
			B.C.	

2353 Wt. W2544/1454 700,000 5/15 D. D. & L. A.D.S.S./Forms/C. 2118.

Instructions regarding War Diaries and Intelligence Summaries are contained in F. S. Regs., Part II. and the Staff Manual respectively. Title pages will be prepared in manuscript.

WAR DIARY
or
~~INTELLIGENCE SUMMARY.~~

(*Erase heading not required.*) 93rd Field Ambulance

Army Form C. 2118.

Place	Date	Hour	Summary of Events and Information	Remarks and references to Appendices
BOIS LALEAU.	25/10/16		Received the following Operation Orders. Secret. D.D.M.S. XIII Corps. No 457/48. Medical Arrangements XIII Corps. Operation No 3. 1. The following will be the medical arrangements for the evacuation of wounded during active operations on the 31st Divisional Front extending from John Copse as far north as K29. c 6.2 Two Battalions will be engaged. 2. Position of medical Units The Field Ambulances of the 31st Division will be located as follows Couin — one Field Ambulance COIGNEUX — one tent division BOIS LALEAU — one tent division In Line — Two bearer divisions In addition to the above, the following will be established	

2353 Wt. W2544/1454 700,000 5/15 D. D. & L. A.D.S.S./Forms/C. 2118.

Instructions regarding War Diaries and Intelligence Summaries are contained in F. S. Regs., Part II. and the Staff Manual respectively. Title pages will be prepared in manuscript.

WAR DIARY
or
~~INTELLIGENCE~~ SUMMARY.
(Erase heading not required.) 93rd Field Ambulance

Army Form C. 2118.

Place	Date	Hour	Summary of Events and Information	Remarks and references to Appendices
			(a) Walking Wounded Collecting Station J.10. c.2.3 (b) Walking Wounded Collecting Post SAILLY Cemetery (c) Control Post about K20 d 9.7. (d) Car Changing Station at a point to be fixed by A.D.M.S. 31st Division on COURCELLES - COIGNEUX Road for cases evacuated from K20. c 2.2. The personnel for (a) will be provided as laid down in this office No 457/21. dated 10th inst with the addition of a water cart with horses, driver and orderly. The personnel for b and c. will be detailed by A.D.M.S. 31st Division as he considers necessary. (3) Evacuations from the Line Cases will be conveyed via Home trench to K20. c.2.2 or through PAPIN trench to the Advanced dressing Station at HEBUTERNE but every endeavour must be made to evacuate as far as possible by the Southern route.	

A6

Army Form C. 2118.

Instructions regarding War Diaries and Intelligence Summaries are contained in F. S. Regs., Part II. and the Staff Manual respectively. Title pages will be prepared in manuscript.

WAR DIARY
or
~~INTELLIGENCE SUMMARY.~~
(Erase heading not required.) 93rd Field Ambulance

Place	Date	Hour	Summary of Events and Information	Remarks and references to Appendices
			From HEBUTERNE cases will be conveyed in Motor Ambulances direct to COIGNEUX, and from K20c32 in Ford Cars via COLINCAMPS to the Car Changing Station, and from there in Ambulance cars to the Main dressing Stations at COINGNEUX and COIN, the latter being used as a place of overflow.	
			From the end of home trench (K20d97.) all walking cases will be directed to proceed by a cross country track suitably marked by boards to the Cemetery at SAILLY-AU-BOIS. From there they will be conveyed in horsed ambulance wagons to the Walking Wounded Collecting Station at J10.c32.	
			(4). Evacuations to Casualty Clearing Stations.	
			(a) Lying Wounded. From the dressing Stations lying cases will be evacuated to No 20 and 43 Casualty Clearing Stations, WARLINCOURT HALTE. in cars of No. Motor Ambulance Convoy.	
			(b) Walking Wounded. Walking Wounded will be sent to the	

47

Army Form C. 2118.

Instructions regarding War Diaries and Intelligence Summaries are contained in F. S. Regs., Part II. and the Staff Manual respectively. Title pages will be prepared in manuscript.

WAR DIARY
or
~~INTELLIGENCE~~ SUMMARY.

(*Erase heading not required.*) 93rd Field Ambulance

Place	Date	Hour	Summary of Events and Information	Remarks and references to Appendices
			same Casualty Clearing Stations as lying and sitting cases. Four buses will be available for this purpose. Walking cases that do not require immediate redressing will have an O put on the right hand bottom corner of the envelope of the Field Medical Card.	
			(c). Shell Shock. All cases of shell shock will be sent to the Field Ambulance at COUIN where they will be dealt with as laid down in D.M.S. Reserve Army No 11/22 dated 24/8/16 forwarded under this Office No 2432 dated 13th inst.	
			(d) Gas Cases all gassed cases will be sent lying down to the Field Ambulance at COUIN.	
			(e). Sick. All Sick will be sent to the Field Ambulance at COUIN. During active operations only very urgent cases will be evacuated, these will be sent to Nos 20 and 43 Casualty Clearing Stations. WARLINCOURT HALTE.	
			(f) Cases of defective vision. During active operations	

2353 Wt. W2544/1454 700,000 5/15 D. D. & L. A.D.S.S./Forms/C. 2118.

48

Army Form C. 2118.

Instructions regarding War Diaries and Intelligence Summaries are contained in F. S. Regs., Part II. and the Staff Manual respectively. Title pages will be prepared in manuscript.

WAR DIARY

or

~~INTELLIGENCE SUMMARY.~~

(Erase heading not required.) 93rd Field Ambulance

Place	Date	Hour	Summary of Events and Information	Remarks and references to Appendices
			the treatment of cases of this nature will be in abeyance. The only cases to be sent to AMIENS are those of disease of the eye of an urgent nature. (g) Infectious disease Cases. These will be sent to 2/1st South Midland ~~Field Ambulance~~ C.C.S at Recmenil Farm. (h). Self inflicted Wounds. All cases of Self inflicted Wounds will be evacuated to 2/1st South Midland C.C.S Recmenil Farm. (j) German Wounded. Wounded prisoners of war will be dealt with in exactly the same manner as laid down for British Wounded. (k) Indian Sick and Wounded. Any Indian Sick and wounded who may be admitted to Field Ambulances or Dressing Stations will be sent to 35 CCS Doullens. (5.) Antitetanic Serum.	

2353 Wt. W2544/1454 700,000 5/15 D. D. & L. A.D.S.S./Forms/C. 2118.

147

Army Form C. 2118.

Instructions regarding War Diaries and Intelligence Summaries are contained in F. S. Regs., Part II. and the Staff Manual respectively. Title pages will be prepared in manuscript.

WAR DIARY
or
~~INTELLIGENCE SUMMARY.~~
(Erase heading not required.)

93rd Field Ambulance

Place	Date	Hour	Summary of Events and Information	Remarks and references to Appendices
			Arrangements will be made for antitetanic Serum to be given in the Dressing Stations at COIGNEUX and COIN and at Walking Wounded Collecting Station. Under no circumstances must it be administered in Regimental Aid Posts or Advance Dressing Stations.	
			(6) Motor Ambulance Cars.	
			The motor Ambulance cars at the disposal of the Corps for all purposes will be the divisional Ambulance cars and one section (15 cars) of 31 Motor Ambulance Convoy. Ambulance cars must move off as soon as loaded and they must on no account travel in Convoy.	
			(7) Reports.	
			The present routine reports and returns will continue to be sent to D.M.S. Reserve Army and to this Office. In addition the following messages are required to be sent daily by wire:	

2353 Wt. W2544/1454 700,000 5/15 D. D. & L. A.D.S.S./Forms/C. 2118.

Instructions regarding War Diaries and Intelligence Summaries are contained in F. S. Regs., Part II. and the Staff Manual respectively. Title pages will be prepared in manuscript.

WAR DIARY
or
~~INTELLIGENCE SUMMARY.~~
(Erase heading not required.) 93rd Field Ambulance

Army Form C. 2118.

Place	Date	Hour	Summary of Events and Information	Remarks and references to Appendices
			(a) As soon after 6 AM and 5 pm as possible the numbers of wounded only (1) admitted to Field Ambulances in the intervals between 6 am and 5 pm and 5 pm and 6 am Officers, other ranks, Indians and Prisoners of War to be distinguished, and (ii) remaining in the whole Field Ambulances distinguishing lying and sitting cases thus:—	
			"To DDMS 13th Corps No 111. 5th AAA. Admitted since 6 am Officers 10 other ranks 120. Indians 6. Germans 47. AAA Remaining lying 78 sitting 120 AAA.	
			From ADMS 31st Division	
			(b) The wire re Shell Shock and gassed cases referred to in this Office No 432 dtd 13th inst at 6 am daily	
			(C) Notification of change of position of any Field Ambulance or that portion of it forming a main dressing	

2353 Wt. W2544/1454 700,000 5/15 D. D. & L. A.D.S.S./Forms/C. 2118.

51

Army Form C. 2118.

Instructions regarding War Diaries and Intelligence Summaries are contained in F. S. Regs., Part II. and the Staff Manual respectively. Title pages will be prepared in manuscript.

WAR DIARY
or
~~INTELLIGENCE SUMMARY.~~

(*Erase heading not required.*) 93rd Field Ambulance

Place	Date	Hour	Summary of Events and Information	Remarks and references to Appendices
			Station.	
			The Officer i/c Walking Wounded Collecting Station will render his returns to A.D.M.S 31st Division, who will combine them with the figures received from the Field Ambulances.	
			(8). Medical Arrangements XIII Corps Operations now are hereby cancelled.	
			Acknowledge	
			J. Cree. Col DDMS XIII Corps	
			24 Oct 1916.	
			BC	
BOIS LALEAU	26/10/16.		In Compliance with the above I detailed Capt R S CUNNINGHAM and LIEUT C.E. MERRYON to reconnoitre the trenches on the 31st Divisional front.	

2353 Wt. W2544/1454 700,000 5/15 D. D. & L. A.D.S.S./Forms/C. 2118.

Instructions regarding War Diaries and Intelligence Summaries are contained in F. S. Regs., Part II. and the Staff Manual respectively. Title pages will be prepared in manuscript.

Army Form C. 2118.

WAR DIARY
or
~~INTELLIGENCE~~ SUMMARY.
(Erase heading not required.) 93rd Field Ambulance

Place	Date	Hour	Summary of Events and Information	Remarks and references to Appendices
BOIS LALEAU	27/10/16		Sent 1 N.C.O and 30 men to assist 95th Field Ambulance in improving the dugout at the A.D.S HEBUTERNE. Sent 1 N.C.O and 10 men to hold huts at the DELL as rest Station for the Bearer division on the outbreak of hostilities B.C.	
BOIS LALEAU	28/10/16		Nothing important to record B.C.	
BOIS LALEAU	29/10/16		Nothing important to record B.C.	

2353 Wt. W2544/1454 700,000 5/15 D. D. & L. A.D.S.S./Forms/C. 2118.

Army Form C. 2118.

Instructions regarding War Diaries and Intelligence Summaries are contained in F. S. Regs., Part II. and the Staff Manual respectively. Title pages will be prepared in manuscript.

WAR DIARY
or
~~INTELLIGENCE SUMMARY.~~

(*Erase heading not required.*) 93rd Field Ambulance

Place	Date	Hour	Summary of Events and Information	Remarks and references to Appendices
BOIS LALEAU	30/10/16.		The D.D.M.S. XIII Corps made an inspection of this camp today	
		7 pm.	Received the following message: Secret. S. 238. O.C. 93rd Field Ambulance Proposed operations will take place on 5th November 1916. ZERO hour will be communicated later. This memo not to pass through the hands of clerks Please acknowledge G. W. Ware Major for Col A.D.M.S. 31st Division D.H.Q. 30/10/16	
BOIS LALEAU	31/10/16		Nothing important to record.	

B. Connell Lieut Col
O.C. 93rd Field Ambulance

2353 Wt. W2544/1454 700,000 5/15 D. D. & L. A.D.S.S./Forms/C. 2118.

Confidential

Volume XI

Vol 9

War Diary

93rd Field Ambulance

31st Division

November 1916.

Nov. 1916

31st Div.

140/1762

5

93rd Field Ambulance

Instructions regarding War Diaries and Intelligence Summaries are contained in F. S. Regs., Part II. and the Staff Manual respectively. Title pages will be prepared in manuscript.

WAR DIARY
or
~~INTELLIGENCE SUMMARY.~~

(*Erase heading not required.*) 93rd Field Ambulance

Army Form C. 2118.

Place	Date	Hour	Summary of Events and Information	Remarks and references to Appendices
BOIS LALEAU.	1/11/16		The unit has been busily employed repairing the huts in the BOIS LALEAU. Most of which are in a very bad state of repair and scarcely fit for the reception of sick in Winter. BC	
BOIS LALEAU.	2/11/16		Capt C.E. NERYON was posted to the 165 Bgde RFA and was struck off the strength of this unit in compliance with orders. I made a careful inspection of the trenches today with a view to locating the medical Aid Posts during the coming operations. I found two battle support trenches but the Aid posts for the Right and left Battalions attacking the attack would not be discovered anywhere. I reported the matter to the ADMS 31st Division	
BOIS LALEAU	3/11/16		Nothing important to record BC	
BOIS LALEAU	4/11/16		Received the following message S.257. Secret OC 93rd F Ambulance The operations by 5th Army N+S of ANCRE are postponed	

2353 Wt. W2544/1454 700,000 5/15 D. D. & L. A.D.S.S./Forms/C. 2118.

Instructions regarding War Diaries and Intelligence Summaries are contained in F. S. Regs., Part II. and the Staff Manual respectively. Title pages will be prepared in manuscript.

WAR DIARY
or
~~INTELLIGENCE SUMMARY.~~

(*Erase heading not required.*) 93rd Field Ambulance

Army Form C. 2118.

Place	Date	Hour	Summary of Events and Information	Remarks and references to Appendices
			till indefinite date. Warning of date eventually fixed will be notified not later than noon on W day.	
			Sd. G. W. Ware Major for Col ADMS 31st Div	
			~~B C Lieut Col~~ ~~OC 93rd Field Ambulance~~	
			4/11/16. B.C.	
BOIS LALEAU	5/11/16		The following is an extract from letter M/1538/10. dated 4/11/16 Lieut McDOUGALL has been appointed O/C Baths in the divisional area. For the present your personnel should remain, but this Office will in future be responsible for all arrangements.	
			4/11/16. Sd. A. W. Beeley. Col ADMS 31st Div	
			B.C.	
BOIS LALEAU	6/11/16		Nothing important to record B.C.	

Instructions regarding War Diaries and Intelligence Summaries are contained in F. S. Regs., Part II. and the Staff Manual respectively. Title pages will be prepared in manuscript.

WAR DIARY
or
~~INTELLIGENCE SUMMARY~~.
(Erase heading not required.) 93rd Field Ambulance

Army Form C. 2118.

Place	Date	Hour	Summary of Events and Information	Remarks and references to Appendices
BOIS LALEAU.	7/11/16.		In Compliance with orders Lieut H.S.C. BLACKMORE was reported to the 94th Field Ambulance and struck off the strength of this unit.	
BOIS LALEAU.			Captain R. McKinnon RAMC (S.R.) joined this unit for duty from No 4 CCS. B.C.	
BOIS LALEAU	8/11/16.		Inspected the Working party working at the Collecting Post at HEBUTERNE. The trenches were in an extremely bad condition and the men were working without gum boots which are most essential under these conditions. As this work is not as urgent as it was a fortnight ago, I have issued instructions that the party should return to headquarters and have informed the OC 95th Field Ambulance to relieve them, with men from his own unit the work of Construction being under his Charge. B.C.	

2353 Wt. W2544/1454 700,000 5/15 D. D. & L. A.D.S.S./Forms/C. 2118.

Instructions regarding War Diaries and Intelligence Summaries are contained in F. S. Regs., Part II. and the Staff Manual respectively. Title pages will be prepared in manuscript.

WAR DIARY
or
~~INTELLIGENCE~~ SUMMARY.
(Erase heading not required.) 93rd Field Ambulance

Army Form C. 2118.

Place	Date	Hour	Summary of Events and Information	Remarks and references to Appendices
BOIS LALEAU	9/11/16.		I was informed that about 10 huts would be appropriated by the Corps for the accommodation of troops in the BOIS LALEAU. B.C.	
BOIS LALEAU	10/11/16.		The Camp was inspected by the D.D.M.S XIII Corps who suggested that the huts should be removed out of the wood into the open fields adjoin. I recalled the working party from the trenches and reported to the A.D.M.S 31st division the necessity of supplying these men with gum boots if this work must be continued. I also represented ~~that~~ this matter to the D.D.M.S XIII Corps. B.C.	
BOIS LALEAU	11/11/16		Received the following message. O.C. 93rd Field Ambulance. Proposed operations will take place on the 13th inst.	

Army Form C. 2118.

Instructions regarding War Diaries and Intelligence Summaries are contained in F. S. Regs., Part II. and the Staff Manual respectively. Title pages will be prepared in manuscript.

WAR DIARY
or
~~INTELLIGENCE SUMMARY.~~
(Erase heading not required.) 93rd Field Ambulance

Place	Date	Hour	Summary of Events and Information	Remarks and references to Appendices
			ZERO hour will be communicated later. This memo is not to pass through the hands of Clerks Acknowledge. Sd. G. W. Ware. Major for Col A.D. M.S. 31st Division DHQ 10/11/16. S 257. B C.	

2353 Wt. W2544/1454 700,000 5/15 D. D. & L. A.D.S.S./Forms/C. 2118.

Instructions regarding War Diaries and Intelligence Summaries are contained in F. S. Regs., Part II. and the Staff Manual respectively. Title pages will be prepared in manuscript.

WAR DIARY
or
~~INTELLIGENCE~~ SUMMARY.

(*Erase heading not required.*) 93rd Field Ambulance

Army Form C. 2118.

Place	Date	Hour	Summary of Events and Information	Remarks and references to Appendices
BOIS. LALEAU.	10/11/16		Received the following Secret. D D M S No 457/55 dtd 10/11/16 The A D M S 40th Division Please detail a bearer division of one of your Field Ambulances to take over from the 49th Division on the morning of the 13th inst. the following places. Advanced Dressing Station HEBUTERNE (K9 d 3 3). Dugouts for Personnel at K 15. a. 7. 9. west of HEBUTERNE. Advanced Dressing Station at SAILLY DELL (J 16. b 9 2.) You should instruct an officer to proceed to the above places at the earliest opportunity to arrange for the taking over Evacuations from the line will be to the 95th Field Ambulance COIGNEUX. Please arrange details direct with A D M S	

2353 Wt. W2544/1454 700,000 5/15 D. D. & L. A.D.S.S./Forms/C. 2118.

Army Form C. 2118.

Instructions regarding War Diaries and Intelligence Summaries are contained in F. S. Regs., Part II. and the Staff Manual respectively. Title pages will be prepared in manuscript.

WAR DIARY
or
~~INTELLIGENCE SUMMARY.~~
(Erase heading not required.)

93rd Field Ambce

Place	Date	Hour	Summary of Events and Information	Remarks and references to Appendices
			31st Division	
			Sd. G. Cree	
			Col.	
			10th Nov 1916	
			DDMS XIII Corps	
			In Connection with the above the following memorandum was received from ADMS 31st Division	
			S 260	
			OC. 93rd Field Ambulance.	
			Reference attached order from DDMS XIII Corps which has been since modified by wire detailing this division for the duty instead of the 40th Division	
			(1). The bearer division of your Field Ambulance is detailed for this duty.	
			(2) The Advance party should proceed on the morning of the 13th inst. to take over and the remainder of the	

2353 Wt. W2544/1454 700,000 5/15 D. D. & L. A.D.S.S./Forms/C. 2118.

Instructions regarding War Diaries and Intelligence Summaries are contained in F. S. Regs., Part II. and the Staff Manual respectively. Title pages will be prepared in manuscript.

WAR DIARY
or
~~INTELLIGENCE~~ SUMMARY.

(*Erase heading not required.*) 93rd Field Ambulance

Army Form C. 2118.

Place	Date	Hour	Summary of Events and Information	Remarks and references to Appendices
			Division will proceed on the morning of the 14th inst (3) All bearers at present working in the line should be withdrawn for 24 hours rest. (4). The dugouts, at present held by you in the DELL should be retained Sd G. W. Ware Major for Col ADMS 31st Div DHQ 11/11/16. In compliance with the above orders I detailed Capt R. S. CUMMING to proceed to HEBUTERNE and arrange for the taking over of the posts detailed in these orders. BC	

Army Form C. 2118.

WAR DIARY
or
~~INTELLIGENCE~~ SUMMARY.
(Erase heading not required.)

93rd Field Ambce

Instructions regarding War Diaries and Intelligence Summaries are contained in F. S. Regs., Part II. and the Staff Manual respectively. Title pages will be prepared in manuscript.

Place	Date	Hour	Summary of Events and Information	Remarks and references to Appendices
BOIS LA DEAU	13/11/16		In connection with the following memoranda received from the ADMS 31st Division Urgent O.C. 93rd Field Ambulance Please arrange to send 2 bearer subdivisions to the Main Dressing Station at COIGNEUX by 11 am tomorrow 13 11 16 stretchers and equipment should be taken with one days rations S. R W Bewley Col ADMS 31st Division D.H.Q. 12/11/16 7.25 P.M. The above order was complied with. The following was received from ADMS 31st Division O.C. 93 Field Ambulance You will take over the Advanced Dressing Station in	

2353 Wt. W2544/1454 700,000 5/15 D. D. & L. A.D.S.S./Forms/C. 2118.

Instructions regarding War Diaries and Intelligence Summaries are contained in F. S. Regs., Part II. and the Staff Manual respectively. Title pages will be prepared in manuscript.

WAR DIARY
or
INTELLIGENCE SUMMARY.
(Erase heading not required.)

Army Form C. 2118.

93rd Field Ambulance

Place	Date	Hour	Summary of Events and Information	Remarks and references to Appendices
BOIS LALEAU	13/11/16		HEBUTERNE and the collecting Post in SAILLY on BOIS from 1/2 W.R. Field Ambulance. Relief to be completed by noon on 15th inst. The following personnel will be sent: A.D.S. HEBUTERNE. 1 Officer, 1 Sergt 18 Other Ranks at SAILLY in the Dell 1 Sergt 2 Other Ranks Relieving party to report to O.C. 1/2 W Riding Field Ambulance at D26 central on morning of 14th inst. Sd. J. W. Weare for Colonel A.D.M.S. 31st Division D.H.Q. 12.11.16 In compliance with the above orders Capt R. MacKinnon was detailed with 1 Sergt + 20 other Ranks and took over as arranged. The following memoranda was received from the A.D.M.S. 31st Urgent O.C. 93 Field Ambulance	

2353 Wt. W2544/1454 700,000 5/15 D. D. & L. A.D.S.S./Forms/C. 2118.

Instructions regarding War Diaries and Intelligence Summaries are contained in F. S. Regs., Part II. and the Staff Manual respectively. Title pages will be prepared in manuscript.

WAR DIARY
or
~~INTELLIGENCE SUMMARY.~~
(Erase heading not required.)

93rd Field Amb[ulan]ce

Army Form C. 2118.

Place	Date	Hour	Summary of Events and Information	Remarks and references to Appendices
BOIS LALEAU	13/11/16		Please detail an officer to proceed forthwith to main Dressing Station COIGNEUX to assist OC 93 Field Ambulance // Please send four hours reliefs for the horses and drivers of your horsed ambulance. Sd Geo W Ware Maj for Colonel A DMS 31st Div DA2 13/11/16 Capt J.N. Pooley was sent to COIGNEUX. Part II of the order was also complied with. The following wire was received from A.D.M.S. 31st Division OC 93 Field Ambulance Detail fourteen other Ranks R.A.M.C. to proceed forthwith to No 44 C.C. Station PUCHEVILLERS for temporary duty AAA report departure AAA MEDICAL 31st Division 14/11/16 (11.45 P.M.) DA7 Sd A W Bewley Col ADMS 31st Division	

2353 Wt. W2544/1454 700,000 5/15 D. D. & L. A.D.S.S./Forms/C. 2118.

Instructions regarding War Diaries and Intelligence Summaries are contained in F. S. Regs., Part II. and the Staff Manual respectively. Title pages will be prepared in manuscript.

WAR DIARY
or
~~INTELLIGENCE SUMMARY.~~
(Erase heading not required.)

93rd Field Ambce

Army Form C. 2118.

Place	Date	Hour	Summary of Events and Information	Remarks and references to Appendices
BOIS LALEAU	15/11/16		This wire was complied with Reference B27 dated 14/11/16 To O.C. 44 C.C.S. Herewith 14 men detailed for temporary duty with you Please notify me arrival Sd B. Connell Lt Col O.C. 93 Field Ambulance signed R. MacKinnon Capt RAMC SR for Lt Col H.B. Connell O.C. 93 Field Ambulance.	
BOIS LALEAU	15/11/16		I have to report that Lt Col H. B. Connell R.A.M.C. O.C. 93 Field Ambulance whilst visiting the Advanced Dressing Station at HEBUTERNE was wounded. Acting under instructions from the A.D.M.S. 31st division I took over temporary command of the 93rd F. Ambulance. RMacKinnon Capt. R.A.M.C (S.R.)	

2353 Wt. W2544/1454 700,000 5/15 D. D. & L. A.D.S.S./Forms/C. 2118.

Instructions regarding War Diaries and Intelligence Summaries are contained in F. S. Regs., Part II. and the Staff Manual respectively. Title pages will be prepared in manuscript.

WAR DIARY
or
~~INTELLIGENCE SUMMARY.~~
(Erase heading not required.)

93rd Field Ambce

Army Form C. 2118.

Place	Date	Hour	Summary of Events and Information	Remarks and references to Appendices
BOIS LALEAU	15/11/16		The following letter was sent to A.D.M.S 31st Division. Lt Col H.B. Connell R.A.M.C. is reported wounded, Capt. R. Mackinnon, R.A.M.C (S.R.) taking duty. R Mackinnon Capt. R.A.M.C. (S.R.)	
	~~16/11/16~~ Rm 16/11/16		Nothing to report. The following telegram was received from A.D.M.S. 31st Division. "I regret to report that Lieut. Col. H.B. CONNELL. R.A.M.C. died from wounds" Rm. 16/11/16. D.D.M.S. XIII CORPS. He is deeply regretted by all ranks of the unit he commanded.	
	17/11/16		Nothing to report Rm.	
	18/11/16		On instructions from D.D.M.S. XIII CORPS. I assumed command of 93rd F.A. vice late Lieut. Col. H. B. CONNELL died of wounds received in action 16.11.16. [illegible] Capt. RAMC	
	19.11.16.		I completed taking over unit from Capt. R. MACKINNON and notified A.D.M.S. 31st DIVISION of the procedure [illegible]	
	20/11/16.		Following order appeared in DIVISION ORDERS:—	

2353 Wt. W2544/1454 700,000 5/15 D. D. & L. A.D.S.S./Forms/C. 2118.

Instructions regarding War Diaries and Intelligence Summaries are contained in F. S. Regs., Part II. and the Staff Manual respectively. Title pages will be prepared in manuscript.

WAR DIARY
or
~~INTELLIGENCE~~ SUMMARY.
(Erase heading not required.)

Army Form C. 2118.

93rd Field Ambce

Place	Date	Hour	Summary of Events and Information	Remarks and references to Appendices
BOIS LALEAU			STRENGTH.	
	19. 11. 16.		CAPT. A.M. POLLARD. R.A.M.C. reported for duty with this division 18.11.16 & assumed command of 93rd F.A. from that date vice LIEUT. COL. H.B. CONNELL R.A.M.C. (died of wounds)	AMP
	20.11.16.		~~I inspected A.D.S. at HEBUTERNE. Also posts at SAILLY DELL. In accordance with permission from A.D.M.S. I handed over (temporarily & to be vacated immediately if required) 2 huts & 1 cookhouse to O.C. 94 MACHINE GUN COY, belonging to the post on SAILLY - COURCELLES ROAD.~~	
			(TY.) Capt. L.C. E. MURPHY and (Ty.) Capt. J.M. MACPHAIL joined this unit for duty this day	AMP
	21.11.16.		I inspected A.D.S. at HEBUTERNE & A.D.S. at SAILLY DELL. Also collecting post on SAILLY - COURCELLES RD. With permission of A.D.M.S. I handed over two huts and a cookhouse of this last to O.C. 94. MACHINE GUN COY., to be returned immediately, should the necessity arise.	AMP

Instructions regarding War Diaries and Intelligence Summaries are contained in F. S. Regs., Part II. and the Staff Manual respectively. Title pages will be prepared in manuscript.

WAR DIARY
or
INTELLIGENCE SUMMARY.
(Erase heading not required.)

93rd Field Ambce

Army Form C. 2118.

Place	Date	Hour	Summary of Events and Information	Remarks and references to Appendices
BOIS LALEAU.				
	22. 11. 16.		I inspected the holding post in WARNIMONT WOOD.	
			Capt. T. MULLING rejoined from detached duty at 95. F.A.	
			Capt. R.S. CUMMINS rejoined with 18 rank & file from ADS. HEBUTERNE. (A Sectn)	
			Capt. H.M. JOSEPH with 18 rank & file (B. Sectn). proceeded for duty to above in relief.	
			Party at A.D.S. SAILLY DELL was relieved, & one additional man sent. Party at collecting post on SAILLY-COURCELLES RD. relieved & replaced by one corporal & one man (all B. Sectn)	
			14 Rank & file rejoined from temporary duty at 44 C.C.S. PUCHEVILLERS.	AW.
	23. 11. 16.		CAPT. CONNELL R.A.M.C joined this unit for duty from 94. F.A.	
			Under instructions from ADMS. M. 3717. I detailed Capt. T. MULLING. R.A.M.C. for temporary duty with 12th Bn. YORKS & LANCASTER Rt. He reported to 94th Bde Hqrs SAILLY au BOIS.	AW.
	24. 11. 16,		I have now managed to obtain some wood & wire netting for bunking & flooring the huts. Adjt. D.W. R.E. has promised to send his skilled workmen to assist,	

2353 Wt. W2544/1454 700,000 5/15 D. D. & L. A.D.S.S./Forms/C. 2118.

Instructions regarding War Diaries and Intelligence Summaries are contained in F. S. Regs., Part II. and the Staff Manual respectively. Title pages will be prepared in manuscript.

WAR DIARY
or
~~INTELLIGENCE SUMMARY.~~

(Erase heading not required.)

Army Form C. 2118.

93rd Field Ambce

Place	Date	Hour	Summary of Events and Information	Remarks and references to Appendices
BOIS LALEAU			CAPT. HUMPHRIES R.A.M.C. rejoined from temporary duty with 12th Bn YORK & LANCASTER Regt.	
9	25.11.16.		Nothing to report.	[illegible]
	26.11.16		Under instructions from ADMS 31 Divn I detailed CAPT. L. MURPHY to see the sick of 31 SUPPLY COLn at FAMECHON daily. The Engineer workmen have now been attached & a start has been made on flooring & bunking the huts. This afternoon D.M.S. & ARMY inspected the camp.	[illegible]
	27.11.16.		Under instructions from D.D.M.S. XIII CORPS, I detailed Capt. HUMPHRIES to see the sick daily at MARIEUX.	[illegible]
	28.11.16.		I inspected ADS at HEBUTERNE & at SAILLY au BOIS. Also the collecting post at last named place. During this inspection, I made ~~[illegible]~~ arrangements for a Soup kitchen at HEBUTERNE to be placed at the RAMC dugouts, on the SAILLY-HEBUTERNE Rd, at entrance to the village.	

2353 Wt. W2544/1454 700,000 5/15 D. D. & L. A.D.S.S./Forms/C. 2118.

Instructions regarding War Diaries and Intelligence Summaries are contained in F. S. Regs., Part II. and the Staff Manual respectively. Title pages will be prepared in manuscript.

WAR DIARY
or
INTELLIGENCE SUMMARY.
(Erase heading not required.)

93rd Field Ambce

Army Form C. 2118.

Place	Date	Hour	Summary of Events and Information	Remarks and references to Appendices
BOIS WARNIMONT	28.11.16 (cont)		Transport & horse lines were inspected today by Major PHILLIMORE A.S.C. for O.C. 31st DIVISIONAL TRAIN. DADMS 31st Divn. also inspected the camp.	
			Capt. R.S. CUMMINGS proceeded on leave this day	[initials]
	29.11.16.		Posts at HEBUTERNE, SAILLY au BOIS & WARNIMONT woods relieved today by detachments of C SECTION. Capt. J. POOLEY relieved Capt. J. JOSEPH at HEBUTERNE.	
			Capt. T MELLING rejoined from detached duty with 12 York & Lancaster Regt.	
"	30.11.16.		under instructions from D.D.M.S. XIII CORPS Capt. HUMPHRIES is detailed to see sick of XIII CORPS SIEGE ARTILLERY PARK daily	[initials]

[signature]
O.C. 93. F.A.

2353 Wt. W2544/1454 700,000 5/15 D. D. & L. A.D.S.S./Forms/C. 2118.

Confidential Volume XII.

140/1903

Dec 1916

Vol 10

War Diary

93rd Field Ambulance 31st Division

December 1916

Instructions regarding War Diaries and Intelligence Summaries are contained in F. S. Regs., Part II. and the Staff Manual respectively. Title pages will be prepared in manuscript.

WAR DIARY
or
~~INTELLIGENCE~~ SUMMARY.

(Erase heading not required.)

93rd. Field Ambce — Army Form C. 2118. — 1

Place	Date	Hour	Summary of Events and Information	Remarks and references to Appendices
BOIS LALEAU	1st Dec. 1916		One hut is now floored & bunked. Two others are floored. Under instructions from ADMS 31st DIVISION, I detailed Capt. M. JOSEPH RAMC for duty at DIVISIONAL (BOMB) SCHOOL, VAUCHELLES.	
			[signature] Capt.	
	2nd Dec 1916		Nothing to report.	
	3rd Dec.		A.D.M.S. 31 DIVISION visited & inspected the camp. Two huts have now been boarded & bunked, two others have been boarded.	
	4th Dec.		In accordance with instructions received from ADMS 31 DIVISION I submitted name of Capt. H.M. JOSEPH R.A.M.C. as officer to be withdrawn from unit. In 1282/23 d. 3.11.16.	
			No. 60360 Q.M.S. BRENTNALL F. RAMC proceeded to No 11 C.C.S. in exchange of duty with No. 12266 Q.M.S. PARKER H. who arrives here for duty. On authority (per A.D.M.S. 31 DIVISION) D.M.S. 4th ARMY M.2/134 d. 29.11.16.	

2353 Wt. W2544/1454 700,000 5/15 D. D. & L. A.D.S.S./Forms/C. 2118.

Instructions regarding War Diaries and Intelligence Summaries are contained in F. S. Regs., Part II. and the Staff Manual respectively. Title pages will be prepared in manuscript.

WAR DIARY
or
~~INTELLIGENCE SUMMARY.~~
(Erase heading not required.)

93rd Field Ambce

Army Form C. 2118. 2

Place	Date	Hour	Summary of Events and Information	Remarks and references to Appendices
BOIS LALEAU	Dec 5th 1916		I inspected A.D.S. HEBUTERNE & SAILLY au BOIS. Soup kitchen is now in progress & 800 men received soup yesterday. I sent a Thomas Sawyer stone Kettle from A.D.S. at SAILLY. No [illegible] are yet being delivered by [illegible].	
			This afternoon, I received following letter:–	
			Secret. S.281.	
			O.C. 93. F.A.	
			(1) In accordance with instructions received from D.D.M.S. VIII CORPS, you will arrange with O.C. 95 F.A. to take over the Advanced Dressing Station at HEBUTERNE (Ref Trench Map Sh. 57D N.E. 3 & 4 parts) at K.15.b.6.2. forthwith.	
			(2) Following [illegible] for stretchers should be completed in all A.D.S's at HEBUTERNE. Indent for timber required should be submitted HERE. [illegible] this Office.	
			(3) Report to this Office when the relief has been effected & when the work mentioned in (2) has been commenced.	
			Sd. A. Bewley Col. D.M.O. 4.12.16 ADMS. 31 Div	

2353 Wt. W2544/1454 700,000 5/15 D. D. & L. A.D.S.S./Forms/C. 2118.

Instructions regarding War Diaries and Intelligence Summaries are contained in F. S. Regs., Part II. and the Staff Manual respectively. Title pages will be prepared in manuscript.

WAR DIARY ~~or~~ ~~INTELLIGENCE SUMMARY.~~ 93rd Field Ambce

(*Erase heading not required.*)

Army Form C. 2118. 3

Place	Date	Hour	Summary of Events and Information	Remarks and references to Appendices
			I accordingly proceeded to 95 F.A. & made arrangements to take over ADS. on 6/12/16.	
			Under instructions from ADMS. S.284. I arranged to hand over 3 G.S. wagons, horses & personnel for duty at 95 F.A. to be taken on their ration strength & accommodated there.	
			[illegible signature]	
BOIS LALEAU	Dec. 6th.		Capt. R. McKINNON & advance party of 6 men proceeded to take over ADS. HEBUTERNE from 95 F.A. at 8.30 AM.	
			Capt. L.C. MURPHY & remainder of B section proceeded to same ADS. at 12.30 p.m. All sectional equipment was taken.	
			In instructions item (1) to occupy ADS. & billets S. 26. 80 & at Soap kitchen – which was also taken over.	
			(2) To send a holding party to COLLECTING POST HOME AVENUE. (6 men)	
			(3) To send 6 stretcher bearers for duty at FORT BRIGGS, to be relieved daily	

Instructions regarding War Diaries and Intelligence Summaries are contained in F. S. Regs., Part II. and the Staff Manual respectively. Title pages will be prepared in manuscript.

WAR DIARY 93rd Field Ambce

or

~~INTELLIGENCE~~ SUMMARY.

(*Erase heading not required.*)

Army Form C. 2118. 4

Place	Date	Hour	Summary of Events and Information	Remarks and references to Appendices
Dec 6th (contd)			To undertake such improvements + repairs as possible.	
BOIS LA LEAU.			Capt. A. McPHAIL + 19 O.R. relieved Capt. J. POOLEY at No 1. (N). ADS. AEBOTERNE. Measurements for fitting up folding stretcher ... were taken. No bones are yet supplied the soup kitchen under instruction from A.D.M.S. Capt. T. MILLING RAMC left this unit for duty with 2nd DIVISION, + is struck off strength.	McPhail Capt
"	Dec 7th		Nothing to report: save that the taking over of new ADS has been accomplished. G.O.C. XXXI Div. has given permission for Capt. A.M. POLLARD. RAMC. to assume rank + insignia of LIEUT. COL. whilst in command of 93 F.A.	AP.
"	Dec 8th		Nothing to report.	AP.
"	Dec 9th		Nothing to report	AP.

2353 Wt. W2544/1454 700,000 5/15 D. D. & L. A.D.S.S./Forms/C. 2118.

Instructions regarding War Diaries and Intelligence Summaries are contained in F. S. Regs., Part II. and the Staff Manual respectively. Title pages will be prepared in manuscript.

WAR DIARY ~~or~~ ~~INTELLIGENCE~~ ~~SUMMARY~~. 93rd Field Ambce

(*Erase heading not required.*)

Army Form C. 2118. 5

Place	Date	Hour	Summary of Events and Information	Remarks and references to Appendices
BOIS LA HEAU	DEC. 10th.		~~Under~~ With permission of ADMS. ~~XXX~~ 7 Div. I have decreased my personnel at the ADS. (nos 1 & 2) at HEBUTERNE, as follows.	
			Capt. L. MURPHY & 22 men rejoined from ADS no 2.	
			8 O. Ranks rejoined from ADS. no. 1.	
			Operations being expected for 11-13th inst., I received the following letter & acted upon it.	
			O.C. 93. F.A. S. 269.	
			In accordance with instructions from G. Branch Surplus personnel will be withdrawn from the A. D Stations at HEBUTERNE, during Artillery Bombardment commencing at 8. a.m. 11th inst. until 13th inst.	
			The strength at the ADS (N.) during this period will be	

2353 Wt. W2544/1454 700,000 5/15 D. D. & L. A.D.S.S./Forms/C. 2118.

Instructions regarding War Diaries and Intelligence Summaries are contained in F. S. Regs., Part II. and the Staff Manual respectively. Title pages will be prepared in manuscript.

WAR DIARY ~~or~~ ~~INTELLIGENCE SUMMARY.~~

93rd Field Ambulance

(Erase heading not required.)

Army Form C. 2118. 6

Place	Date	Hour	Summary of Events and Information	Remarks and references to Appendices
BOIS EN LEAU 10th Dec (cont).			1 officer & 6 men: at the ADS. (S.) 1 officer + 12 men. Remainder of personnel to be kept at ADS. SAILLY DELL.	
			10. 12. 16. A. Bewley Col. ADMS. 31 Div.	
			Takes over the soup kitchens. Movements completed by 7. 30 p.m.	A. Bewley Col.
Dec. 11th.			Received following this morning.	
			O.C. 93 F.A. S. 292.	
			Notification has been received that the Operation will not take place as arranged between 11th & 13th inst. The personnel withdrawn to ADS at	

Instructions regarding War Diaries and Intelligence Summaries are contained in F. S. Regs., Part II. and the Staff Manual respectively. Title pages will be prepared in manuscript.

WAR DIARY or ~~INTELLIGENCE SUMMARY.~~

9 3rd. Field Ambce

(Erase heading not required.)

Army Form C. 2118.

7

Place	Date	Hour	Summary of Events and Information	Remarks and references to Appendices
BOIS LALEAU	Dec 11th (cont).		SAILLY DELL should be returned to the A.D.S. HEBUTERNE please.	
"			R.W. Bewley Col. ADMS 31. Div.	
			10.12.16.	
			Necessary instructions were given: also orders to reopen Soup kitchen at once.	
			Capt. R.S. COMMINGS. returned from leave. R.H. Pollard Lt. Col.	
"	Dec 12th.		Nothing to report.	R.P.
"	Dec 13th.		Nothing to report, save usual weekly reliefs at the two A.D.S HEBUTERNE Capt J. POOLEY & Capt R. COMMINGS being relieving officers.	R.P.
"	Dec 14th		Under instructions from ADMS. I recalled Capt H. JOSEPH from DIVISIONAL SCHOOL and relieved him by Capt. J. McPHAIL.	R.P.

2353 Wt. W2544/1454 700,000 5/15 D. D. & L. A.D.S.S./Forms/C. 2118.

Instructions regarding War Diaries and Intelligence Summaries are contained in F. S. Regs., Part II. and the Staff Manual respectively. Title pages will be prepared in manuscript.

WAR DIARY
~~or~~
~~INTELLIGENCE~~ SUMMARY.
(*Erase heading not required.*)

93rd Field Ambce

Army Form C. 2118.

Place	Date	Hour	Summary of Events and Information	Remarks and references to Appendices
BOIS LALEAU			Nothing of importance to record	
	Dec. 15th.		Permission received from O/C A.S.C. Section; ~~[illegible]~~ a/Sgt HARRIS A.S.C. H.T. to be A/Staff (Sergt) Major	
"	Dec. 16th.		I inspected the A.D.S. (N & S) at HEBUTERNE.	
			A.D.S. (N). A good deal of work is being done here. Big sick parade each morning. Everything seems satisfactory. Soup kitchen is unable to prepare as it should, as units will not supply boxes. The continued wet has caused the trench leading from billets to A.D.S. to fall in; it is in a bad state of repair & apparently needs skilled labour.	
			A.D.S. (S). Practically no work is being done here. 1 wounded & 5 or 6 sick seen in 3 days. The kitchen is being strengthened. Soup kitchen is not supplying a great deal of soup: as here again units will not supply boxes.	
			The pump at HEBUTERNE is still unmended & all water has to be brought in petrol tins from SAILLY.	
			A.D.S. (SAILLY) everything satisfactory.	

2353 Wt. W2544/1454 700,000 5/15 D. D. & L. A.D.S.S./Forms/C. 2118.

Instructions regarding War Diaries and Intelligence Summaries are contained in F. S. Regs., Part II. and the Staff Manual respectively. Title pages will be prepared in manuscript.

WAR DIARY
or
~~INTELLIGENCE SUMMARY.~~
(*Erase heading not required.*)

9th Field Ambulance

Army Form C. 2118.

9

Place	Date	Hour	Summary of Events and Information	Remarks and references to Appendices
BOIS LALEAU	Dec. 17th.		Nothing of importance to record, save that Capt HUMPHRIES proceeded on leave.	[illegible] Lt Col.
"	Dec 18th.		Nothing to report.	
"	Dec 19th.		Camp was inspected this morning by G.O.C. 31 Division, he suggested that more canvas should be used in the horse lines.	
			Capt. H.M. JOSEPH proceeded on leave	
"	Dec 20th.		I submitted name of Capt. R. MACKINNON to be posted as Divisional Gas Officer according to ADMS instructions. Usual weekly relief of detachments at ADS. (S.R.) HEBUTERNE took place. Capt. MACKINNON & Capt. MURPHY relieved Capts. POOLEY & CUMMINGS.	

2353 Wt. W2544/1454 700,000 5/15 D. D. & L. A.D.S.S./Forms/C. 2118.

Instructions regarding War Diaries and Intelligence Summaries are contained in F. S. Regs., Part II. and the Staff Manual respectively. Title pages will be prepared in manuscript.

WAR DIARY
~~or~~
~~INTELLIGENCE SUMMARY.~~
(Erase heading not required.)

93rd Field Ambce

Army Form C. 2118.

10

Place	Date	Hour	Summary of Events and Information	Remarks and references to Appendices
BOIS LA LEAU.	Dec 21st		Nothing of importance to report [signature] Lt Col.	
"	Dec 22nd		Nothing to report. [initials]	
			I reported to ADMS this day. He gave me permission to withdraw one	
"	Dec 23rd		~~Nothing to report~~ Officer from ADS, HEBUTERNE [initials]	
"	Dec 24th		Nothing to report. [initials]	
"	Dec 25th		Xmas Day. The camp was inspected by ADMS 31 Div: also later in the day by G.O.C. 31 Div., who saw the unit on parade. Inspected ADS (N & S) HEBUTERNE.	
			ADS (S). Trench leading to ADS, is falling in & is with difficulty kept clear. The two dugouts are leaking & it is impossible to keep them decently clean. The subway connecting these two is	

2353 Wt. W2544/1454 700,000 5/15 D. D. & L. A.D.S.S./Forms/C. 2118.

Instructions regarding War Diaries and Intelligence Summaries are contained in F. S. Regs., Part II. and the Staff Manual respectively. Title pages will be prepared in manuscript.

WAR DIARY
~~or~~
~~INTELLIGENCE SUMMARY.~~
(Erase heading not required.)

93rd Field Ambce

Army Form C. 2118.

11

Place	Date	Hour	Summary of Events and Information	Remarks and references to Appendices
BOIS LALEAU	Dec 25th (cont)		also giving way. Apparently two heavy batteries are close to the ADS, the constant concussion from the firing of the guns & constant close shell fire from enemies guns, combined with the very wet weather are causing very considerable damage to the ADS. It is also very exposed and situated in a most dangerous locality. Very little work is being done. Withdrew Capt. R. M. KINNON from ADS. (N) & left Capt. L. MURPHY in charge of both this by permission of ADMS 31 Div.	
"	Dec 26th		Capt R. CUMMING relieved Capt. MacPHAIL as M.O. to DIVISIONAL SCHOOL VAUCHELLES 3 DAIMLER cars of this unit were sent to 31 Div. Sup. Column for exchange for SUNBEAM cars. Replaced been temporarily relieved by cars	

[signature] Lt Col

Instructions regarding War Diaries and Intelligence Summaries are contained in F. S. Regs., Part II. and the Staff Manual respectively. Title pages will be prepared in manuscript.

WAR DIARY ~~or~~ ~~INTELLIGENCE SUMMARY.~~ 93rd Field Ambce

(Erase heading not required.)

Army Form C. 2118. 12

Place	Date	Hour	Summary of Events and Information	Remarks and references to Appendices
			from 31 M.A.C	Chas Pollard Lieut Col
BOIS LA LEAU	Dec 27th		Under instructions from ADMS 31 Div. I detailed Capt R. McKINNON for daily duty at ORVILLE & SARTON, in relief of M.O. NORTHUMBERLAND HUSSARS, who is on the sick list. Capt. McPHAIL & detachment of B Sectn. relieved Capt. MURPHY & detacht. C Section at ADS's SAILLY DELL & HEBUTERNE. Five SUNBEAM Cars were received today from O/c 53 SUP. COL. in exchange for DAIMLER Cars. The cars from 31 M.A.C. will rejoin as soon as relieved at SAILLY DELL.	CP
"	Dec 28th		A & C Sections & ASC (M.T. & H.T.) were issued with Box Respirators today, and were passed thro' a hut filled with lachrymatory gas fumes. Two heavy draught horses were drawn to make good deficiencies.	CP

2353 Wt. W2544/1454 700,000 5/15 D. D. & L. A.D.S.S./Forms/C. 2118.

Instructions regarding War Diaries and Intelligence Summaries are contained in F. S. Regs., Part II. and the Staff Manual respectively. Title pages will be prepared in manuscript.

WAR DIARY 93rd Field Ambulance
or
~~INTELLIGENCE~~ **SUMMARY.**
(Erase heading not required.)

Army Form C. 2118.

Place	Date	Hour	Summary of Events and Information	Remarks and references to Appendices
BOIS LALEAU	Dec 29th.		Nothing of importance to report. A W Sladen Lt Col	
"	Dec 30th.		Under instructions from ADMS 31 Div. I detailed Capt. L. MURPHY for temporary duty with 15th Bn. W. Yorks Regt., in place of Capt. McCAWLEY who is proceeding on leave on JAN 1st 1917	
"	Dec 31st.		Inspected post at VARVICHONT WOOD, this morning. Nothing of importance to report.	

A W Sladen Lt Col
O.C. 93 F.A.

Confidential

140/1743 Volume XIII.

Jan. 1917

S

Vol XI

War Diary

93rd Field Ambulance, 31st Division

January. 1917

PAGE I

WAR DIARY
or
~~INTELLIGENCE SUMMARY.~~
(Erase heading not required.)

93rd FIELD AMBULANCE

Army Form C. 2118.

Instructions regarding War Diaries and Intelligence Summaries are contained in F. S. Regs., Part II. and the Staff Manual respectively. Title pages will be prepared in manuscript.

Place	Date	Hour	Summary of Events and Information	Remarks and references to Appendices
BOIS LALEAU.	JAN 1st 1917.		New Years Day. Inspected ADS's at SAILLY DELL & at HEBUTERNE. A.D.S. (S). HEBUTERNE. Practically no medical work during the last week. A lot of work was done by the detachment upon the trenches. No work has yet been done by R.E. SOUP KITCHEN (S). Good supply of bones. Soup given daily to about 300 men. The wall of the room adjoining that used as the kitchen was blown in by a shell last night. ADS (N) HEBUTERNE. A large number of sick has been here. Not many wounded. Everything satisfactory. SOUP KITCHEN (N). Supply of bones now satisfactory. About 150-200 men fed daily. Trench at back is very wet except near the kitchen, which was almost under water. The ablution bench at Hqrs. of the unit has now been installed. Capt L. MURPHY left for temporary duty with 15th Bn W. YORKS Regt. [illegible]	

Page II

Instructions regarding War Diaries and Intelligence Summaries are contained in F. S. Regs., Part II. and the Staff Manual respectively. Title pages will be prepared in manuscript.

WAR DIARY
or
~~INTELLIGENCE SUMMARY.~~
(Erase heading not required.)

93rd FIELD AMBULANCE.

Army Form C. 2118.

Place	Date	Hour	Summary of Events and Information	Remarks and references to Appendices
BOIS LALEAU.	JAN. 2nd 1917.		Under instructions from ADMS 31st DIV. I have ceased to send an officer daily to see sick of ORVILLE & SARTON. Transport & horse lines were inspected by Major PHILLIMORE ASC, for O.C. 31 DIVISIONAL TRAIN. Capt HUMPHRIES returned from leave this day.	[signature]
"	JAN 3rd '17		Usual weekly relief at A.D.S: took place today. C section relieved B. Sectn. & Capt J. HUMPHREYS relieved Capt J.M. PHAIL. Capt. R. McKINNON proceeded on leave from 3/1/17 to 15/1/17.	[initials]
"	JAN 4th "		The remainder of the unit has today been fitted with Box Respirators. Capt. J. McPHAIL assumed medical charge of PRISONERS CAMP, THIEVRES. One G.S. wagon & 2 horses returned from duty with 95 F.A. Capt H. M. JOSEPH returned from leave this day.	[initials]
"	JAN 5th "		Under instructions from ADMS. 31 DIV. I detailed Capt H. JOSEPH	

2353 Wt. W2544/1454 700,000 5/15 D. D. & L. A.D.S.S./Forms/C. 2118.

PAGE III

Instructions regarding War Diaries and Intelligence Summaries are contained in F. S. Regs., Part II. and the Staff Manual respectively. Title pages will be prepared in manuscript.

WAR DIARY
or
~~INTELLIGENCE SUMMARY.~~
(Erase heading not required.)

Army Form C. 2118.

93rd FIELD AMBULANCE

Place	Date	Hour	Summary of Events and Information	Remarks and references to Appendices
BOISLALEAU				
	JAN 5th 17 (cont).		for temporary duty with 169th Brigade R.F.A.	[illegible] Maj
"	JAN 6th '17		The following instructions were received from ADMS 31 Div. under RAMC OPERATION ORDER no 8 by Col. A.W. BEWLEY Commandt. RAMC 31 Div. D. 6.1.17.	
			Ref. Map 57D 1/40000.	
			(1) The 31st DIVISION will be relieved between 9th & 11th inst. by the 19th Divisn & will move into billets in the BEAUVAL area.	
			(2) Personnel of the 93rd Field Ambulance holding Advanced Dressing Stations at HEBUTERNE & collecting post in SAILLY DELL will be relieved by a detachment of 57th Field Ambulance on Jan 10th. On completion of relief, the personnel & transport to rejoin Hqrs at BOISLALEAU.	
			On 11th inst. this unit will hand over the camp at BOIS LALEAU to 58th Field Ambulance & will march to billets in BRETEL	
			(3) Units to march independently under orders of O.C. Route Areas	

2353 Wt. W2544/1454 700,000 5/15 D. D. & L. A.D.S.S./Forms/C. 2118.

PAGE IV

Instructions regarding War Diaries and Intelligence Summaries are contained in F. S. Regs., Part II. and the Staff Manual respectively. Title pages will be prepared in manuscript.

WAR DIARY
or
~~INTELLIGENCE~~ SUMMARY.
(Erase heading not required.)

93rd FIELD AMBULANCE

Army Form C. 2118.

Place	Date	Hour	Summary of Events and Information	Remarks and references to Appendices
BOIS LALEAU.	Jan 6th (contd)		follows. FAMECHON - XRDs. B23. d.9.1. - X RDs. H4 a.3.3 - AMPLIER - AUTHIEULE - DOULLENS - BRETEL. (4) 93rd Field Ambulance at BRETEL to remain closed, until further orders. [signature]	[initials]
"	Jan 7th 1917.		Nothing to report.	[initials]
"	Jan 8th 1917.		An Officer of 58th Fd. Ambulance reported here with a view to taking over ADS. at HEBUTERNE on 10th inst.	[initials]
"	Jan 9th		Under instructions from ADMS 31st Div. - S.319 d. 8.1.17 - Capt. J. POOLEY proceeded to VALHEUREUX for duty with V ARMY TRENCH MORTAR SCHOOL	[initials]
	JAN. 10th		The 58th F.A. took over from us the ADS's at HEBUTERNE & SAILLY DELL; also the soup kitchens. The detachment of C section under Capt. J. HUMPHRY rejoined headquarters of the unit.	

2353 Wt. W2544/1454 700,000 5/15 D. D. & L. A.D.S.S./Forms/C. 2118.

Page V

Instructions regarding War Diaries and Intelligence Summaries are contained in F. S. Regs., Part II. and the Staff Manual respectively. Title pages will be prepared in manuscript.

WAR DIARY
or
~~INTELLIGENCE~~ SUMMARY.
(*Erase heading not required.*)

Army Form C. 2118.

93rd Field Ambulance

Place	Date	Hour	Summary of Events and Information	Remarks and references to Appendices
	1917			
BRETEL	JAN. 11		The 93rd F.A. vacated the camp at BOIS LALEAU and proceeded to BRETEL, where they billeted. The men & N.C.O's are in barns. Horses on a made stone standing, but in the open. Unit left at 9. A.M & arrived ~~without~~ without mishap at BRETEL at 3 p.m. A fatigue party under Lt & Qmr. ALLEN remained behind. As no advance party was sent by incoming unit, this party did not arrive in billets till 7.30 p.m. having journeyed there in motor ambulances. The 58th F.A. took over the camp at BOIS LALEAU.	
"	JAN 12th		The Day was spent in building latrines, incinerators & general cleaning up of billets, which are dirty & insanitary. At 8.30 p.m. a wire was received from ADMS 31st Div. ordering me to detail Capts. J. HUMPHREYS & J. MACPHAIL to proceed forthwith to 29 C.C.S. for temporary duty. ~~[illegible]~~	

PAGE VI

Instructions regarding War Diaries and Intelligence Summaries are contained in F. S. Regs., Part II. and the Staff Manual respectively. Title pages will be prepared in manuscript.

WAR DIARY
or
~~INTELLIGENCE SUMMARY.~~
(Erase heading not required.)

Army Form C. 2118.

93rd FIELD AMBULANCE.

Place	Date	Hour	Summary of Events and Information	Remarks and references to Appendices
BRETEL	1917 JAN 12th (cont).		~~[illegible]~~ CR	Arnold Pollard [illegible]
"	JAN. 13th		Under instructions from ADMS 31st Div. I detailed 3 large motor ambulances to proceed to BEAUVAL for duty with 95th F.A.	CR
			I proceeded this afternoon to LE MEILLARD & took over a quantity of equipment & stores left behind by O.C. 59 F.A. I placed these under the charge of the N.C.O sent in advance as 11th unit	CR
"	JAN. 14th		Under instructions, all sick of 31st DIV. are to be sent to 94 F.A at BEAUVAL and not to CORPS REST STATION.	
			Capt. L.C. MURPHY returned from temporary duty with 15th W. YORKS Regt.	CR
"	JAN 15th		The men of this unit are now being trained. Two sections are sent out daily for a route march, of about 3 hrs. duration. Squad & stretcher drill is being practised in the early part of the morning, & the afternoons devoted to Athletic Games	CR

2353 Wt. W2544/1454 700,000 5/15 D. D. & L. A.D.S.S./Forms/C. 2118.

PAGE VII

Instructions regarding War Diaries and Intelligence Summaries are contained in F. S. Regs., Part II. and the Staff Manual respectively. Title pages will be prepared in manuscript.

WAR DIARY
or
~~INTELLIGENCE SUMMARY.~~
(Erase heading not required.)

Army Form C. 2118.

93rd FIELD AMBULANCE

Place	Date	Hour	Summary of Events and Information	Remarks and references to Appendices
BRETEL.	JAN. 16th 1917.		Under instructions from ADMS. 31st Div. I despatched 23 O.R. for duty with Special Operating Centre AUTHIE, to replace detachments from 19th + 32nd Divs. Capt. R. McKINNON arrived back from leave this night. [illegible] Lt Col.	
"	JAN. 17th 1917		Under instructions from ADMS 31 Div. I detailed Capt. L. MURPHY to proceed to 19th Div. SCHOOL of INSTRUCTn. at Mt RENAULT FARM. A very heavy fall of snow last night. I have managed to obtain permission to exercise the horses in a neighbouring field. [initials]	
"	JAN. 18th "		Nothing of importance to report save a memo from ADMS. 31 Div. notifying me, that this unit would proceed to new billets at LE MEILLARD, on the 22nd inst. Unit to be clear of HEM by 10.a.m. on that day. [initials]	

2353 Wt. W2544/1454 700,000 5/15 D. D. & L. A.D.S.S./Forms/C. 2118.

PAGE VIII

Instructions regarding War Diaries and Intelligence Summaries are contained in F. S. Regs., Part II. and the Staff Manual respectively. Title pages will be prepared in manuscript.

WAR DIARY
or
~~INTELLIGENCE SUMMARY.~~
(Erase heading not required.)

Army Form C. 2118.

93rd FIELD AMBULANCE.

Place	Date	Hour	Summary of Events and Information	Remarks and references to Appendices
BRETEL	JAN. 19th 1917.		Under instructions received from ADMS 31st DIV. – OPERATION ORDER no. 9 d. 18.1.17 – this unit is to proceed to LE MEILLARD on 22nd inst. and to billet there.	
			The unit will then [illegible] and receive sick from the following units:–	
			93 INF. BDE. & TRENCH MORTAR BTY. & MACHINE GUN COY.	
			DIVIS. ARTILLERY and AMMUNIT. COL. & TRENCH MORTAR BTY.	
			31st DIVIS. TRAIN (less 279th Coy. ASC)	A.W. Pollard Lt Col.
	" JAN 20th "		I sent on an advance party of 1 N.C.O. & 15 men to clean and prepare the chateau at LEMEILLARD, which is to be used for reception of sick.	
	" JAN 21st "		Nothing to report.	A.W.P.
	" JAN. 22nd "		The unit paraded at 8.30 AM & marched to LE MEILLARD, via OCCOCHES, OUTREBOIS & MEZEROLLES. Unit arrived at new billets	

PAGE IX

Instructions regarding War Diaries and Intelligence Summaries are contained in F. S. Regs., Part II. and the Staff Manual respectively. Title pages will be prepared in manuscript.

WAR DIARY
or
~~INTELLIGENCE SUMMARY.~~
(Erase heading not required.)

Army Form C. 2118.

93rd FIELD AMBULANCE

Place	Date	Hour	Summary of Events and Information	Remarks and references to Appendices
LE MEILLARD	JAN 22nd 1917 (contd)		at 11.30 A.M. The hospital was opened for reception of sick and 6 cases were admitted yesterday. Under instructions from ADMS 31st Div. All serious cases are to be evacuated to C.C.S. (29 or AUSTRALIAN); all diarrhoea and Scabies cases to be evacuated to C.R.S. (95 F.A)	[signature]
"	JAN 23rd "		I have detailed Capt. H. JOSEPH to act as O.C. i/c Wards B section & Officer personnel	[initials]
"	JAN. 24th		Under instructions from ADMS. 31 DIV. I detailed Capt. R. CUMMING for temporary duty with 170th Bde. R.F.A.	[initials]
"	JAN. 25th		The ADMS. 31 DIV. inspected the hospital this morning. I proceeded on leave & handed over charge to Capt. R. McKINNON.	[initials]

Instructions regarding War Diaries and Intelligence Summaries are contained in F. S. Regs., Part II. and the Staff Manual respectively. Title pages will be prepared in manuscript.

PAGE X

WAR DIARY
or
~~INTELLIGENCE~~ SUMMARY.
(Erase heading not required.)

Army Form C. 2118.

93rd Field Ambulance

Place	Date	Hour	Summary of Events and Information	Remarks and references to Appendices
LE MEILLARD	Jan 26th		Nothing to report. R Mackinnon Capt	
"	27th		Nothing to report RM	
"	" 28th		Nothing to report RM	
"	" 29		The D.A & Q.M.G. XIII Corps visited the Field Ambulance this morning RM	
"	" 30		Nothing to report RM	
	" 31		Under instructions received from the A.D.M.S. 31st Division the unit will collect sick daily from the 93rd Infantry Brigade area and I detailed 1 large motor ambulance for duty with the 94th Field Ambulance	

R Mackinnon
Capt RAMC (SR)
for Lt Col. Commanding 93rd Field Amb.

2353 Wt. W2544/1454 700,000 5/15 D. D. & L. A.D.S.S./Forms/C. 2118.

140/1997

Confidential

Volume XIV.

Feb 1917

S

Vol 12

War Diary.

93rd Field Ambulance 31st Division

February 1917

PAGE II

Instructions regarding War Diaries and Intelligence Summaries are contained in F. S. Regs., Part II. and the Staff Manual respectively. Title pages will be prepared in manuscript.

WAR DIARY
or
~~INTELLIGENCE SUMMARY.~~
(Erase heading not required.)

Army Form C. 2118.

93 FIELD AMBULANCE

Place	Date	Hour	Summary of Events and Information	Remarks and references to Appendices
	1917.			
LE MEILLARD	FEB	9th	Nothing to report. A.W. Pollard Lt Col	
"	"	10th	Nothing of importance to report. The number of sick are now decidedly lessening, especially the diarrhoeal cases. A.P.	
"	"	11th	LIEUT. + QMR. G. READ arrived for duty with this unit. The severe frost does not yet show signs of abating A.P.	
"	"	12th	Nothing to report. A.P.	
"	"	13th	Nothing to report. A.P.	
"	"	14th	Inspection by actg/A.D.M.S. Number of sick are lessening. Barn used by A section has now been bunked. A.P.	
"	"	15th	Nothing to report A.P.	
"	"	16th	Nothing to report A.P.	
"	"	17th	Number of sick is 33 in Hospital. Considerable lessening A.P.	

A5834 Wt. W4973/M687 750,000 8/16 D. D. & L. Ltd. Forms/C.2118/13.

PAGE III

Instructions regarding War Diaries and Intelligence Summaries are contained in F. S. Regs., Part II. and the Staff Manual respectively. Title pages will be prepared in manuscript.

WAR DIARY
or
~~INTELLIGENCE SUMMARY.~~
(Erase heading not required.)

Army Form C. 2118.

93rd FIELD AMBULANCE

Place	Date	Hour	Summary of Events and Information	Remarks and references to Appendices
LE MEILLARD	Feb 18th '17		I received a preliminary notice from ADMS. 31 Div. to hold the unit in readiness to move.	
			Later I received detailed orders, containing copy of DDMS XIII CORPS order no. IV (Medical Arrangements) dated 17.2.17, the number of ADMS. 31 DIV. RAMC operation order was no 9 d. 19.2.17	
			This unit is to proceed to forward area & take over camp at BOIS LALEAU: the ADS's at HEBUTERNE & SAILLY DELL.	
			The unit to move to BEAUVAL on 19th inst. & to BOIS LALEAU on 20th inst.	
			[illegible] Lt Col.	
BEAUVAL	Feb 19th		Unit came under orders of 93rd INF BDE as regards march. Unit moved off at 11.30 A.M. & arrived at BEAUVAL at 3.30 p.m. Route BERNAVILLE – FIENVILLERS – CANDAS – BEAUVAL.	

PAGE I

Instructions regarding War Diaries and Intelligence Summaries are contained in F. S. Regs., Part II. and the Staff Manual respectively. Title pages will be prepared in manuscript.

WAR DIARY
or
~~INTELLIGENCE~~ ~~SUMMARY.~~

(Erase heading not required.)

93rd Field Ambulance

Army Form C. 2118.

Place	Date	Hour	Summary of Events and Information	Remarks and references to Appendices
LE MEILLARD	Feb	1st	Under instructions from A.D.M.S. 31st Division I detailed Lieut and Qr Mr A. ALLEN to report for duty to D.G.T.	
"		~~2nd~~	~~Nothing~~ MECHELON. G.H.Q. R. McKinnon Capt. R.A.M.C. (S.R)	
		2nd	Nothing to report this day. RM	
"		3rd	43 Other Ranks were inoculated with T.A.B. this afternoon RM	
"	"	4th	Nothing to report. RM	
"	"	5th	Nothing to report RM	
"	"	6th	I rejoined from leave in England & reassumed command from Capt. R.S. McKinnon. [illegible] Lt Col	
"	"	7th	Frost is still very severe. Nothing to report. A.R.	
"	"	8th	I have received a new Nissen Hut, which is now being erected and will increase the accommodation for sick.	
"	"	9th	Capt R.S. CUMMING A.R. rejoined for duty.	

A5834 Wt. W4973/M687 750,000 8/16 D. D. & L. Ltd. Forms/C.2118/13.

Page ~~10~~

Instructions regarding War Diaries and Intelligence Summaries are contained in F. S. Regs., Part II. and the Staff Manual respectively. Title pages will be prepared in manuscript.

WAR DIARY
or
~~INTELLIGENCE SUMMARY.~~
(Erase heading not required.)

93rd FIELD AMBULANCE

Army Form C. 2118.

Place	Date	Hour	Summary of Events and Information	Remarks and references to Appendices
BEAUVAL	19.2.17 (contd).		Capt. R. CUMMING + a billeting party had proceeded ahead, + conducted unit to the billets assigned to it.	
			I sent forward Capt. H. JOSEPH + 16. O.R. as an advance party to take over ADS's at HEBUTERNE + SAILLY DELL. They proceeded in motor ambulances on arrival at BEAUVAL, + reported to O.C. 57 F.A. at COIGNEUX.	AW Holland LtCol.
BOIS LALEAU.	20.2.17.		Unit received orders from 93rd INF. BDE, + marched to BOIS LALEAU. Route. BEAUVAL - X roads 1100 yds. S.S.E of L in BEAUVAL - BEAUQUESNE - MARIEUX - AUTHIE.	
			The road from X rds. 1100 yds SSE of L in BEAUVAL - BEAUQUESNE was found to be impassable. Waggons sank up to the axle in mud, after about 1 mile was traversed, and men over their knees. The unit had to turn, + proceed via VERT GALAND. Two hours were lost and men + horses arrived in an exhausted condition at BOIS LALEAU at 3.p.m.	

Instructions regarding War Diaries and Intelligence Summaries are contained in F. S. Regs., Part II. and the Staff Manual respectively. Title pages will be prepared in manuscript.

PAGE V.

WAR DIARY
or
~~INTELLIGENCE SUMMARY.~~

(Erase heading not required.)

93rd FIELD AMBULANCE

Army Form C. 2118.

Place	Date	Hour	Summary of Events and Information	Remarks and references to Appendices
BOIS LALEAU	Feb. 20th (contd).		I sent forward 2 Cpls. & 14 O.R. for duty at HEBUTERNE & SAILLY DELL. This included 2 cooks for duty at Soup kitchens. I also detailed 2 SUNBEAM cars & 1 FORD car to relieve the ambulances of 57. F.A. This party proceeded to HEBUTERNE in the above cars. I took over the camp from a small holding party of 2/1st W. RIDING F.A. The huts, latrines, cookhouses etc were left clean. The camp, however, was in the hands of a party of FORESTRY DEPT. (as far as I could ascertain) V CORPS troops. German prisoners were engaged in felling & cutting trees, & a large party of the above troops were engaged collecting wood cut, and dragging ~~felled~~ trees & logs away with horse teams. The state of the camp was indescribably dirty, due to this work & the late thaw. In addition, refuse etc was thrown about by this party: many of the huts are damaged, the felt of nearly every door being torn away, and the woodwork in many cases damaged by falling trees. The 2/1st W. RIDING F.A. were in no way to blame for the condition of affairs: they had done all they	

A5834 Wt. W4973/M687 750,000 8/16 D. D. & L. Ltd. Forms/C.2118/13.

PAGE VI

Instructions regarding War Diaries and Intelligence Summaries are contained in F. S. Regs., Part II. and the Staff Manual respectively. Title pages will be prepared in manuscript.

WAR DIARY
or
~~INTELLIGENCE SUMMARY.~~

(*Erase heading not required.*)

Army Form C. 2118.

93rd FIELD AMBULANCE

Place	Date	Hour	Summary of Events and Information	Remarks and references to Appendices
BOIS LALEAU	Feb. 20th (contd)		to cope with the difficulty. I reported the condition to the ADMS. 31st Div.	[illegible] Lt Col.
BOIS LALEAU	Feb. 21st		The morning was spent in unpacking and storing away sectional equipt. also a large amount of straw, palliasses, stretchers & medical stores taken over. Men were also employed in trying to restore some order to the camp, but the FORESTRY detacht. are still at work.	AB.
" "	Feb 22nd		Nothing to report.	AB.
"	Feb 23rd		I opened up the ambulance for reception of sick: orders from ADMS being to detain all cases pending further orders.	AB
"	Feb. 24th		Nothing to report. Am detaining all sick collected locally. Wood cutting has ceased, but the camp is still very dirty.	AB
"	Feb 25th		I received orders from ADMS to evacuate the detachment in the ADS's at HEBUTERNE, as on information received the	

Page VII

Instructions regarding War Diaries and Intelligence Summaries are contained in F. S. Regs., Part II. and the Staff Manual respectively. Title pages will be prepared in manuscript.

WAR DIARY
or
~~INTELLIGENCE~~ SUMMARY.

(*Erase heading not required.*)

Army Form C. 2118.

R3 FIELD AMBULANCE

Place	Date	Hour	Summary of Events and Information	Remarks and references to Appendices
BOIS LALEAU	1917 Feb. 25th (Contd)		evening was retiring on our front. I detailed Capt. R COMMING & 30 O.R. for duty at ADS.(S): 8 men for duty at FORT BRIGGS & 8 men at FORT SUSSEX the remainder for duty at the ADS, & as bearers if required at other places. I also sent forward [illegible] 2 more SUNBEAM CARS to SAILLY DELL	
"	Feb 26th.		In company with D.D.M.S, I visited ADS's at HEBUTERNE. I found most things satisfactory. At each ADS there is in the area around a dugout, capable of taking 12-14 lying cases. Trenches need to be made from the ADS to each dugout.	
"	Feb 27th		I visited ADS's at HEBUTERNE. Acting on instructions from ADMS. 31 DIV. I detailed a collecting post of 1 N.C.O + 12 bearers at a dugout in our (old) front line at K.17 C.2.3. I also made arrangements for two other collecting posts	

A5834 Wt. W4973/M687 750,000 8/16 D. D. & L. Ltd. Forms/C.2118/13.

PAGE VIII

Instructions regarding War Diaries and Intelligence Summaries are contained in F. S. Regs., Part II. and the Staff Manual respectively. Title pages will be prepared in manuscript.

WAR DIARY
or
~~INTELLIGENCE~~ SUMMARY.

(*Erase heading not required.*)

Army Form C. 2118.

93 FIELD AMBULANCE

Place	Date	Hour	Summary of Events and Information	Remarks and references to Appendices
BOIS LALEAU	1917 Feb 27th (cont)		at K.11.D.3.1. (12 bearers) & K.18.A.0.5 (16 bearers). This latter has already been set up by a party from 95 F.A. As the enemy has retired some distance, the collecting posts are necessary to enable Field Ambulance bearers to relieve regimental bearers, & it is possible more such may be required. At my request the ADMS. has detailed a bearer ~~at road between SAILLY~~ section from 95 F.A. to assist in the collection of wounded on our front line. The road between HEBUTERNE & SAILLY is in such a terrible condition that motor transport is impossible. I have detailed 2 horsed ambulances, & one detailed from 95 F.A., to evacuate wounded from HEBUTERNE to SAILLY VILLAGE where they will be transferred to motor ambulances. [illegible signature]	

A5834 Wt. W4973/M687 750,000 8/16 D. D. & L. Ltd. Forms/C.2118/13.

PAGE IX

WAR DIARY
or
INTELLIGENCE SUMMARY.
(*Erase heading not required.*)

Instructions regarding War Diaries and Intelligence Summaries are contained in F. S. Regs., Part II. and the Staff Manual respectively. Title pages will be prepared in manuscript.

Army Form C. 2118.

93 FIELD AMBULANCE

Place	Date	Hour	Summary of Events and Information	Remarks and references to Appendices
BOIS LALEAU.	Jul. 26th.	1917	Wounded are still coming in pretty fast, and the horsed ambulances are feeling the strain. I have detailed 4 light draught horses to assist with permission of ADMS. 31st Div. I have established a third collecting post at K.11.d.1.5. in conjunction with the left battalion. I have also withdrawn all bearers, save 2, from K.17.c.2.3, as this post is being little used.	
			[illegible] Lt Col	

A5834 Wt. W4973/M687 750,000 8/16 D. D. & L. Ltd. Forms/C.2118/13.

140/2042

Confidential

Volume X

Mar. 1917.

S

Vol 13

War Diary.

93rd Field Ambulance.

31st Division

March 1917.

Instructions regarding War Diaries and Intelligence Summaries are contained in F. S. Regs., Part II. and the Staff Manual respectively. Title pages will be prepared in manuscript.

PAGE I

WAR DIARY
or
~~INTELLIGENCE SUMMARY~~.

(Erase heading not required.)

Army Form C. 2118.

93 FIELD AMBULANCE

Place	Date	Hour	Summary of Events and Information	Remarks and references to Appendices
BOIS LALEAU.	MARCH 1st 1917		Capt. L.C. MURPHY relieved Capt. H. JOSEPH today at ADS. HEBUTERNE. Wounded are less now, but the condition of roads still renders the evacuation very difficult. I regret that No. 79586 Pte. POLLEY C. died of wounds received in action 28/2/17.	A.R. [illegible] Lt Col
"	MARCH 2nd.		I received information from ADMS. 31 Div. that the 31st Div. was extending their line towards the left, replacing 19th Div.; that the ADS's at COLINCAMPS & EUSTON would be taken over by this unit and the evacuation from the line, later, upon receipt of detailed orders. I made arrangements with OC 95 F.A. to withdraw my personnel from the HEBUTERNE sector and to hand over the ADS's there, as well as the soup kitchens and the ADS at SAILLY. My bearer section was relieved by a section from 94 FA	A.R.
"	March 3rd		Following upon the Operation orders of ADMS 31st Div. I arranged	

A5834 Wt. W4973/M687 750,000 8/16 D. D. & L. Ltd. Forms/C.2118/13.

Army Form C. 2118.

WAR DIARY
or
~~INTELLIGENCE SUMMARY.~~
(*Erase heading not required.*)

Instructions regarding War Diaries and Intelligence Summaries are contained in F. S. Regs., Part II. and the Staff Manual respectively. Title pages will be prepared in manuscript.

PAGE II

93rd FIELD AMBULANCE

Place	Date	Hour	Summary of Events and Information	Remarks and references to Appendices
BOIS LALEAU	1917 March 3rd (cont'd)		with O.C 59. F.A. and sent up Capt McKINNON & one bearer subdivision with 10 men of a tent subdivision to take over ADS's at COLINCAMPS & EUSTON. This was done in the evening, and the bearers posted with the bearers of above F.A. during the night, at the various collecting posts	A.D. [illegible]
"	March 4th		Capt. L MURPHY with a bearer subdivision proceeded to COLINCAMPS & EUSTON this morning, and the ADS's were finally taken over. Following are the instructions contained in RAMC OPERATION ORDER no 10 for 31st Div: All sick to be evacuated to 59 F.A. BUS. All wounded to be evacuated to CORPS MAIN DRESSING STATN P.17.b.1.9. The sick are collected at COLINCAMPS & evacuated by Horsed ambulance. The wounded are evacuated by motor ambulance from EUSTON. A trolley tramway runs from ADS EUSTON to STAR WOOD, where there is a RAP	

A5834 Wt. W4973/M687 750,000 8/16 D. D. & L. Ltd. Forms/C.2118/13.

Army Form C. 2118.

WAR DIARY
or
~~INTELLIGENCE SUMMARY.~~
(*Erase heading not required.*)

Instructions regarding War Diaries and Intelligence Summaries are contained in F. S. Regs., Part II. and the Staff Manual respectively. Title pages will be prepared in manuscript.

PAGE III

92nd FIELD AMBULANCE

Place	Date	Hour	Summary of Events and Information	Remarks and references to Appendices
BOIS LALEAU	1917 MARCH 4th (contd)		Collecting posts for stretcher bearers are at ~~K.6.~~ K.23.b.3.5. and K.23.c.3.3.	
			Stores have been collected at posts at OBSERVATION WOOD and at FLAG AVENUE, SACKVILLE STREET. Bearers are stationed at these two points to guard stores.	[signature] Lt Col
"	March 5th		I proceeded to COLINCAMPS & inspected A.D.S. there. Everything seemed satisfactory. An incinerator is being put up.	
			I also inspected A.D.S. EUSTON. There are 3 dugouts here, 1 used as a dressing room, 1 for sick & 1 for wounded. Another dugout alongside has been taken over & is being repaired. An incinerator is being built.	
			I also inspected the posts at OBSERVATION WOOD, at K.23.c.2.3 & at K.23.b.5.8. There is a mass of all sorts of material at OBSERVATION WOOD & this I am having collected as far as possible.	
			I met O.C. 1/4 Y. & LANCS. REGT who informed me ~~that~~	

A5834 Wt. W4973/M687 750,000 8/16 D. D. & L. Ltd. Forms/C.2118/13.

Army Form C. 2118.

WAR DIARY
or
INTELLIGENCE SUMMARY.
(*Erase heading not required.*)

Instructions regarding War Diaries and Intelligence Summaries are contained in F. S. Regs., Part II. and the Staff Manual respectively. Title pages will be prepared in manuscript.

PAGE IV. 93rd FIELD AMBULANCE.

Place	Date	Hour	Summary of Events and Information	Remarks and references to Appendices
BOIS LALEAU.	1917 March 5th (cont.)		his regiment & 11 E. LANCS. were taking over line PUISIEUX & to the South from 7th DIV. I sent forward another post to the RAP (about) L. 20 a 4.6., with instructions to evacuate wounded to tramway at BOX WOOD.	AMPollard Maj
	11 March 6th		I reported to ADMS 31 DIV my dispositions of yesterday, and from him received orders to take over from 3rd FA. the line of evacuation from PUISIEUX along the SERRE Rd. but not the ADS. at SUCRERIE. This consists of a line of posts along the PUISIEUX-SERRE rd., at which bearers are stationed & which evacuates back from the RAP. PUISIEUX to ADS. SUCRERIE. I am arranging to evacuate by tramway & merely to hold these posts with small holding parties. At 5 p.m. I received a further order from ADMS. 31 DIV. to send a party of bearers to RAP. of left battalion at WUNDT WERK L. 32. b. 5. 8. and arrange for evacuation: either to SERRE Rd. to EUSTON or else to PUISIEUX & so to the tramway at BOX WOOD.	

A5834 Wt. W4973/M687 750,000 8/16 D. D. & L. Ltd. Forms/C.2118/13.

Instructions regarding War Diaries and Intelligence Summaries are contained in F. S. Regs., Part II. and the Staff Manual respectively. Title pages will be prepared in manuscript.

PAGE V

WAR DIARY
or
~~INTELLIGENCE SUMMARY~~.
(Erase heading not required.)

Army Form C. 2118.

93rd FIELD AMBULANCE

Place	Date	Hour	Summary of Events and Information	Remarks and references to Appendices
BOIS LALEAU	1917 March 6th (contd)		I sent up the necessary instructions to Capt. R. McKINNON, O/c ADS EUSTON, & received communication from him at 11.30 p.m. ~~that~~ he had this matter in hand. A W Pollard Lt Col	
"	March 7th		The ADMS 31 Div. visited the camp & held a board upon [illegible] P.B. men. AP	
"	March 8th		As a considerable number of wounded are collected from Artillery, Ration carrying parties, in the vicinity of the SERRE–PUISIEUX Rd., I detailed Capt. CUMMING & a party of 8 O.R. to proceed to an advanced ADS in [illegible] region, K35a.88. There is also a collecting post [illegible] ¾ mile up this road, where carrying [illegible] down to this ADS. Wounded are [illegible] evacuated by [illegible] to EUSTON [illegible] by motor [illegible]. I inspected this ADS & ADS EUSTON to-day. AP	
"	March 9th		I received orders from ADMS 31st Div. last night to take over [illegible] from [illegible] 5? [illegible] BUS: and to	

A5834 Wt. W4973/M687 750,000 8/16 D. D. & L. Ltd. Forms/C.2118/13.

Instructions regarding War Diaries and Intelligence Summaries are contained in F. S. Regs., Part II. and the Staff Manual respectively. Title pages will be prepared in manuscript.

PAGE VI

WAR DIARY
or
INTELLIGENCE SUMMARY

(*Erase heading not required.*)

93rd FIELD AMBULANCE

Army Form C. 2118.

Place	Date	Hour	Summary of Events and Information	Remarks and references to Appendices
BOIS LALEAU	March 9th (contd) 1917		hand over the camp stores etc. BOIS LALEAU to O.C. 35th F.A. These moves to take place on 10th inst. I sent a small advance party to BUS this afternoon. Capt W. CRABTREE joined for duty.	A.W.P.
"	March 10th		I took over the camp & stores at BUS from O.C. 59 F.A. this day. Duplicate receipt sent to ADMS. 52 sick were in hospital. I handed over the camp at BOIS LALEAU to O.C. 35 F.A. I also sent 1 N.C.O. & 2 men to take over sick & stores from 57 F.A. at LOUVENCOURT.	A.W.P.
BUS	March 11th		I received preliminary notice from ADMS 31 Div, that the division was coming out of line.	A.W.P.
"	March 12th		I received orders from ADMS 31 Div to hand over forward line of evacuation to O.C. 22 F.A. 7th Div. I conferred with this officer, & arranged details of relief, which is to be completed by noon 13th inst.	A.W.P.
"	March 13th		The detachment arrived back from the forward area, some parties at ADS. EUSTON & COLINCAMPS	A.W.P.

A5834 Wt. W4973/M687 750,000 8/16 D. D. & L. Ltd. Forms/C.2118/13.

Army Form C. 2118.

WAR DIARY
or
~~INTELLIGENCE SUMMARY.~~

(Erase heading not required.)

Instructions regarding War Diaries and Intelligence Summaries are contained in F. S. Regs., Part II. and the Staff Manual respectively. Title pages will be prepared in manuscript.

PAGE VII

93rd FIELD AMBULANCE

Place	Date	Hour	Summary of Events and Information	Remarks and references to Appendices
	1917			
BUS	MARCH 14th		Detachment at ADS EUSTON returned on relief by 22nd F.A. I received notice that division was to proceed to 1st ARMY, & to collect at BOUQUE MAISON by 20th inst.	A.R. Martin Maj
"	MARCH 15th		This afternoon I received message from ADMS 31 Div. that the Division might be called upon to move Eastwards at any time: & to be ready to move at 4 hours notice. I have had 4 G.S. wagons packed. A kit inspection was held & deficiencies made good.	A.R.
"	MARCH 16th		On instructions from ADMS 31 Div. I detached Capts. CRABTREE & JOSEPH & proceed to 29 C.C.S. in relief of Capts MACPHAIL & HUMPHREYS, who rejoined.	A.R.
"	MARCH 17th		I received preliminary notice that this unit would be attached to 94 INF. BGDE. for administration during the march Northwards, and would move on 19th inst.	A.R.

A5834 Wt. W4973/M687 750,000 8/16 D. D. & L. Ltd. Forms/C.2118/13.

Instructions regarding War Diaries and Intelligence Summaries are contained in F. S. Regs., Part II. and the Staff Manual respectively. Title pages will be prepared in manuscript.

PAGE VIII

WAR DIARY
or
~~INTELLIGENCE SUMMARY.~~
(*Erase heading not required.*)

Army Form C. 2118.

93rd FIELD AMBULANCE

Place	Date 1917	Hour	Summary of Events and Information	Remarks and references to Appendices
BUS	MARCH 18th		Following upon instructions received from ADMS 31 DIV, I evacuated all the sick to REST STATION, VAUCHELLES. The camp & stores were handed over to a detachment (1 NCO + 2 O.R.) of 2/1st N. MIDLAND. F.A.	
			The stores at WARNIMONT WOOD were collected & the holding party rejoined	
			The ADS. COLINCAMPS was relieved by a F.A. of 7th DIVISION and rejoined.	[signature] Lt Col OC 93 F.A.
BEAUVAL	MARCH 19th		The three horse ambulances were detached today, and handed over for duty with the various battalions of the 94th Bgde. Capt. HUMPHREY was detailed as billeting officer, with a party of 1 NCO + 1 man proceeded last afternoon to take over billets for the following day, in advance of the unit. Capt MACPHAIL was detailed as transport officer for the march.	
			The unit left BUS at 10.15 a.m. and reached billets at 2.45 p.m. at BEAUVAL. Sick were evacuated to No. 33 F.A.	[initials]
			The detachments from LE MEILLARD & from OPERATING CENTRE, AUTHIE rejoined this evening.	
REBREUVE	MARCH 20th		Unit left billets at BEAUVAL at 8.A.M. and marched to REBREUVE (near FREVENT)	

A5834 Wt. W4973/M687 750,000 8/16 D. D. & L. Ltd. Forms/C.2118/13.

Instructions regarding War Diaries and Intelligence Summaries are contained in F. S. Regs., Part II. and the Staff Manual respectively. Title pages will be prepared in manuscript.

PAGE IX

WAR DIARY
or
~~INTELLIGENCE SUMMARY.~~
(Erase heading not required.)

Army Form C. 2118.

93rd FD AMBULANCE.

Place	Date	Hour	Summary of Events and Information	Remarks and references to Appendices
	1917 MARCH 20th (contd)		reaching that place about 3.15 p.m. March was much delayed by constant halts in the region of DOULLENS: the roads about BOUQUEMAISON were bad, men and horses arrived very tired. Sick evacuated to 6 STATIONARY H'PTAL. Capts. CRABTREE & JOSEPH rejoined from 29 C.C.S.	[signature] Lt Col
GAUCHIN	MARCH 21st		The unit left billets at 9.15 a.m. and marched to GAUCHIN, near St POL. The roads were good, and billets were reached at 12.15 p.m. Sick were evacuated to no 12 ~~GENERAL~~ STATIONARY HOSPITAL, St POL.	[initials]
FLORINGHEM	MARCH 22nd		Billets were left at 8 a.m. and unit marched to FLORINGHEM, near PERNES. Short march, good roads & billets were reached at 11.15 a.m. Sick were evacuated as on previous day	[initials]
FLORINGHEM	MARCH 23rd		The unit rested in their billets today. Wagons were cleaned. Capt. MURPHY was evacuated with measles.	[initials]
BOURECQ.	MARCH 24th.		Unit left billets at 9 a.m. and marched to BOURECQ near LILLERS. Arrived at 11.45 a.m. Time was put on 1hr, at midnight, as summer time. Sick evacuated to 57 C.C.S. St VENANT.	[initials]

A5834 Wt. W4973/M687 750,000 8/16 D. D. & L. Ltd. Forms/C.2118/13.

Instructions regarding War Diaries and Intelligence Summaries are contained in F. S. Regs., Part II. and the Staff Manual respectively. Title pages will be prepared in manuscript. PAGE X

WAR DIARY
or
INTELLIGENCE SUMMARY.
(*Erase heading not required.*)

93rd FD. AMBULANCE

Army Form C. 2118.

Place	Date	Hour	Summary of Events and Information	Remarks and references to Appendices
	1917			
CALONNE	MARCH 25th.		Unit left billets at 8 a.m. and reached CALONNE at 12.30 p.m, where it is to remain pending further orders.	
			Men are billetted at the MILL, and in a barn near the Railway station.	
			Horses & transport at the MILL, but the horses are on made standings in the open.	
			Accommodation for sick in (1) Two rooms of a house, on ground floor, accommodation 8-10 men, these for the more serious cases. (2) For lighter cases, a barn; accommodation about 50.	
			C Section is detailed for hospital duties, & Capt. JOSEPH to take charge of the sick.	
			Evacuations to 57 C.C.S. & 2/1st LONDON C.C.S. MERVILLE. Infectious cases to No 8 GENERAL HOSPITAL, St OMER.	[signature] Lt Col
CALONNE	MARCH 26th.		ADMS. 31 Div. visited the village & inspected site of the hospital.	
			I have detailed Capt. HUMPHREY as transport officer.	
			A despatch rider goes round to units of 94th BGDE, to collect number of sick for hospital, which are then collected.	AWO
CALONNE	MARCH 27th		Sectional equipment is being thoroughly overhauled & cleaned.	AWO

A5834 Wt. W4973/M687 750,000 8/16 D. D. & L. Ltd. Forms/C.2118/13.

Army Form C. 2118.

Instructions regarding War Diaries and Intelligence Summaries are contained in F. S. Regs., Part II. and the Staff Manual respectively. Title pages will be prepared in manuscript.

PAGE X

WAR DIARY
or
~~INTELLIGENCE SUMMARY.~~
(Erase heading not required.)

93rd FD. AMBULANCE

Place	Date	Hour	Summary of Events and Information	Remarks and references to Appendices
	1917			
CALONNE	MARCH 28th		Nothing to report. I have been able to get 10 horses under cover. There have been 2 cases of sickness amongst the horses, due to exposure	A.R. [illegible] Lt Col
"	MARCH 29th		Nothing to report.	A.R.
"	MARCH 30th		Nothing to report.	A.R.
"	MARCH 31st		Number of sick remaining in Hospital is 33: daily number of admissions is 15-20. Majority of cases are P.U.O.; practically no diarrhoeal diseases.	A.R.

A.R. [illegible] Lt Col R.A.M.C.
O.C. 93rd F.A.

A5834 Wt. W4973/M687 750,000 8/16 D. D. & L. Ltd. Forms/C.2118/13.

April 1917.

Confidential.

140/2086

Volume XVI

Vol 14

S

War Diary.

93rd Field Ambulance 31st Division

April 1917.

Instructions regarding War Diaries and Intelligence Summaries are contained in F. S. Regs., Part II. and the Staff Manual respectively. Title pages will be prepared in manuscript.

PAGE I

WAR DIARY
or
~~INTELLIGENCE SUMMARY.~~
(Erase heading not required.)

93rd FIELD AMBULANCE

Army Form C. 2118.

Place	Date	Hour	Summary of Events and Information	Remarks and references to Appendices
CALONNE.	1917 APRIL 1st		Capt L.C. MURPHY returned from No 7 STATIONARY HOSPITAL, after suffering from an attack of measles. Capt. J. MACPHAIL proceeded on leave.	A W Pollard Lt Col
" "	APRIL 2nd		Nothing to report.	AWP
" "	APRIL 3rd.		A case of CEREBRO SPINAL MENINGITIS was admitted from 12th Bn KOYLI & transferred to No 12 STATIONARY HOSPITAL St OMER.	AWP
" "	APRIL 4th.		Under instructions received from A.D.M.S. 31 DIV., Capt W. CRABTREE + 10 O.R. (including 2 N.C.O.s as steward & pack storekeeper) were detached for temporary duty at No 18 C.C.S. LAPUGNOY.	AWP.
" "	APRIL 5th		Nothing to report. Attended conference at A.D.M.S. 31 Div.	AWP

A5834 Wt. W4973/M687 750,000 8/16 D. D. & L. Ltd. Forms/C.2118/13.

Army Form C. 2118.

Instructions regarding War Diaries and Intelligence Summaries are contained in F. S. Regs., Part II. and the Staff Manual respectively. Title pages will be prepared in manuscript.

WAR DIARY
or
~~INTELLIGENCE SUMMARY.~~
(Erase heading not required.)

PAGE II — 92nd Fd AMBULANCE

Place	Date	Hour	Summary of Events and Information	Remarks and references to Appendices
	1917			
CALONNE	APRIL 6th		Received notice that unit would move to ANNEZIN on 8th inst to march with 94th BDE, the unit therefore to be ready to move at 4 hrs. notice.	A... Lt Col
"	APRIL 7th		Nothing to report.	A.
"	APRIL 8th		Unit paraded at 11.30 a.m. & moved off en route for ANNEZIN. Unit marched in rear of 94th INF. BDE. Billets reached at 2.15 p.m.	
			A large ward – containing 25 beds – has been put at my disposal for reception of sick, by O.C. 2/1st E. LANCS F.A. This F.A. has its main dressing station in the school room at ANNEZIN.	A.
"	APRIL 9th		About 18 cases in hospital. Evacuated [illegible] today to No 1 CCS	A.

A5834 Wt. W4973/M687 750,000 8/16 D. D. & L. Ltd. Forms/C.2118/13.

Army Form C. 2118.

Instructions regarding War Diaries and Intelligence Summaries are contained in F. S. Regs., Part II. and the Staff Manual respectively. Title pages will be prepared in manuscript.

PAGE III.

WAR DIARY
or
~~INTELLIGENCE SUMMARY.~~

(*Erase heading not required.*)

93rd Fd AMBULANCE.

Place	Date	Hour	Summary of Events and Information	Remarks and references to Appendices
	1917			
ANNEZIN	APRIL 10th.		Nothing to report.	A.W. Sellard Lt Col
"	APRIL 11th		At 2.30 a.m. I received message from 94th INF. BDE. Hqrs. that the brigade would move about 11 a.m. & that further orders would be issued.	
			At 11.30 a.m. received orders to march in rear of 94th INF BDE, to billets in RUITZ (near BRUAY). I detached horse ambulances to 12th, 13th & 14th Btns YORK & LANCS Rgt.	
			Unit moved off at 12.30 p.m. & reached billets at 3.30 p.m.	
			Route. FOUQUIÈRES - HESDIGNEUL - LA BUISSIÈRE - HAILLICOURT - RUITZ.	AWS
RUITZ.	APRIL 12th		Have fitted up one room in the chateau as a hospital capable of taking 15 patients. Evacuation to 22 C.C.S.	AWS
"	APRIL 13th.		Warned that the 31st DIVn were to move on 14th inst.	AWS

A5834 Wt. W4973/M687 750,000 8/16 D. D. & L. Ltd. Forms/C.2118/13.

Instructions regarding War Diaries and Intelligence Summaries are contained in F. S. Regs., Part II. and the Staff Manual respectively. Title pages will be prepared in manuscript.

PAGE IV

WAR DIARY
or
~~INTELLIGENCE SUMMARY.~~
(*Erase heading not required.*)

Army Form C. 2118.

93rd FIELD AMBULANCE

Place	Date	Hour	Summary of Events and Information	Remarks and references to Appendices
FREVILLERS	1917 APRIL 14th		According to instructions received from 93rd Inf. Bde., the unit marched into billets at FREVILLERS. Hour of start 12.30 p.m.	
			Route. MAISNIL – ~~HERMIN~~ REBREUVE – HERMIN – FREVILLERS	
			Arrived at 3.45 p.m.	
			Billets very crowded. No site for any hospital.	[illegible]
"	APRIL 15th		Nothing to report. The 93 Machine Gun Coy. has moved – I have been able to obtain further accomodation, and in particular a M. Inspection room.	A.P.
"	" 16th		Nothing to report.	A.P.
"	" 17th		Nothing to report	A.P.
"	" 18th		Nothing to report.	A.P.
"	" 19th		Nothing to report.	A.P.
"	" 20th		Nothing to report	A.P.
"	" 21st		Inspection of billets etc by A.D.M.S. 31st Div.	
"	" 22nd		Under instructions from A.D.M.S. 31st Div. I detailed 2 large motor ambulances & 1 Ford ambulance to report for duty with A.D.M.S. 2nd Div. at St CATHARINE.	A.P.

A5834 Wt. W4973/M687 750,000 8/16 D. D. & L. Ltd. Forms/C.2118/13.

Army Form C. 2118.

WAR DIARY
or
~~INTELLIGENCE SUMMARY~~.
(Erase heading not required.)

Instructions regarding War Diaries and Intelligence Summaries are contained in F. S. Regs., Part II. and the Staff Manual respectively. Title pages will be prepared in manuscript.

PAGE V — 93rd Fd AMBULANCE

Place	Date	Hour	Summary of Events and Information	Remarks and references to Appendices
	1917			
FREVILLERS	APRIL 23rd		Nothing to report	[signature]
"	APRIL 24th		Under instructions from ADMS. 31 DIV. I detailed Capt. H.M. JOSEPH for temporary duty with 16th W. YORKS Regt	[initials]
"	APRIL 25th		I detailed Capt MACKINNON as President & Capts. CUMMING & MACPHAIL as members of a Court of Inquiry to be held to consider circumstances under which the late T Dr. MOORE R. ASC received an injury on 3.2.17.	[initials]
"	APRIL 26th		Nothing to report.	[initials]
"	APRIL 27th		At 11.30 p.m. I received a warning order that 93rd INF BGDE would move next day.	[initials]
"	APRIL 28th		At 2.30 a.m. I received order that 93rd INF. BGDE. would move to ECOIVRES. This unit to remain at present location. I detailed Horse Ambulances to accompany brigade, at request of Brigade [illegible]	[initials]

Instructions regarding War Diaries and Intelligence Summaries are contained in F. S. Regs., Part II. and the Staff Manual respectively. Title pages will be prepared in manuscript.

WAR DIARY
or
~~INTELLIGENCE SUMMARY.~~
(Erase heading not required.)

Army Form C. 2118.

PAGE VI — 93rd Fd. AMBULANCE

Place	Date 1917	Hour	Summary of Events and Information	Remarks and references to Appendices
ECOIVRES	APRIL 24th		Under instructions from ADMS. 31 DIV. the unit moved to ECOIVRES, preliminary to taking over forward evacuation from 2.A. of 63rd DIV.	
IN THE FIELD			I took over this morning A.D.S. at H.1.C.3.8. (Map Ref. 51B)	
			(A) 1 collecting post at B.28.A.1.8. At this place 40 bearers are stationed for collecting cases. R.A.P's at B.22.b.4.6. and at B.30.a.9.9. 2 Ford cars are stationed at B.26.c.2.3. & 3 large cars at ADS. At this post I detailed Capt COMMING & 28 bearers.	
			(B) 1 Collecting post at H.4. Central. Capt HUMPHREY & 26 bearers. 1 Forward Collecting post at B.30.a.6.2. Here I placed Sgt FRANKLIN and 14 bearers. These posts evacuate from R.A.P. at B.29.b.9.1. 2 Cars & 1 Ford are stationed at H.8. Central. These posts & ADS taken over from O.C. 1.F.A. 63rd Div.	[signature] O.C. 93 F.A.

A5834 Wt. W4973/M687 750,000 8/16 D. D. & L. Ltd. Forms/C.2118/13.

B.E.F.

SUMMARY OF MEDICAL WAR DIARIES FOR 93rd F.A. 31st Divn. 13th Corps,

1st Army

3rd Army from 11/4/17.

WESTERN FRONT April-May. '17.

O.C. Lt. Col. A.M. Pollard.

SUMMARISED UNDER THE FOLLOWING HEADINGS

Phase "B" Battle of Arras- April- May. '17.

1st Period Attack on Vimy Ridge April.

2nd Period Capture of Siegfried May.

93rd F.A. 31st Divn. 13th Corps WESTERN FRONT.

O.C. Lt. Col. A.M. Pollard. April. '17.

1st Army.

3rd Army from 11/4/17.

Phase "B" Battle of Arras- April- May. '17.

1st Period Attack on Vimy Ridge April.

1917.		Headquarters. at Calonne.
April.	4th.	Moves Detachment: 1 and 10 detached for temp. duty at No.18 C.C.S. Lapugnoy.
	8th.	Moves: with 94th Inf. Bde. to Annezin.
		Accommodation: Ward 20 beds set aside for reception of sick by 2/2nd E. Lancs. Field Ambulance.
		M.D.S. in school room at Annezin.
	11th.	Moves: with 94th Inf. Bde. to Ruitz (near Bruay)
		Accommodation: Room filled up in Chateau as Hospital. Evacuations to 22nd Casualty Clearing Station.
		Transfer. 3rd Army.

93rd F.A. 31st Divn. 13th Corps. WESTERN FRONT.

O.C. Lt. Col. A.M. Pollard. April. '17.

3rd Army.

Phase "B" Battle of Arras- April- May' '17.

1st Period Attack on Vimy Ridge April.

1917.

April. 11th. Transfer. 3rd Army.

14th. Military Situation: Moves: 31st Divn. and Unit moved into billets at Frevillers.

22nd. Moves Detachment: 2 large Motor Ambulances and 1 Ford Ambulance for duty with A.D.M.S. 63rd Divn. at St Catherine.

28th. Military Situation: 93rd Inf. Bde. moved to Ecoivres.

29th. Moves: Unit moved to Ecoivres.

Medical Arrangements: A.D.S. at H.1.c.3.8. (Map Ref. 51 B.)

(A) Coll. Post at B.28..A.1.8. = 40 brs.
R.A.Ps at B.22.c.4.6. and B/30 a.9.9.-2 Ford Cars, at B.26.c.2.3.- 3 large cars at Advanced Dressing Station.

(B) Coll. Post at H.4 Central 1 and 26 Brs.
1 Forward Coll., Post at B.30.a.6.2. 19 Brs.
These posts evacuate from R.A.P. at B. 29.b.9.1.
2 Cars and 1 Ford at H.8. Central.
These Posts and A.D.S. taken over from 1st Field Ambulance 63rd Divn.

93rd F.A. 31st Divn. 13th Corps — WESTERN FRONT.

O.C. Lt. Col. A.M. Pollard. — April. '17.

1st Army.

3rd Army from 11/4/17.

Phase "B" Battle of Arras- April- May. '17.

1st Period Attack on Vimy Ridge April.

1917. Headquarters. at Calonne.

April. 4th. Moves Detachment: 1 and 10 detached for temp. duty at No.18 C.C.S. Lapugnoy.

8th. Moves: with 94th Inf. Bde. to Annezin.

Accommodation: Ward 20 beds set aside for reception of sick by 2/2nd E. Lancs. Field Ambulance.

M.D.S. in school room at Annezin.

11th. Moves: with 94th Inf. Bde. to Ruitz (near Bruay)

Accommodation: Room filled up in Chateau as Hospital. Evacuations to 22nd Casualty Clearing Station

Transfer. 3rd Army.

93rd F.A. 31st Divn. 13th Corps. WESTERN FRONT.

O.C. Lt' Col. A.M. Pollard. April. '17.

3rd Army.

Phase "B" Battle of Arras- April- May' '17.

1st Period Attack on Vimy Ridge April.

1917.

April. 11th. Transfer. 3rd Army.

14th. Military Situation: Moves: 31st Divn. and Unit moved into billets at Frevillers.

22nd. Moves Detachment: 2 large Motor Ambulances and 1 Ford Ambulance for duty with A.D.M.S. 63rd Divn. at St Catherine.

28th. Military Situation: 93rd Inf. Bde. moved to Ecoivres.

29th. Moves: Unit moved to Ecoivres.

Medical Arrangements: A.D.S. at H.I.c.3.8. (Map Ref. 51 B.)

(A) Coll. Post at B.28 A.1.8. = 40 brs.

R.A.Ps at B.22.c.4.6. and B/30.a.9.9.-2 Ford Cars.

at B.26.c.2.3.- 3 large cars at Advanced Dressing Station.

(B) Coll. Post at H.4 Central 1 and 26 Brs.

1. Forward Coll. Post at B.30.a.6.2. 19 Brs.

These posts evacuate from R.A.P. at B. 29.b.9.1.

2 Cars and 1 Ford at H.8. Central.

These Posts and A.D.S. taken over from 1st Field Ambulance 63rd Divn.

Confidential 14 | Volume XVII

May 1917 | 140/2230 | Vol 15

5

War Diary.

93rd Field Ambulance | 31st Division

May 1917.

Instructions regarding War Diaries and Intelligence Summaries are contained in F. S. Regs., Part II. and the Staff Manual respectively. Title pages will be prepared in manuscript.

WAR DIARY

~~or INTELLIGENCE SUMMARY.~~

(Erase heading not required.)

Army Form C. 2118.

PAGE I. 93rd FD. AMBULANCE

Place	Date	Hour	Summary of Events and Information	Remarks and references to Appendices
A.D.S. H.1.C.38 (Map. Ref. 51 B).	1917 MAY 1st		Visited COLLECTING POST at B 28. a. 28. yesterday afternoon. Good position & good dugouts, but very exposed to shell fire. This morning LIEUT. GATT of 94th F.A. + 26 O.R. joined Capt. CUMMING there to relieve a party of 1st F.A. 63rd F.A. Many wounded are collected from this area. I have now arranged that ~~Capt. Cumm~~ this post shall evacuate 13. E. YORKS (B. M. C. 63) and 12th K.O.Y.L.I. (B. 21. C. 8.2). 11 E. YORKS are also in line & using same R.A.P. as 13th Bn.	
			Visited COLLECTING POST at H.4. Central. CAPT. KING of 94th FA + 24 O.R. joined Capt. HUMPHREY to relieve party of 1st F.A. 63rd Div. These collect cases from following :- 18th W. YORKS (B. 30. a. 8.9.), 16th W. YORKS (B. 30. a. 4.4.) + 15th W. YORKS (B. 29. C. 9.0.). Their R.A.P.'s are close to the Forward Collecting Post at B. 29. D 8.8.	
"	MAY 2nd		O.C. 94 F.A. took over from me the GUN PIT Collecting Post (H 4 Central), on instructions from ADMS. 31 Div. Capt. HUMPHREY and his party joined Capt. CUMMING at B. 28. a. 28.; + Lieut. GATT's party from 94 F.A. joined O.C. 94 F.A. at GUN PITS.	A W Ollis [illegible]

A5834 Wt. W4973/M687 750,000 8/16 D. D. & L. Ltd. Forms/C.2118/13.

Instructions regarding War Diaries and Intelligence Summaries are contained in F. S. Regs., Part II. and the Staff Manual respectively. Title pages will be prepared in manuscript. PAGE II

WAR DIARY
or
~~INTELLIGENCE SUMMARY.~~
(*Erase heading not required.*)

93rd FD. AMBULANCE.

Army Form C. 2118.

Place	Date	Hour	Summary of Events and Information	Remarks and references to Appendices
A.D.S (11.c.3.8)	1917 May 2nd (cont).		I was warned that 31st Div. would attack tomorrow. 92nd Bgde being on left & 93rd Bgde on right. 94th Bgde to be in support. My duty here was the forward line of evacuation from 93rd Bgde. I made the following arrangements with Hqrs. 93rd Bgde.	
			(1) R.A.P. B.17 d 4.4. for 10th & 12th E. Yorks Regt. 1 N.C.O & 18 bearers sent there from Collecting Post at B.28. a.2.8. These evacuate back to Collecting Post.	
			(2) R.A.P. B.16 a.8.7. (SUGAR FACTORY). These to evacuate for 11th E. Yorks directly back to MAISON de la CÔTE (B.26.b.8.9), without calling at Collecting Post. 1 N.C.O & 24 men stationed here.	
			Runners to keep touch between R.A.P.'s & Collecting Post.	
			The Ford cars & 1 heavy car are to be massed up as near MAISON de la CÔTE as is reasonably safe.	
			I have to note with great regret the death in action of Sergt. QUAYLE and of Pte BREENAN killed this evening. The former displayed great devotion to duty and gallantry & had he not been killed, I should have forwarded his name to Divisional Commander as being worthy of immediate reward. [illegible signature]	

A5834 Wt. W4973/M687 750,000 8/16 D. D. & L. Ltd. Forms/C.2118/13.

Army Form C. 2118.

Instructions regarding War Diaries and Intelligence Summaries are contained in F. S. Regs., Part II. and the Staff Manual respectively. Title pages will be prepared in manuscript. PAGE III

WAR DIARY
or
~~INTELLIGENCE SUMMARY.~~
(Erase heading not required.)

93rd F.A. AMBULANCE.

Place	Date	Hour	Summary of Events and Information	Remarks and references to Appendices
A.D.S. (H.1.C.3.8)	1917 MAY 3rd		Wounded began to come in at about 6.30 a.m. this morning. I was able to use empty lorries along the road to evacuate lightly wounded to M.D.S. On application, the ADMS 31 Div. sent up 3 heavy motor ambulances for use here. Between 6.30 am + 11.30 am, about 220 cases passed through. After that hour, the flow of wounded very considerably slackened off, and during the afternoon cases came in slowly.	
			At 7 p.m. I handed over 100 stretcher bearers (officer detailed by Hqr. 92nd Bde.) for the purpose of clearing the battle area. About 11.30 p.m. these cases began to arrive, and between that hour and 7.30 a.m. we dealt with 70 stretcher cases, all serious wounds + many very collapsed, a certain number belonged to 2nd + 63rd Div. units that have lain out for some days.	
			[illegible signature]	
~	MAY 4th		As my bearer parties are extremely exhausted, I asked the ADMS, 31 Div. to relieve my bearers in line if possible.	
			The ADMS. inspected my arrangements here and has also detailed	

A5834 Wt. W4973/M687 750,000 8/16 D. D. & L. Ltd. Forms/C.2118/13.

Instructions regarding War Diaries and Intelligence Summaries are contained in F. S. Regs., Part II. and the Staff Manual respectively. Title pages will be prepared in manuscript. PAGE IV.

WAR DIARY
or
~~INTELLIGENCE~~ SUMMARY.
(*Erase heading not required.*)

Army Form C. 2118.

93rd FD AMBULANCE

Place	Date	Hour	Summary of Events and Information	Remarks and references to Appendices
A.D.S (H.I.C.3.8)	1917 May 4th (cont'd)		50 bearers under Capt. ANDERSON of 95th F.A. to relieve my bearers in line. I have arranged for the entire party to be relieved; & am sending them to Hqrs. at St. CATHERINE, less 30 bearers & Capts. HUMPHREY & CUMMINS, who will remain here. Capts. McKINNON & MURPHY will proceed to Hqrs. at St. CATHERINE.	
			Capt. J. MacPHAIL was this day evacuated to M.D.S., suffering from P.U.O.	
			The relieving party arrived here at 1.30 p.m.	[illegible]
A.D.S.	May 5th.		A good many wounded are still being dealt with, among Artillery and Ration Parties, & working parties on the roads.	AP
A.D.S	May 6th.		Nothing to report.	AP.
St. CATHERINES	May 7th		I returned to Unit Hqrs. today.	AP.
"	May 8th		Nothing to report. Capt. L.C. MURPHY proceeded to Collecting Post for duty.	AP.
"	May 9th.		I inspected A.D.S. this morning. The big dugout for personnel is almost cleaned out.	AP.

Instructions regarding War Diaries and Intelligence Summaries are contained in F. S. Regs., Part II. and the Staff Manual respectively. Title pages will be prepared in manuscript.

WAR DIARY
or
~~INTELLIGENCE SUMMARY.~~
(Erase heading not required.)

Army Form C. 2118.

PAGE V

93rd FD. AMBULANCE.

Place	Date	Hour	Summary of Events and Information	Remarks and references to Appendices
	1917.			
ST. CATHERINE	MAY 10th.		Nothing to report.	R Pollard Lt Col
"	MAY 11th		Inspection of horses & transport by O.C. 31st Div. TRAIN.	RP.
"	MAY 12th.		My bearers in line were relieved by bearers from 95th F.A. Capt. R. MACKINNON relieved Capt. L. MURPHY.	RP.
"	MAY 13th.		I inspected A.D.S. everything is satisfactory. Latrines have been covered in. A more suitable kitchen has been erected.	RP.
"	May 14th.		Nothing to report.	RP.
"	May 15th.		Extract from 31st D.R.O. d. 14.5.17. REWARDS The Corps Commander has awarded the Military Medal to the undermentioned for Gallantry in the Field:— No 60559 Pte A. FRANCIS } 93rd FD. AMBULANCE. date of award. 12.5.17. No 60493. Pte. E. HUMPHRIES. } The unit paraded this evening and the ribbon of the medal was presented to the above mentioned men by ADMS. 31st DIV.	RP.

A5834 Wt. W4973/M687 750,000 8/16 D. D. & L. Ltd. Forms/C.2118/13.

Army Form C. 2118.

WAR DIARY

or

~~INTELLIGENCE SUMMARY.~~

(Erase heading not required.)

Instructions regarding War Diaries and Intelligence Summaries are contained in F. S. Regs., Part II. and the Staff Manual respectively. Title pages will be prepared in manuscript.

PAGE VI

93rd FD. AMBULANCE.

Place	Date 1917	Hour	Summary of Events and Information	Remarks and references to Appendices
ST CATHERINE	MAY 16th.		According to instructions received from D.M.S. 1st ARMY, via usual channels, Capt. W. CRABTREE and party rejoined last night from no. 18 C.C.S. 2 N.C.O's & 48 men of my unit relieved similar party of 95th F.A. at Collecting Post. Capt. HUMPHREY relieved Capt MacKINNON at Collecting post; latter rejoined Hqrs. Capt. MURPHY relieved Capt. HUMPHREY at A.D.S.	[signature]
"	MAY 17th		Nothing to report.	[initials]
"	MAY 18th		Nothing to report.	[initials]
"	MAY 19th		I received a copy of R.A.M.C. Operation Orders No 17 d. 18.5.17. by A.D.M.S. 31st Div. The unit is to be relieved in line and at St CATHERINE by 2nd F.A. 63rd DIV. On the 21st inst. Unit will proceed to CAMBLIGNEUL and open for the reception of sick.	[initials]

A5834 Wt. W4973/M687 750,000 8/16 D. D. & L. Ltd. Forms/C.2118/13.

Instructions regarding War Diaries and Intelligence Summaries are contained in F. S. Regs., Part II. and the Staff Manual respectively. Title pages will be prepared in manuscript.

PAGE VII

WAR DIARY
or
~~INTELLIGENCE SUMMARY.~~

(Erase heading not required.)

Army Form C. 2118.

93rd Fd. AMBULANCE.

Place	Date	Hour	Summary of Events and Information	Remarks and references to Appendices
	1917			
ST. CATHERINE	MAY 20th.		According to the instructions of ADMS. 31st DIV. I sent Capt. JOSEPH. and 4 O.R., as an advance party, to take over from O.C. 2nd F.A. 63rd DIV. at CAMBLIGNEUL.	A.W. Pollard Lt Col
			The bearers were relieved in the line this evening & returned at 7 p.m.	
CAMBLIGNEUL	MAY 21st.		Unit proceeded to CAMBLIGNEUL today. Route via ST. POL – ARRAS Rd. to ACQ & ~~thence~~ via CAMBLIN. Hour of start 10 a.m. Hour of arrival 2.30 p.m.	
			4 patients were left behind & taken over. The unit being now open for reception of sick.	AWP.
"	MAY 22nd		Nothing to report.	AP.
"	MAY 23rd		Nothing to report	AP.
"	MAY 24th.		Capt. H.M. JOSEPH left for duty with O.C. 2nd OPTHALMIC CENTRE.	AWP.
"	MAY 25th.		~~[illegible]~~ Inspection of transport by G.O.C. 31st DIVISION.	AWP.

A5834 Wt. W4973/M687 750,000 8/16 D. D. & L. Ltd. Forms/C.2118/13.

Army Form C. 2118.

WAR DIARY
or
~~INTELLIGENCE SUMMARY.~~
(Erase heading not required.)

Instructions regarding War Diaries and Intelligence Summaries are contained in F. S. Regs., Part II. and the Staff Manual respectively. Title pages will be prepared in manuscript.

PAGE VIII

93rd Fd. AMBULANCE.

Place	Date	Hour	Summary of Events and Information	Remarks and references to Appendices
CAMBLIGNEUL	1917 MAY 26th.		Capt. J. MacPHAIL joined this unit for duty.	[illegible] Lt Col
"	MAY 27th.		Capt. S.A. HONY joined this unit for duty	[illegible]
"	MAY 28th.		Nothing to report.	[illegible]
"	MAY 29th.		LIEUT & QMR. READ departed on leave to England	[illegible]
"	MAY 30th.		Capt. W. CRABTREE left for temporary duty with no. 2. C.C.S., under instructions from ADMS 31st Div.	[illegible]
"	MAY 31st		Number of patients in hospital on last day of month is 17.	[illegible] Lt Col O.C. 93 F.A.

B.E.F.

SUMMARY OF MEDICAL WAR DIARIES FOR 93rd F.A. 31st Divn. 13th Corps, 1st Army
3rd Army from 11/4/17.

WESTERN FRONT April-May. '17.

O.C. Lt. Col. A.M. Pollard.

SUMMARISED UNDER THE FOLLOWING HEADINGS

Phase "B" Battle of Arras- April- May. '17.

1st Period Attack on Vimy Ridge April.

2nd Period Capture of Siegfried May.

B.E.F.

93rd F.A. 31st Divn. 13th Corps. WESTERN FRONT.

O.C. Lt. Col. A.M. Pollard. May. '17.

3rd Army.

Phase "B" Battle of Arras- April. May. 1917.

2nd Period Capture of Siegfried Line May.

1917.

May. 2nd. Casualties R.A.M.C. 0 and 2 killed.

3rd Operations. 31st Division attacked - 92nd Bde. on.L. 93rd Bde. on R. 94th Bde. in support.

Medical Arrangements:-

(1) R.A.P. B.17.d.4.4.

(2) R.A.P. B.16.a.8.7. (Sugar Factory) to evacuate back to Maison de la Cote (B.26.b.8.9.) without calling out Coll. Post.

Runners keeping touch between R.A.Ps/ and coll. Post. Ford Cars and 1 Heavy Car moved up as near as reasonably safe.

Casualties: Evacuation: W. began to come in about 6.30. a.m. empty lorries used to evacuate lightly wounded to M.D.S.

3 Heavy Motor Ambulances sent up.

Between 6.30. and 11.30 a.m. about 220 wounded passed through. Afterwards the flow of wounded very considerably slackened off and during afternoon wounded came in slowly.

At 7.p.m. 100 stretchers handed over to 92nd Bde. for purpose of clearing battle area.

Between 7.30 p.m. and 11.30 p.m. 70 stretcher cases dealt with- all serious wounds- a certain number belonged to 2nd and 63rd Divisions Units/ and had been lying out for some days.

4th. Medical Arrangements: Operations R.A.M.C. Br. Parties being extremely exhausted, 50 Brs. of 95th Field Ambulance relieved Brs. in line. The entire party later relieved/ and sent

93rd F.A. 31st Divn. 13th Corps. WESTERN FRONT.

O.C. Lt. Col. A.M. Pollard. May. '17.

3rd Army.

Phase "B" cont.

2nd Period cont.

1917.

May. 4th cont. Medical Arrangements: Operations R.A.M.C. to Headquarters at St. Catherine.

5th. Casualties. A good many wounded still being dealt with mainly Artillery and Ration Parties and Working parties on the road.

12th. Operations R.A.M.C. Brs. in line relieved by Brs. 95th F.A.

13th. Sanitation: Latrines at A.D.S. covered in. Suitable kitchen erected.

15th. Decorations: Pte. A. Francis and Pte E. Humphries awarded M.M.

20th. Moves: Unit relieved by 2nd Field Ambulance 63rd Divn. and moved to Cambligneul being now open for reception of sick.

31st. Casualties. 0 and 17 sick in Hospital.

B.E.F.

93rd F.A. 31st Divn. 13th Corps. WESTERN FRONT.

O.C. Lt. Col. A.M. Pollard. May. '17.

3rd Army.

Phase "B" Battle of Arras- April. May. 1917.

2nd Period Capture of Siegfried Line May.

1917.

May. 2nd. Casualties R.A.M.C. 0 and 2 killed.

3rd Operations. 31st Division attacked - 92nd Bde. on.L. 93rd Bde. on R. 94th Bde. in support.

Medical Arrangements:-

(1) R.A.P. B.17.d.4.4.

(2) R.A.P. B.16.a.8.7. (Sugar Factory) to evacuate back to Maison de la Cote (B.26.b.8.9.) without calling out Coll. Post.

Runners keeping touch between R.A.Ps and coll. Post. Ford Cars and 1 Heavy Car moved up as near as reasonably safe.

Casualties: Evacuation: W. began to come in about 6.30. a.m. empty lorries used to evacuate lightly wounded to M.D.S.

3 Heavy Motor Ambulances sent up.

Between 6.30. and 11.30 a.m. about 220 wounded passed throug

Afterwards the flow of wounded very considerably slackened off and during afternoon wounded came in slowly.

At 7.p.m. 100 stretchers handed over to 92nd Bde. for purpose of clearing battle area.

Between 7.30 p.m. and 11.30 p.m. 70 stretcher cases dealt with- all serious wounds- a certain number belonged to 2nd and 63rd Divisions Units and had been lying out for some days.

4th. Medical Arrangements: Operations R.A.M.C. Br. Parties being extremely exhausted, 50 Brs. of 95th Field Ambulance relieved Brs. in line. The entire party later relieved and sent

93rd F.A. 31st Divn. 13th Corps. WESTERN FRONT.

O.C. Lt. Col. A.M. Pollard. May. '17.

3rd Army.

Phase "B" cont.

2nd Period cont.

1917.

May. 4th cont. Medical Arrangements: Operations R.A.M.C. to Headquarters at St. Catherine.

5th. Casualties. A good many wounded still being dealt with mainly Artillery and Ration Parties and Working parties on the road.

12th. Operations R.A.M.C. Brs. in line relieved by Brs. 95th F.A.

13th. Sanitation: Latrines at A.D.S. covered in. Suitable kitchen erected.

15th. Decorations: Pte. A. Francis and Pte E. Humphries awarded M.M.

20th. Moves: Unit relieved by 2nd Field Ambulance 63rd Divn. and moved to Cambligneul being now open for reception of sick.

31st. Casualties. 0 and 17 sick in Hospital.

21

Confidential

June 1917

VF 16

Volume XVIII

140/2230

War Diary

93rd Field Ambulance 31st Division

June 1917

Instructions regarding War Diaries and Intelligence Summaries are contained in F. S. Regs., Part II. and the Staff Manual respectively. Title pages will be prepared in manuscript.

PAGE I.

WAR DIARY
or
~~INTELLIGENCE SUMMARY.~~
(Erase heading not required.)

93rd Fd. AMBULa.

Army Form C. 2118.

1

Place	Date 1917	Hour	Summary of Events and Information	Remarks and references to Appendices
CAMBLIGNEUL	JUNE 1st.		Nothing to report.	A. R. Pollard Lt Col. A.R.
"	JUNE 2nd		Nothing to report.	A.R.
"	JUNE 3rd		Nothing to report.	A.R.
"	JUNE 4th		Nothing to report.	A.R.
"	JUNE 5th		Nothing to report.	A.R.
"	JUNE 6th.		Capt. L. C. MURPHY returned from leave	A.R.
"	JUNE 7th.		D.M.S. 1st ARMY visited the camp. Capt. S. A. KUNY proceeded to relieve M.O. i/c 18. DURHAM. Lt. Inf. Capt. R. McKINNON proceeded on leave	A.R.
"	JUNE 8th		Nothing to report, save the receipt of Operation Orders no 18. by A.D.M.S. 31st Divn. This unit is to take over M.D.S. at St. CATHERINE from 1st F.A. 63rd DIV. Relief to be completed by 9 a.m. 11th inst. Advance Party of 1 officer, 1 N.C.O + 4 men to proceed on 10th inst.	A.R.

Instructions regarding War Diaries and Intelligence Summaries are contained in F. S. Regs., Part II. and the Staff Manual respectively. Title pages will be prepared in manuscript. PAGE II

WAR DIARY
or
INTELLIGENCE SUMMARY.
(Erase heading not required.)

93rd FD. AMBULANCE

Army Form C. 2118. 2

Place	Date	Hour	Summary of Events and Information	Remarks and references to Appendices
	1917			
CAMBLIGNEUL	JUNE 9th.		Nothing to report.	[illegible]
"	JUNE 10th		Capt. J. MacPHAIL and an advance party were sent over to ST. CATHERINE to take over M.D.S.	
ST. CATHERINE	JUNE 11th		The unit moved to ST. CATHERINE to-day and replaced 1st F.A. 63rd Div. Time of start 6. A.M. Route CAMBLAIN – MT. ST. ELOI – ST. CATHERINE. Arrived 9.45 A.M.	
			Few wounded came in during the day.	
			Took over 31 sick from 1st F.A. 63rd Div. These men I am retaining, and am notifying O.C. of above unit & ADMS 63rd Div. of their disposal, daily.	
			Scabies cases of the whole Corps are being retained here, & I have taken over the FODEN LORRY.	
			Future cases of sick of 63rd Div. will be sent to 2nd F.A. 63rd Div. at CAMBLIGNEUL.	[illegible]

A5834 Wt. W4973/M687 750,000 8/16 D. D. & L. Ltd. Forms/C.2118/13.

PAGE III | Army Form C. 2118. | 3

WAR DIARY
or
INTELLIGENCE SUMMARY.
(Erase heading not required.)

Instructions regarding War Diaries and Intelligence Summaries are contained in F. S. Regs., Part II. and the Staff Manual respectively. Title pages will be prepa[illegible] manuscript.

93rd Fd. AMBULANCE

Place	Date	Hour	Summary of Events and Information	Remarks and references to Appendices
M.D.S. ST. CATHERINE	1917 JUNE 11th (contd.)		Sick & wounded are evacuated to C.C.S. at AUBIGNY by cars of No. 6 M.A.C., which is adjacent. Severely severely wounded cases are sent to C.C.S. at DUISANS.	[illegible]
"	JUNE 12th		Lt. GEN. SIR W. CONGREVE V.C., Commandant XIII CORPS was admitted today, suffering from severe shell injuries to left hand, he was evacuated to 19 C.C.S. DUISANS.	[illegible]
			All sick of 31st DIV. are now sent to 95 F.A. at ANZIN.	
"	JUNE 13th		Nothing to report. Lt. & Qrmr. READ returned from leave last evening.	[illegible]
"	JUNE 14th		D.M.S. 1st ARMY visited the M.D.S.	[illegible]
"	JUNE 15th		Nothing to report	[illegible]
"	JUNE 16th		A/Sgt. TEW returned to the unit, after being evacuated wounded 30/4/17. There are 2 officers & 84 O.R. in hospital with [illegible] SCABIES. In addition there are 45 O.R. sick. No. of wounded is less than 20 per diem. Stretcher bath. One being made for the main ward.	[illegible]

Instructions regarding War Diaries and Intelligence Summaries are contained in F. S. Regs., Part II. and the Staff Manual respectively. Title pages will be prepared in manuscript.

WAR DIARY
or
~~INTELLIGENCE SUMMARY.~~
(*Erase heading not required.*)

Army Form C. 2118.

PAGE IV — 93rd Fd AMBULANCE — 4

Place	Date	Hour	Summary of Events and Information	Remarks and references to Appendices
M.D.S.	1917		Tanks have been cleared out from the near end, which was separated	
St CATHERINE	JUNE 16th		off, and this place has been cleaned out & is reserved only for cutting	
	(contd).		up food. The whole ward has been re-whitewashed.	[illegible]
			Capt. CUMMING attended a course of Gas Instruction at DIVISIONAL SCHOOL. This	
			course commenced today and finishes on 18th inst.	
"	JUNE 17th		Nothing to report	AR
	JUNE 18th		Capt. R.M. DAVIES (O.C. No 12 M.A.C.) reported here for instructional	
			purposes & is taken on the strength	AR
"	JUNE 19th		A French Interpreter — M FAUVEAU — joined this unit	AR
"	JUNE 20th		Inspection of M.D.S. by G.O.C. 1st ARMY.	AR
"	JUNE 21st		Inspection of M.D.S. by G.O.C. 3rd Divn	AR
"	JUNE 22nd		Capt. R.M. DAVIES proceeded to A.D.S. for instructional purposes. Capt. S.A.	
			HUNT having reported sick, I detailed Capt J HUMPHREYS to relieve him	
			with the 18th D.L.I.	AR
			The CORPS REST STATn has now opened. I have transferred the	
			majority of sick — & all SCABIES cases — to that place.	

A5834 Wt. W4973/M687 750,000 8/16 D. D. & L. Ltd. Forms/C.2118/13.

Instructions regarding War Diaries and Intelligence Summaries are contained in F. S. Regs., Part II. and the Staff Manual respectively. Title pages will be prepared in manuscript.

WAR DIARY
or
~~INTELLIGENCE SUMMARY.~~

(Erase heading not required.)

PAGE V. 93rd Fd AMBULANCE

Army Form C. 2118.

Place	Date	Hour	Summary of Events and Information	Remarks and references to Appendices
M.D.S. ST CATHERINE.	1917 June 23rd		Capt. HUNT having reported sick, I detailed Capt J. HUMPHREYS in relief for duty with 18th D.L.I.	
			12 reinforcements arrived from the base this day and are taken on strength	
			In accordance with instructions from ADMS 31st Div. I detailed a N.C.O. for duty with 31st Div. BATHS.	
" "	JUNE 24th		H. H. Prince AMORODHAT of Siam inspected the M.D.S.	
			CAPT. J. HUMPHREYS returned from temporary duty with 18th D.L.I.	
" "	JUNE 25th		Nothing to report.	
" "	June 26th		Inspection by D.D.M.S. XIII CORPS.	
			I received information that the 31st DIVISION would attack on 28th inst, a line running from C19.a.75.65 to C19.c.8.9 (WINDMILL TRENCH) & CADORNA TRENCH at C19.c.45.65 along CADORNA TRENCH to its junction with WOOD ALLEY, WOOD ALLEY & from this trench to OPPY TRENCH. Estimated casualties 350.	
			Capt. C. CRABTREE returned from duty at No 2 C.C.S.	

A5834 Wt. W4973/M687 750,000 8/16 D. D. & L. Ltd. Forms/C.2118/13.

Instructions regarding War Diaries and Intelligence Summaries are contained in F. S. Regs., Part II. and the Staff Manual respectively. Title pages will be prepared in manuscript.

WAR DIARY
or
~~INTELLIGENCE SUMMARY.~~
(Erase heading not required.)

Army Form C. 2118. 6

PAGE VI

93rd Fd. AMBULANCE

Place	Date	Hour	Summary of Events and Information	Remarks and references to Appendices
M.D.S. St. CATHERINE	1917 June 27th		Under instructions from A.D.M.S. 3rd Div. (R.A.M.C. Operation Order no. 20) I am to hold a party of 60 stretcher bearers and 2 Officers ready to relieve the bearers in the line of the 95th F.A.	
			Wounded from the GAVRELLE sector are evacuated in cars. Wounded from BAILLEUL sector are evacuated by the light railway running past the A.D.S. direct to St. CATHERINES. A small branch line has been run into the 3rd Div. SALVAGE location; and cases will be evacuated from here to the M.D.S. – a distance of about 300 yds. The Div. SALVAGE OFFICER is sending 20 men to act as bearers.	[illegible] Lt Col
"	June 28th		I detailed Capts. MURPHY and MacPHAIL to hold themselves ready to proceed with bearers on 29th inst. should these be required.	
			At the railhead in the SALVAGE location, I detailed 1 N.C.O. and 1 R.A.M.C. orderly for duty with the SALVAGE stretcher party. An Operation tent was erected here, and extra blankets, hot water bottles and stimulants kept there. I detailed Capt MURPHY to superintend the unloading and also to superintend the loading of the Ambulance cars at the M.D.S. and the	

Army Form C. 2118. 7

WAR DIARY
or
INTELLIGENCE SUMMARY.
(*Erase heading not required.*)

Instructions regarding War Diaries and Intelligence Summaries are contained in F. S. Regs., Part II. and the Staff Manual respectively. Title pages will be prepared in manuscript.

PAGE VII — 93rd Fd. AMBULANCE.

Place	Date	Hour	Summary of Events and Information	Remarks and references to Appendices
M.D.S. ST. CATHERINE	1917 June 28th		(contd). General comfort & feeding of patients.	
			I placed 3 med. officers in each station i.e. walking wounded and stretcher station.	
			Capt. S. A. HUNT repaired to O.C. 95 F.A. to replace Capt. YOUNG wounded.	
			Wounded began to come in about 9.30 p.m. Between that hour and 4. A.M. they came in steadily, though not in a rush. Total wounded were from 5 p.m. 28th – 9 p.m. 29th inst. 9 officers. 114 O.R. 13 German wounded.	
" "	JUNE 29th		D.D.M.S. XIII CORPS inspected M.D.S. this morning.	A. W. Pollard Lt Col.
			Wounded are still coming in slowly. Two cases died in M.D.S. in early hours of morning.	
			I detailed Capt HUMPHREY to proceed to GUNPITS COLLECTG POST for duty there under instructions from A.D.M.S.	
			Capt. HUNT returned from temporary duty with 95th F.A.	
			The COMMANDER XIII CORPS inspected the M.D.S this evening.	
"	JUNE 30th		Nothing to report.	A. W. Pollard Lt Col. O.C. 93 F.A.

A5834 Wt. W4973/M687 750,000 8/16 D. D. & L. Ltd. Forms/C.2118/13.

Confidential

July 1917

140/2298

Volume x

Vol 17

War Diary.

93rd Field Ambulance — 31st Division

July 1917

Instructions regarding War Diaries and Intelligence Summary are contained in F. S. Regs., Part II. and the Staff Manual respectively. Title pages will be prepared in manuscript.

PAGE I

WAR DIARY
or
INTELLIGENCE SUMMARY.
(Erase heading not required.)

93rd Fd AMBUL

Army Form C. 2118.

Place	Date	Hour	Summary of Events and Information	Remarks and references to Appendices
	1917			
M.D.S. ST. CATHERINE	JULY 1st.		Nothing to report, save that the reinforcements arrived today	[illegible]
"	JULY 2nd		Nothing to report. Capt. R. CUMMING proceeded on leave. I received preliminary notice that the Division would move into rest on 3rd–4th inst. this unit to proceed to CAMBLIGNEUL the relieved by 2nd F.A. (R.N.).	AP
	JULY 3rd.		I received a copy of RAMC OPERATION ORDER no 21 by ADMS 51st Div. Accordingly I sent on Capt. J. MacPHAIL with 1 N.C.O. & 6 men as an advance party to take over Fd Amb. site and hospital from 2nd FA (RN). A similar advance party arrived here. I detailed Capt. L. MURPHY to relieve Capt. THOMPSON temporarily, duty with R.E.s.	
"	JULY 4th		Unit marched out at 6.30 a.m. to CAMBLIGNEUL, via ANZIN – Mt ST ELOI – CAMBLIN. Arrived 10 a.m. Weather extremely wet and the camp is very muddy. Men are in billets at the Chateau. I am using one hut as men's dining room: one hut as patients ward: the Nissen hut as patients dining room. The men were employed in cleaning & clearing the camp.	AP

A5834 Wt. W4973/M687 750,000 8/16 D. D. & L. Ltd. Forms/C.2118/13.

Instructions regarding War Diaries and Intelligence Summaries are contained in F. S. Regs., Part II. and the Staff Manual respectively. Title pages will be prepared in manuscript.

PAGE 11

WAR DIARY
or
INTELLIGENCE SUMMARY.
(Erase heading not required.)

Army Form C. 2118.

93rd FD. AMBULce.

Place	Date	Hour	Summary of Events and Information	Remarks and references to Appendices
	1917			
CAMBLIGNEUL	JULY 5th		I detailed Capt. W. CRABTREE to proceed in relief of Capt. ROCHE, for temporary duty with 15th W. YORKS.	
			I detailed Capt. KUNY to visit 31st DIV. SIGNALS & 4th LABOUR Coy daily under instructions from ADMS.	
			There is a great deal required in the way of repairing huts, clearing away refuse and rubbish heaps. This work is being proceeded with.	A.H. Pollard Lt Col
" "	JULY 6th.		Nothing to report	A.P.
" "	JULY 7th		Nothing to report.	A.P.
" "	JULY 8th		Capt. L.C. MURPHY returned from temporary duty with 31st DIV. R.E.	A.P.
" "	JULY 9th		Nothing to report.	A.P.
" "	JULY 10th.		Received preliminary notice that the 31st DIV. would probably relieve 1st CANADIAN DIV. in line on 12th inst.	A.P.
"	July 11th.		I handed over to Capt. R. MACKINNON, prior to proceeding on leave. A.H. Pollard Lt Col.	
"	July 12th		Lt Col A.H. POLLARD proceeded on leave to ENGLAND and Capt R. MACKINNON R.A.M.C. assumed temporary command of the unit. R Mackinnon Capt R.A.M.C	

A5834 Wt. W4973/M687 750,000 8/16 D. D. & L. Ltd. Forms/C.2118/13.

Instructions regarding War Diaries and Intelligence Summaries are contained in F. S. Regs., Part II. and the Staff Manual respectively. Title pages will be prepared in manuscript.

PAGE III

WAR DIARY
or
~~INTELLIGENCE~~ SUMMARY.
(*Erase heading not required.*)

93rd Fd AMBULANCE

Army Form C. 2118.

Place	Date	Hour	Summary of Events and Information	Remarks and references to Appendices
CAMBLIGNEUL	JULY 12.		I received a copy of R.A.M.C. Operation order No 22 by A.D.M.S 31st DIV. In accordance with above order I detailed Capt J. M. MACPHAIL and 30 other ranks to report to O.C. 95th Field Ambulance for duty in the forward area; and I detailed an advance party of 1 N.C.O and [illegible] men to take over from No 3 Canadian Field Ambulance. R Mackinnon Capt RAMC	
"	JULY 13		Unit marched at 6.30 A.M. to VILLERS-AU-BOIS via CAMBLIN ABBAYE arrived at 10 A.M. Men are in billets in the Field Ambulance site. Accomodation for patients 40 beds. I detailed Capt J. N. HUMPHREYS and 1 Tent Sub-division to take over the accomodation for sick at NEUVILLE-ST-VAAST. Rmackinnon Capt R.A.M.C	
"	JULY 14th		The men were employed in general fatigues about the camp. Capt. R. S. CUMMING returned from leave. Rmackinnon Capt RAMC	
	JULY 15		I detailed Capt L. L. E. MURPHY to take over temporary medical charge of 13th Batt East Yorkshire Regiment in relief of Capt H. E. P. YORKE. The D.A.D.M.S 31st Division inspected the camp.	
	~~JULY 16~~		Rmackinnon Capt R.A.M.C	

A5834 Wt. W4973/M687 750,000 8/16 D. D. & L. Ltd. Forms/C.2118/13.

Instructions regarding War Diaries and Intelligence Summaries are contained in F. S. Regs., Part II. and the Staff Manual respectively. Title pages will be prepared in manuscript.

Vol IV

WAR DIARY
or
~~INTELLIGENCE SUMMARY.~~
(Erase heading not required.)

93rd FD AMBULANCE

Army Form C. 2118.

Place	Date	Hour	Summary of Events and Information	Remarks and references to Appendices
VILLERS-AU-BOIS	JULY 16		Acting under instructions from A D M S 31st I detailed 2 N C O's and 1 Large Motor Ambulance to 95th Field Ambulance. Capt. H.E.P. YORKE M.C. reported here for temporary duty from 13th East Yorkshire Regiment. R.M.	
"	" 17		I inspected the Tent Subdivision at NEUVILLE-ST-VAAST. R.M.	
"	" 18		Capt S.A. KUNY reported his departure on the completion of his contract. R.M.	
"	" 19		Capt H.E.P. YORKE M.C. has been detailed to visit sick vice Capt S.A. KUNY. Capt R.S. CUMMING M.C. and 32 Other ranks have been detailed to relieve Capt J.M. MACPHAIL and 32 other ranks ~~[illegible]~~ 93rd Field Ambulance in the forward area. R.M.	
"	" 20		Nothing to report to day. R.M.	
"	" 21.		I visited the Tent sub division at NEUVILLE ST-VAAST. R.M.	

Instructions regarding War Diaries and Intelligence Summaries are contained in F. S. Regs., Part II. and the Staff Manual respectively. Title pages will be prepared in manuscript.

PAGE XV

WAR DIARY
or
INTELLIGENCE SUMMARY.
(Erase heading not required.)

Army Form C. 2118.

93rd Fd. AMBULANCE

Place	Date	Hour	Summary of Events and Information	Remarks and references to Appendices
VILLERS-AU-BOIS	JULY 22		Capt. W. CRABTREE rejoined from temporary duty with the 16th W. YORKS REGT. The following is an extract from D.M.S 1st ARMY No 865/29 dated 21st July 1917. "Each D.D.M.S Corps must be prepared in the near future to provide Medical Officers at the rate of three per Division in the Corps to proceed at 24 hours notice to another area for temporary duty" A.D.M.S. No S326 dated 22/7/17 "Please submit name of Officer selected from your unit to this Office as soon as possible" Name of officer submitted Capt R MACKINNON. The following was received from ADMS 31st Division No S529 In the event of an enemy retirement on the 31st Divisional front the following Medical arrangements will come into force. OC 93rd Field Ambulance will reinforce the Advanced Dressing Station at LA CHAUDIERE (S 18 C 9.3) sheet 36C by one Bearer sub-division. R Mackinnon Capt RAMC	
"	JULY 23rd		I returned from leave this day and assumed command of the unit from Capt. R. MACKINNON. Capt. J. HUMPHREY proceeded on leave to CANADA + is struck off strength.	

[signature] Lt Col

A5834 Wt. W4973/M687 750,000 8/16 D. D. & L. Ltd. Forms/C.2118/13.

Instructions regarding War Diaries and Intelligence Summaries are contained in F. S. Regs., Part II. and the Staff Manual respectively. Title pages will be prepared in manuscript. PAGE VI

WAR DIARY
or
~~INTELLIGENCE SUMMARY.~~
(Erase heading not required.)

Army Form C. 2118.

9 2nd Fd AMBULANCE

Place	Date	Hour	Summary of Events and Information	Remarks and references to Appendices
VILLERS AU BOIS	1917 July	24th	Nothing to report.	A.W. Pollard Lt Col.
"	"	25th	I inspected ADS at NEUVILLE St. VAAST. New latrines require to be made and a new incinerator. I am also sending up utensils for the cook	A.W.P.
"	"	26th	I detailed Capt. CRABTREE, 32 Q.R. of C. section to proceed to ADS. LA CHAUDIERE in relief of Capt. CUMMING and party, who rejoined HQrs.	A.W.P.
"	"	27th	Capt. MacKINNON proceeded to ADS. NEUVILLE St. VAAST in relief of Capt. MacPHAIL, who returned to HQrs. In accordance with instructions from ADMS 3rd DIV. I detailed Capt. R. CUMMING M.C. to proceed for temporary duty with 3rd DIV TRAIN.	A.W.P.
"	"	28th	According to orders received from ADMS. 3 Div., I sent all available ranks this evening for a route march, under Gas Conditions. Route march lasted 1½ hrs. and the men marched for alternate periods with mask in the alert position and with it on.	A.W.P.
"	"	29th	Nothing to report.	A.W.P.

A5834 Wt. W4973/M687 750,000 8/16 D. D. & L. Ltd. Forms/C.2118/13.

Instructions regarding War Diaries and Intelligence Summaries are contained in F. S. Regs., Part II. and the Staff Manual respectively. Title pages will be prepared in manuscript. PAGE ~~VIII~~

WAR DIARY
or
~~INTELLIGENCE SUMMARY.~~
(Erase heading not required.)

93RD FD AMBULANCE

Army Form C. 2118.

Place	Date	Hour	Summary of Events and Information	Remarks and references to Appendices
		JULY 1917		
VILLERS-AU-BOIS		30th	Nothing to report	A M Pollard Lt Col
"		31st	G.O.C. 31st Div. inspected the unit today.	
			Visited the A.D.S. NEUVILLE St VAAST; new latrines have been dug and a new incinerator is being built	A M Pollard Lt Col O.C. 93 FA.

21

Confidential | Volume XX

Aug 1917 | 140/2364 | Vol 18

War Diary.

93rd Field Ambulance | 31st Division

August 1917

Instructions regarding War Diaries and Intelligence Summaries are contained in F. S. Regs., Part II. and the Staff Manual respectively. Title pages will be prepared in manuscript.

PAGE I.

WAR DIARY
or
~~INTELLIGENCE~~ SUMMARY.
(Erase heading not required.)

Army Form C. 2118.

93rd FIELD AMBULANCE

Place	Date	Hour	Summary of Events and Information	Remarks and references to Appendices
VILLERS AU-BOIS	1917 AUGUST 1st		Nothing to report. A. W. Sutherland Lt Col	
	AUG. 2nd		Capt. H. YORKE M.C. returned to duty with 13th Bn. E. YORKS Regt.	
			Capt. L. MURPHY returned to Hqrs. unit. | Two new reinforcements - heavy draught horses - drawn today.	
			Capt R. McKINNON + 30 O.R. relieved Capt. CRABTREE and party at A.D.S. LA CHAUDIÈRE. Capt. CRABTREE took over charge of A.D.S. at NEUVILLE St. VAAST vice Capt McKINNON. A.W.	
"	AUG. 3rd		Weather has been very wet: horse lines are very muddy and it is difficult to find any dry ground.	
			Capt. MacPHAIL has taken over Capt. YORKE'S duties at the CHINESE and LABOUR CAMPS. A.W.	
"	AUG. 4th		Nothing to report. A.W.	
"	AUG. 5th		Nothing to report. A.W.	

A5834 Wt. W4973/M687 750,000 8/16 D. D. & L. Ltd. Forms/C.2118/13.

Instructions regarding War Diaries and Intelligence Summaries are contained in F. S. Regs., Part II. and the Staff Manual respectively. Title pages will be prepared in manuscript.

PAGE II

WAR DIARY
or
~~INTELLIGENCE SUMMARY.~~
(Erase heading not required.)

Army Form C. 2118.

93rd F. AMBOL^CE.

Place	Date	Hour	Summary of Events and Information	Remarks and references to Appendices
VILLERS AU BOIS	1917 AUG. 6th.		Under instructions from ADMS. 31st DIV. Capt. R CUMMING rejoined from temporary duty with 31st DIV. TRAIN.	
			Capt. E. BARNES. R.A.M.C. and Lieut. A. SNAPE having reported their arrival for duty, are taken on the strength of the unit	A.D. MacD. Lt.Col.
"	AUG. 7th.		The ADMS. 31st DIV. inspected the campound hospital today	A.D.
"	AUG. 8th.		I inspected ADS. NEUVILLE St. VAAST today. A new Soyer stove has been sent up; some of the gas curtains require renewing.	A.D.
"	AUG. 9th.		Capt. MacPHAIL and party of 30 O.R. relieved Capt. McKINNON and detachment at ADS. LA CHAUDIÈRE.	
			Capt. E. BARNES relieved Capt. CRABTREE at NEUVILLE St. VAAST	A.D.
"	AUG. 10th.		I detailed Capt. W. CRABTREE to the sick of the Chinese Camp, & the 4th INF. LABOUR BN. I have sent a carpenter to the ADS. LA CHAUDIÈRE & NEUVILLE St. VAAST to fit the doorways with proper gas curtains	A.D.

Army Form C. 2118.

WAR DIARY
or
~~INTELLIGENCE SUMMARY.~~
(*Erase heading not required.*)

Instructions regarding War Diaries and Intelligence Summaries are contained in F. S. Regs., Part II. and the Staff Manual respectively. Title pages will be prepared in manuscript.

PAGE III

93rd Fd. AMBULANCE.

Place	Date	Hour	Summary of Events and Information	Remarks and references to Appendices
VILLERS AU BOIS.	1917 Aug	11th	Horse lines inspected by O.C. Hqr. Coy. Div. TRAIN. A. W. Pollard Lt Col	
"	Aug	12th	I inspected the ADS. at NEUVILLE St. VAAST. AWP	
"	Aug	13th	Capt. L. C. MURPHY, on expiration of contract, proceeded to LONDON and is struck off the strength of the unit.	
			Capt W. CRABTREE proceeded on leave. AWP.	
"	Aug	14th	I inspected the ADS at NEUVILLE St VAAST. I gave instructions that the road way for the entrance of motor ambulances should be repaired. AWP	
"	Aug	15th	Under instructions from ADMS 31st DIV. I took over charge of the ADS at LA CHAUDIÈRE. Issued up the necessary equipment. AWP	
"	Aug	16th	Capt. BARNES relieved Capt. MACPHAIL at LA CHAUDIÈRE. Capt MACPHAIL took charge of the ADS at NEUVILLE St VAAST. Lt SNAPE proceeded to XIII CORPS SCHOOL of SANITATION for a course, under instructions received from ADMS 31st DIV. AWP	

A5834 Wt. W4973/M687 750,000 8/16 D. D. & L. Ltd. Forms/C.2118/13.

Instructions [illegible]ding War Diaries and Intelligence Summaries are contained in F. S. Regs., Part II. and the Staff Manual respectively. Title pages will be prepared in manuscript.

PAGE IV

WAR DIARY
or
INTELLIGENCE SUMMARY.
(*Erase heading not required.*)

Army Form C. 2118.

93rd Fd. AMBULANCE

Place	Date	Hour	Summary of Events and Information	Remarks and references to Appendices
	1917			
VILLERS AU BOIS.	Aug. 17th		The ADMS. inspected here today. I received his instructions. Commence work upon the horse standings for winter.	[illegible] Lt. Col.
"	Aug 18th		I inspected ADS. at NEUVILLE St. VAAST. The road has been improved, but still requires some work.	AP
"	Aug. 19th		Nothing to report.	AP
"	Aug 20th		I inspected ADS. at LA CHAUDIERE. New steps require to be made for this ADS. Some walking wounded shelters require to be placed en route to RAP. One air shaft requires to be re-curtained & the outlet protected by a bursting charge and sandbags. Kitchen and Dressing room require thorough cleaning and whitewashing. More cupboards required for food. There is an excess of drugs, also A.T.S. which I have given instructions to have sent down.	

A5834 Wt. W4973/M687 750,000 8/16 D. D. & L. Ltd. Forms/C.2118/13.

Instructions regarding War Diaries and Intelligence Summaries are contained in F. S. Regs., Part II. and the Staff Manual respectively. Title pages will be prepared in manuscript.

WAR DIARY
or
~~INTELLIGENCE SUMMARY~~

(Erase heading not required.)

Army Form C. 2118.

Page V — 93rd Fd. AMBULANCE

Place	Date 1917	Hour	Summary of Events and Information	Remarks and references to Appendices
VILLERS AU BOIS	Aug 20th (cont.)		I went over the railway system in the neighbourhood. At present 1 Car is kept there all day & night, the evacuation being done, as far as possible at night time. A trolley depot at R.A.P. (36.C.) 19.B.8.7. would be useful as the carry is a long one. Evacuation by trolley could be carried out from LA CHAUDIERE, but only via PEGGY DUMP, which is near the R.A.P above, & evacuation would be better from the R.A.P. direct.	[illegible] Lt Col.
"	Aug 21st		Nothing to report. With permission of A.D.M.S. I withdrew 8 men from A.D.S. at CHAUDIERE & transferred them to the A.D.S. at NEUVILLE St. VAAST.	A.P.
"	Aug 22nd		Nothing to report.	A.P.
"	Aug 23rd.		Capt. McKINNIN relieved Capt. MACPHAIL at NEUVILLE St. VAAST. Capt. CUMMING relieved Capt. DARVES at LA CHAUDIÈRE.	A.P.
	Aug 24th		Nothing to report.	A.P.
	Aug 25th		Nothing to report.	A.P.

A5834 Wt. W4973/M687 750,000 8/16 D. D. & L. Ltd. Forms/C.2118/13.

Army Form C. 2118.

WAR DIARY
or
INTELLIGENCE SUMMARY.
(*Erase heading not required.*)

Instructions regarding War Diaries and Intelligence Summaries are contained in F. S. Regs., Part II. and the Staff Manual respectively. Title pages will be prepared in manuscript.

PAGE VI

93rd FD. AMBULANCE.

Place	Date	Hour	Summary of Events and Information	Remarks and references to Appendices
	1917			
VILLERS AU BOIS	Aug 26th		I inspected A.D.S. at NEUVILLE St. VAAST. A new kitchen has been erected, present building turned into a dining room. Some work has been done in improving the road.	A.W. Ward Lt Col.
"	Aug 27th		Capt. J.S. LYONS. RAMC. joined for duty.	A.W.
			I detailed Lt. H. SNAPE for duty with Capt. CUMMING at ADS LA CHAUDIÈRE.	A.W.
"	Aug 28th		I inspected A.D.S. at NEUVILLE St. VAAST, and ADS at LA CHAUDIÈRE, new trench latrines require to be dug. This ADS is now gas proof.	A.W.
"	Aug 29th		Nothing to report.	A.W.
"	Aug 30th		Nothing to report.	A.W.
"	Aug 31st		Capt. LYONS relieved Capt. MACKINNON at NEUVILLE St. VAAST.	A.W. Ward Lt Col. O.C. 93 F.A.

A5834 Wt. W4973/M687 750,000 8/16 D. D. & L. Ltd. Forms/C.2118/13.

Confidential 27 140/2438 Volume XXI

Sept. 1917 Vol 19

War Diary.

93rd Field Ambulance 31st Division

September 1917.

Instructions regarding War Diaries and Intelligence Summaries are contained in F. S. Regs., Part II, and the Staff Manual respectively. Title pages will be prepared in manuscript.

WAR DIARY
or
~~INTELLIGENCE SUMMARY.~~
(Erase heading not required.)

Army Form C. 2118.

PAGE I   92nd Fd AMBULANCE   1

Place	Date	Hour	Summary of Events and Information	Remarks and references to Appendices
VILLERS AU BOIS	1917 Sept 1st.		I received a preliminary warning from ADMS 31st Div. that the 31st Div. would be relieved in the left sector by the 3rd CANADIAN Div. and take over on the right from the V Div. Capt. J.B. BARNES is seeing the sick of 165th & 170th Bgde. R.F.A. (Wagon lines)	A.R. Maxwell
"	Sept. 2nd.		Received copy of ADMS 31st DIV. Operation order No. 23. This unit is to take over the Main Dressing station at ROCLINCOURT and in addition to be responsible for forward evacuation	A.R.
"	Sept 3rd.		I went round the new line to be taken over by this division, visiting the R.A.P.'s and relief posts. Capt. J. BARNES having been appointed as M.O. i/c 31st Div. R.E. is struck off the strength.	A.R.
"	Sept 4th.		I handed over Field Ambulance site at VILLERS au BOIS to 8th CANADIAN FIELD AMBULANCE. I took over the MAIN DRESSING	

A5834 Wt. W4973/M687 750,000 8/16 D. D. & L. Ltd. Forms/C.2118/13.

Instructions regarding War Diaries and Intelligence Summaries are contained in F. S. Regs., Part II. and the Staff Manual respectively. Title pages will be prepared in manuscript.

PAGE II

WAR DIARY
or
~~INTELLIGENCE~~ SUMMARY.

(Erase heading not required.)

Army Form C. 2118.

2

92nd F.A. AMBULANCE

Place	Date	Hour	Summary of Events and Information	Remarks and references to Appendices
ROCLINCOURT	1917 ~~Sept~~ 4th (contd).		STATION at ROCLINCOURT from 15th F.A. A.M. Pollard	[illegible]
"	Sept 5th.		The 15th F.A. vacated the M.D.S. at 11 a.m. At 10 a.m. 4 cases of shell-gas poisoning arrived from LA CHAUDIÈRE, with information ~~that~~ a heavy bombardment of gas shells had occurred the previous night in that vicinity. I sent Capt. LYONS and 12 men to relieve the detachment at LA CHAUDIÈRE. Later in the day, ~~Capt~~ Lt. SNAPE and the whole of his detachment were sent in. During the day about 160 cases came in. Most of the cases were light, suffering from vomiting and conjunctivitis. Patients were stripped, washed with a 3%	

A5834 Wt. W4973/M687 750,000 8/16 D. D. & L. Ltd. Forms/C.2118/13.

Instructions regarding War Diaries and Intelligence Summaries are contained in F. S. Regs., Part II. and the Staff Manual respectively. Title pages will be prepared in manuscript.

PAGE III

WAR DIARY
or
INTELLIGENCE SUMMARY.
(Erase heading not required.)

93rd FD AMBULANCE

Army Form C. 2118.

3

Place	Date	Hour	Summary of Events and Information	Remarks and references to Appendices
ROCLINCOURT	Sept. 5th (cont)	1917	Solution of Sod. Bicarbonate; then eyes with a 1% solution of the same. Vaseline applied to eyelids. No food was given. The clothes were not sent to C.C.S. with them. I was assisted by 4 cars from 94th F.A. Lieut. SNADE did exceptionally good work, under very trying circumstances at the A.D.S.	
			I took over the ADS at WILLERVAL and evacuation from 95th F.A. 50 men from that ambulance are attached to me for duty [illegible]	
"	Sept. 6th		I took over from 13th F.A. (1) ADS. at 51.B. B.14.C.8.6. I detailed Capt. CUMMING + 14 O.R. here (2) B.15.C.4.8. Relay post. 1 N.C.O. + 4 O.R. (3) Relay Post B.10.C.8.6. 1 N.C.O. + 5 O.R. (4) Relay post B.11.d.4.8. a bat post: 4 O.R. (5) R.A.P. B.12.A.6.5. 4 O.R. (6) R.A.P. B.5.a.6.8. 4 O.R. This R.A.P. is the evacuated to ADS at WILLERVAL.	
			The evacuation from the right R.A.P. will be to the A.D.S. BROWN LINE + thence to DAYLIGHT RAILHEAD B.19.central. thence by trolley to M.D.S.	

A5834 Wt. W4973/M687 750,000 8/16 D. D. & L. Ltd. Forms/C.2118/13.

Instructions regarding War Diaries and Intelligence Summaries are contained in F. S. Regs., Part II. and the Staff Manual respectively. Title pages will be prepared in manuscript.

WAR DIARY
or
INTELLIGENCE SUMMARY.
(Erase heading not required.)

Army Form C. 2118.

4

PAGE IV

93rd Fd. AMBULANCE

Place	Date	Hour	Summary of Events and Information	Remarks and references to Appendices
	1917			
ROCLINCOURT	Sept. 6th (contd)		The centre R.A.P. (B.5.A.6.8) and the two left R.A.P.S. (36.C T.29.B.88 and T.29 B.6.8.) evacuate by new Hudson Trench to T.22.D.9.2 thence by wheeled stretcher (or parallel [illegible]) to Vancouver Rd (T.28.a.4.3.7) thence to ADS.	
			This ADS. is cleared nightly. Evacuation is done by [illegible] Ambulance	
			Capt. CRABTREE is sent to this ADS [illegible] of 95th F.A.	
			A new ADS is being constructed at 51.B.S15.c.5.2. I have detailed 12 men for this work.	[illegible]
			Capt. J. LYONS and 8 o.r. were evacuated suffering from shell gas poisoning. A total	
			2 officers 33 o.r. have been evacuated as casualties during past two days. Capt. LYONS and all [illegible] worked extremely well and rendered great assistance.	[illegible]
"	Sept. 7th		A few gassed cases came in today, and were dealt with as before. Some cases had developed blisters	A.P.
"	Sept. 8th		LIEUTS. SMITH, KNAPP and JOHNSON of the U.S.A. Medical Service were posted here for duty this day, and are taken on the strength. The ADMS. inspected the Camp today.	A.P.

A5834 Wt. W4973/M687 750,000 8/16 D. D. & L. Ltd. Forms/C.2118/13.

Instructions regarding War Diaries and Intelligence Summaries are contained in F. S. Regs., Part II. and the Staff Manual respectively. Title pages will be prepared in manuscript.

WAR DIARY
or
INTELLIGENCE SUMMARY.
(Erase heading not required.)

Page V

93rd Fd Ambulance

Army Form C. 2118.

15

Place	Date	Hour	Summary of Events and Information	Remarks and references to Appendices
	1917			
ROCLINCOURT	Sept. 9th.		Another [illegible] 12 cases of gas poisoning, due to [illegible] cylinder of our own gas being struck by an enemy shell, were admitted today. They were treated as before; but the symptoms were more pulmonary. Oxygen was given.	[illegible]
"	Sept. 10th.		I have visited the A.D.S.'s at BROWN LINE and WILLERVAL. Both need better gas protection, and I have sent the carpenter to the latter place. Besides the R.A.P. left [illegible] (36.c T.29 b.6.6.) the camp is too busy, and I am arranging a relief post. A bomb was dropped in the near vicinity and 10 casualties were admitted.	[illegible]
"	Sept. 11th.		Twenty extra men were sent to the Brown ADS. for construction purposes. I have arranged to send rations to A.D.S. WILLERVAL every evening, and that the ration car will bring back sick & wounded from there. Motor ambulances will only be sent there for an emergency.	[illegible]

A5834 Wt. W4973/M687 750,000 8/16 D. D. & L. Ltd. Forms/C.2118/13.

Instructions regarding War Diaries and Intelligence Summaries are contained in F. S. Regs., Part II. and the Staff Manual respectively. Title pages will be prepared in manuscript.

PAGETT

WAR DIARY
or
~~INTELLIGENCE SUMMARY.~~

(Erase heading not required.)

93rd FD AMBULANCE

Army Form C. 2118.

6

Place	Date	Hour	Summary of Events and Information	Remarks and references to Appendices
ROCLINCOURT	1917 Sept 12th		Nothing to report	[illegible]
"	Sept 13th		ADMS. 31st Div. inspected the Camp. Lieut KNAPP. U.S.A. (Med. Service) under instructions from ADMS. is struck off strength & reported to O.C. 94 F.A. for duty. Capt. McKINNON and LIEUT SMITH (U.S.A.) proceeded to BROWN LINE ADS in relief of Capt R. CUMMING. M.C. Capt. McPHAIL & LIEUT. JOHNSON (U.S.A.) proceeded to ADS. WILLERVAL in relief of Capt. H. CRABTREE.	[illegible]
"	Sept 14th		Nothing to report: except. O.C. 31st Div. Train inspected horses & transport.	[illegible]
"	Sept 15th		C.R.E. 31st Div. visited the camp & inspected new horse standings. Seven Nissen Huts have been drawn & are in process of erection	[illegible]

A5834 Wt. W4973/M687 750,000 8/16 D. D. & L. Ltd. Forms/C.2118/13.

Army Form C. 2118.

7

WAR DIARY
or
~~INTELLIGENCE SUMMARY.~~
(*Erase heading not required.*)

Instructions regarding War Diaries and Intelligence Summaries are contained in F. S. Regs., Part II. and the Staff Manual respectively. Title pages will be prepared in manuscript.

PAGE VII — 93rd Fd. AMBULANCE

Place	Date	Hour	Summary of Events and Information	Remarks and references to Appendices
ROCLINCOURT.	1917 Sept. 16th.		G.O.C. 31st Div. inspected the camp: he was kind enough to express himself as very satisfied with the existing conditions. DADMS. 31st Div. inspected the camp.	[initials]
"	Sept 17th.		ADMS. 31st Div. inspected A.D.S. BROWN LINE and new A.D.S. in the Sunken Rd. (51B.B15.C.5.0.). Work is progressing fast at the new A.D.S. Capt. A.L. WALKER is posted to this unit for duty & is taken on the strength.	[initials]
"	Sept 18th		I inspected A.D.S. WILLERVAL & am moving dressing room to a different building. This will give a larger & better protected dressing room. I also visited Relay Post (R.A.P.) at WILLERVAL SOUTH B10.C.8.6. There are two deep dugouts, connected with the R.A.P. About 20 stretcher cases could be accommodated here.	[initials]
"	Sept 19th.		Nothing to report.	[initials]
"	Sept 20th		Capts. CRABTREE & WALKER relieved Capt. MACKINNON & LIEUT. SMITH at BROWN LINE A.D.S. (contd).	

Instructions regarding War Diaries and Intelligence Summaries are contained in F. S. Regs., Part II. and the Staff Manual respectively. Title pages will be prepared in manuscript.

PAGE VIII

WAR DIARY
or
INTELLIGENCE SUMMARY.
(Erase heading not required.)

Army Form C. 2118.

8

93rd Fd. AMBULANCE

Place	Date	Hour	Summary of Events and Information	Remarks and references to Appendices
ROCLINCOURT	1917 Sept. 20th	(contd)	Under instructions from ADMS 3rd Div. Capt. R BURGESS of 95th F.A reported here for duty. He & Capt. CUMMING MC relieved Capt. J. MacPHAIL & Lieut. JOHNSON at ADS. WILLERVAL.	
"	Sept. 21st		Kitchen at ADS. WILLERVAL was blown in by H.E. shell. Two casualties 95th F.A. slight.	[illegible]
"	Sept. 22nd		The ADMS. 3rd Div. has given me permission to try and find a suitable place for an ADS instead of that we now have at WILLERVAL.	
"	Sept 23rd		Five NISSEN huts are now erected. Capt. R. CUMMING MC, i/c ADS. WILLERVAL reports that 94th Bde have taken over R.A.P. in left sector 36.C. T.29.b.5.8 – as a Canteen. I have informed ADMS. 3rd Div. of the procedure.	
"	Sept. 24th		I inspected ADS. at BROWN LINE and the ADS. at TUNNEL DUMP, improvements of construction. A good deal of work has been done	

A5834 Wt. W4973/M687 750,000 8/16 D. D. & L. Ltd. Forms/C.2118/13.

Army Form C. 2118.

9

Instructions regarding War Diaries and Intelligence Summaries are contained in F. S. Regs., Part II. and the Staff Manual respectively. Title pages will be prepared in manuscript.

PAGE IX

~~WAR DIARY~~
or
INTELLIGENCE SUMMARY.

(*Erase heading not required.*)

93rd Fd Ambulance

Place	Date	Hour	Summary of Events and Information	Remarks and references to Appendices
	1917			
ROCLIN-COURT.	Sept 24th (Contd)		Walls & ceilings are being boarded. A large elephant is being erected for the personnel. I also inspected the A.D.S. WILLERVAL. It is a most dangerous locality: very little accommodation for wounded or sick & impossible to render shell or gas-proof.	Arthur Cluny(?) [illegible]
			Capt C.L. ARTHUR reports for duty.	
"	Sept 25th		Twelve C.B. men arrive for duty under instructions from the ADMS. They were sent to 94 & 95 F.A. to replace H.T. A.S.C. personnel under instructions from ADMS. Capt WALKER reports to O.C. 94 F.A. for duty in charge of the strength.	ACP.
"	Sept 26th		Nothing to report.	ACP.
"	Sept 27th		Capt McKeown & Lt Smith relieved Capts CUMMING M.C. & BURGESS at the ADS WILLERVAL.	
			Capt McPhail & Lt Johnson relieved Capt CRABTREE & Capt ARTHUR at the ADS BROWN LINE.	ACP.

A5834 Wt. W4973/M687 750,000 8/16 D. D. & L. Ltd. Forms/C.2118/13.

Instructions regarding War Diaries and Intelligence Summaries are contained in F. S. Regs., Part II. and the Staff Manual respectively. Title pages will be prepared in manuscript.

PAGE I

WAR DIARY
or
~~INTELLIGENCE~~ SUMMARY.
(*Erase heading not required.*)

93rd Fd AMBULANCE

Army Form C. 2118.

10

Place	Date	Hour	Summary of Events and Information	Remarks and references to Appendices
	1917			
ROCLINCOURT	Sept 28th		Nothing to report.	A W Pollard Lt Col
"	Sept 29th		Eight Nissen huts have now been erected. Two more are still to be put up. The R.E.'s are endeavouring to render ADS WILLERVAL wind gas proof	AWP
"	Sept 30th		At 11 p.m. I was notified by ADMS 31st Div. that 50 gassed cases were awaiting removal in the left sector. I sent 3 cars + 20 bearers under Capt. CUMMING, + 4 cars + 20 bearers were sent from 95 F.A. under instructions from ADMS. In all 24 cases were evacuated by trolley.	
			In all 101 cases were evacuated to 42 CCS. The ADS WILLERVAL + RAP were clear by 5 A.M. + the M.D.S. by 6 A.M.	
			The cases came right up VANCOUVER RD. + evacuated direct from HUDSON TRENCH.	A W Pollard Lt Col 5C 93/FA

A5834 Wt. W4973/M687 750,000 8/16 D. D. & L. Ltd. Forms/C.2118/13.

Confidential 27 11

Volume XXV

140/2578

Vol 20

Oct. 1917

War Diary.

93rd Field. Ambulance 31st Division

October 1917.

Army Form C. 2118.

WAR DIARY
or
INTELLIGENCE SUMMARY.
(Erase heading not required.)

Instructions regarding War Diaries and Intelligence Summaries are contained in F. S. Regs., Part II, and the Staff Manual respectively. Title pages will be prepared in manuscript.

PAGE I

93rd Fd AMBULANCE

Place	Date	Hour	Summary of Events and Information	Remarks and references to Appendices
ROCLINCOURT. M.D.S.	1917 Oct. 1st.		About 15 minor cases of gas poisoning were admitted today: one death in the ADS WILLERVAL and four were sufficiently serious to evacuate to No. 19 C.C.S.	
"	Oct 2nd		10 gassed cases admitted today. I inspected ADS BROWN LINE & the bearer posts in front. The new ADS at TUNNEL DUMP is almost complete.	
"	Oct 3rd		I inspected ADS WILLERVAL. The dressing room has been moved to the cellar across the road.	
"	Oct 4th		7 gassed cases during past 24 hrs. Capt ARTHUR & CUMMING relieved Capt McKINNON & LIEUT. SMITH at ADS WILLERVAL. Capt. BURGESS (95th F.A.) & Capt CRABTREE relieves Capt MacPHAIL & Lieut JOHNSON at ADS BROWN LINE.	

A5834 Wt. W4973/M687 750,000 8/16 D. D. & L. Ltd. Forms/C.2118/13.

Army Form C. 2118.

WAR DIARY
or
INTELLIGENCE SUMMARY.
(Erase heading not required.)

Instructions regarding War Diaries and Intelligence Summaries are contained in F. S. Regs., Part II. and the Staff Manual respectively. Title pages will be prepared in manuscript.

Part II [illegible] F. AMBULANCE

Place	Date	Hour	Summary of Events and Information	Remarks and references to Appendices
ROCLINCOURT	1919 Oct	5th	ADMS 3rd Div. inspected the Camp	[illegible] Lt Col.
"	"	6th	7 gassed cases in during the day, owing to a gas bombardment during the night.	
			9 Nissen huts now erected. Horses are moved into the new standings	[illegible]
"	"	7th	New ADS complete. 20 men of 95 F.A. are being relieved	[illegible]
			Sergt Major F. RELF was evacuated sick to 22 C.C.S	
"	"	8th	Nothing to report	[illegible]
"	"	9th	Inspected ADS BROWN LINE and the new one at TUNNEL DUMP. This is almost complete, but the stretcher racks & gas proof curtains are not quite finished. A cook-house has also been built. Inspected the relay posts and RAP's in right and centre sectors & also the ADS. WILLERVAL.	[illegible]

A5834 Wt. W4973/M687 750,000 8/16 D. D. & L. Ltd. Forms/C.2118/13.

Instructions regarding War Diaries and Intelligence Summaries are contained in F. S. Regs., Part II. and the Staff Manual respectively. Title pages will be prepared in manuscript.

PAGE III

WAR DIARY
or
~~INTELLIGENCE SUMMARY.~~
(Erase heading not required.)

93rd Fd. AMBULANCE

Army Form C. 2118.

Place	Date	Hour	Summary of Events and Information	Remarks and references to Appendices
ROCLINCOURT	1917 Oct.	10th	Nothing to report.	[illegible]
"	Oct	11th	Horses & transport inspected by O.C 1 Coy Div. Train	
			Capt. McKINNON & Lt SMITH relieved Capts CUMMING & ARTHUR at ADS. WILLERVAL	
			Capt. McPHAIL & Lt JOHNSON relieved Capts BURGESS & CRABTREE at ADS BROWN LINE	[illegible]
"	Oct	12th	Under instructions from ADMS. 31st Div. Lt JOHNSON is proceeding to 13th Y.&L. Regt. in relief of Capt H. Lins M.C	
			ADMS. inspected the camp.	[illegible]
"	Oct	13th	Capt L.C. ARTHUR reported to O.C 11th E. LANCS for temporary duty in relief of Capt MOELLER. U.S.M.S.	[illegible]
"	Oct	14th	Nothing to report	[illegible]
"	Oct	15th	Nothing to report.	[illegible]

A5834 Wt. W4973/M687 750,000 8/16 D. D. & L. Ltd. Forms/C.2118/13.

Instructions regarding War Diaries and Intelligence Summaries are contained in F. S. Regs., Part II. and the Staff Manual respectively. Title pages will be prepared in manuscript.

WAR DIARY or ~~INTELLIGENCE SUMMARY.~~

(Erase heading not required.)

Army Form C. 2118.

PAGE IV — 93rd Fd AMBULANCE

Place	Date	Hour	Summary of Events and Information	Remarks and references to Appendices
ROCLINCOURT	Oct 16th	1917	The enemy made a big raid on our front line last night. The front line trenches, RED LINE & WILLERVAL were deluged with H.E. & gas shells. About 50 casualties occurred during the 24 hrs. about 20 cases being gassed. Of these gassed cases, 8 cases were from the detachment at ADS WILLERVAL - 3 of 93rd F.A. & 5 of 95th F.A. I relieved Capt. R. MACKINNON in the evening by Capt. CRABTREE. The D.D.M.S. XIII CORPS inspected the dressing station this morning, and a little later, the DIV. COMMANDER and MAJ GENERAL O'RYAN U.S.A. ARMY also inspected.	[signature]
"	Oct 17th		Capt. R. McKINNON was relieved by Capt CRABTREE at WILLERVAL. Capt. McKINNON is admitted as a battle casualty, gassed, but is not sufficiently affected to necessitate removal to a C.C.S. Inspected site for new ADS VANCOUVER RD. and work is being commenced tomorrow.	[initials]
"	Oct 18th		20 men of 95 F.A. are sent for work on new ADS. 20 men of this unit are also required. Capt. DUNKERLEY (95 F.A.) relieved [illegible] at ADS WILLERVAL.	

A5834 Wt. W4973/M687 750,000 8/16 D. D. & L. Ltd. Forms/C.2118/13.

Instructions regarding War Diaries and Intelligence Summaries are contained in F. S. Regs., Part II. and the Staff Manual respectively. Title pages will be prepared in manuscript.

PAGET

WAR DIARY
or
~~INTELLIGENCE SUMMARY.~~
(*Erase heading not required.*)

93rd FIELD AMBULANCE

Army Form C. 2118.

Place	Date	Hour	Summary of Events and Information	Remarks and references to Appendices
	1917			
ROLLINCOURT			Sergt. Major F. RELF returned from 42 CCS today.	
	Oct. 19th		I inspected ADS. BROWN LINE. The new ADS at TUNNEL DUMP is almost ready, only the cookhouse being still unfinished.	A.W.P.
"	Oct 20th		Surg. General BIRMINGHAM. U.S. ARMY, accompanied by DDMS XIII CORPS and ADMS 31st DIV. inspected the Camp today.	A.W.P.
"	Oct 21st		Nothing to report.	A.W.P.
"	Oct 22nd		Nothing to report.	A.W.P.
"	Oct 23rd		Nothing to report.	A.P.
"	Oct 24th		I inspected ADS. BROWN LINE and new ADS at TUNNEL DUMP. The cookhouse is nearly complete. Evacuation will be carried out via TOMMY ALLEY: a relay post is necessary and there is a suitable one at junction Gabriel and RED LINE B.16.d.4.6.	A.W.P.
"	Oct 25th		Capt. MacPHAIL relieved Capts. CRAMMIRGE & DUNKERLEY at WILLERVAL. Capt. MacKINNON & Lt SMITH relieved Capt CUMMING at BROWN LINE	A.W.P.

A5834 Wt. W4973/M687 750,000 8/16 D. D. & L. Ltd. Forms/C.2118/13.

Instructions regarding War Diaries and Intelligence Summaries are contained in F. S. Regs., Part II. and the Staff Manual respectively. Title pages will be prepared in manuscript.

PAGE VI

WAR DIARY
or
INTELLIGENCE SUMMARY.
(Erase heading not required.)

93rd Fd AMBULANCE

Army Form C. 2118.

Place	Date	Hour	Summary of Events and Information	Remarks and references to Appendices
ROCLINCOURT	1917 Oct. 26th.		I inspected ADS WILLERVAL. New ADS in VANCOUVER RD. is being built & satisfactory progress is being made	A. Rolleston Lt Col
"	Oct. 27th.		Nothing to report.	AR
"	Oct. 28th		Nothing to report	AR
"	Oct. 29th		[illegible] The new ADS at TUNNEL DUMP has been taken over & evacuation via TOMMY ALLEY and thence to DAYLIGHT R'HEAD from ADS.	AR
"	Oct. 30th		Nothing to report.	AR
"	Oct. 31st		Nothing to report.	A. Rolleston Lt Col OC 93 F.A.

A5834 Wt. W4973/M687 750,000 8/16 D. D. & L. Ltd. Forms/C.2118/13.

Confidential 26 Volume XXIII

Nov. 1917

140/2578

Vol 21

War Diary.

93rd Field Ambulance. 31st Division

November 1917.

Instructions regarding War Diaries and Intelligence Summaries are contained in F. S. Regs., Part II. and the Staff Manual respectively. Title pages will be prepared in manuscript.

WAR DIARY
or
~~INTELLIGENCE SUMMARY.~~
(Erase heading not required.)

PAGE I.

Army Form C. 2118.

93rd F. AMBULANCE

Place	Date	Hour	Summary of Events and Information	Remarks and references to Appendices
ROLLINCOURT	1917 NOV. 1st		Capt. CRABTREE relieved Capt MacKINNON at ADS. TUNNEL DUMP. Capt. ARTHUR & CUMMING proceeded to ADS. WILLERVAL. Capt. MacPHAIL returned to Hqrs.	[illegible]
"	Nov 2nd		A relay post has been established in HUDSON TRENCH about T 22. D. 8.16.	
"	Nov 3rd		Under instructions from DMS. 1st ARMY, the term MAIN DRESSING STATION is no longer to be employed. A.D.S's are to be known as Advanced R.A.M.C. Post	[initials]
"	Nov 4th.		I inspected A.R.P. at TUNNEL DUMP. New latrines need to be built and several cupboards are required, as well as shelves in the kitchen.	[initials]
"	Nov 5th		I inspected A.R.P. at WILLERVAL. Great progress has been made with the work in VANCOUVER ROAD	[initials]

Instructions regarding War Diaries and Intelligence Summaries are contained in F. S. Regs., Part II. and the Staff Manual respectively. Title pages will be prepared in manuscript.

WAR DIARY
or
INTELLIGENCE SUMMARY.
(Erase heading not required.)

Army Form C. 2118.

PAGE II

93rd Fd. AMBULANCE

Place	Date	Hour	Summary of Events and Information	Remarks and references to Appendices
	1917			
ROCLINCOURT.			Nothing to report.	
"	Nov. 6th		LIEUT. SMITH U.S.M.R. is attached for duty to 13th E YORKS & is struck off our strength.	
"	Nov 7th		In view of the forthcoming raid, on the left sector, the following arrangements were made, according to A.D.M.S. 31st DIV. MEDICAL ARRANGEMENTS d. 31.10.17. 32 bearers are to be placed at R.A.P.S. in the left sector. 32 bearers are to be placed at the Relay Post at junction of HUDSON TRENCH & SASKATCHEWAN RD. 16 O.R. 95th F.A. are to report here for duty and be sent up to WILLERVAL: 3 motor ambulances from same F.A. are also to be attached for duty. Cases to be evacuated to WILLERVAL ADRAMC Post, & thence by car: walking cases to proceed on foot to COMMANDANTS HOUSE & thence by car.	
"	Nov 8th		The proposed raid took place & was, with great success. 50 wounded were evacuated, of whom about 2/3 were stretcher cases: one case died at the A.D.S. R.A.P.S were reported clear by 5 a.m., the raid having occurred at 12 noon(?). LIEUTS. D. EVANS & H.J. BUCHANAN reported for duty & are taken on our strength. CAPT. COMMINS(?) proceeded on 14 days leave of absence to PARIS.	

A5834 Wt. W4973/M687 750,000 8/16 D. D. & L. Ltd. Forms/C.2118/13.

Instructions regarding War Diaries and Intelligence Summaries are contained in F. S. Regs., Part II. and the Staff Manual respectively. Title pages will be prepared in manuscript.

Page III

WAR DIARY
or
~~INTELLIGENCE SUMMARY.~~
(Erase heading not required.)

93rd F. Ambulance

Army Form C. 2118.

Place	Date	Hour	Summary of Events and Information	Remarks and references to Appendices
		1917		
Roclincourt	Nov. 9th		Lieut. Evans relieved Capt. Arthur at Willerval.	Capt. Arthur
"	Nov. 10th		Under instructions from ADMS 31st Div. Lieut. Evans reported for duty to ADMS 48th Div. Lieut. Buchanan relieved him at Willerval.	A.P.
"	Nov. 11th		Nothing to report. Lieut. Moore U.S.A.M.C. reported for duty.	A.P.
"	Nov. 12th		Nothing to report.	A.P.
"	Nov. 13th		I visited Tunnel Dump, also relay posts. A RAMC Post also.	A.P.
"	Nov. 14th		Under instructions from ADMS 31st Div. Capt. Arthur reported to O.C. 1st Army Instruction Camp (33 C.C.S.) for 10 days course.	A.P.
"	Nov. 15th		Inspected Adv. RAMC Post Willerval. The new post at Vancouver Rd. is almost complete and a cook house is being erected. [illegible] needed [illegible]	A.P.
"	Nov. 16th		Under instructions from ADMS 31st Div. Lieut. R.J. Buchanan reported for duty with 31st D.A.C. & is struck off the strength. The old nomenclature of "Main" & "Advanced Dressing Station" is to be resumed.	A.P.

A5834 Wt. W4973/M687 750,000 8/16 D. D. & L. Ltd. Forms/C.2118/13.

Instructions regarding War Diaries and Intelligence Summaries are contained in F. S. Regs., Part II. and the Staff Manual respectively. Title pages will be prepared in manuscript.

PAGE IV.

WAR DIARY
or
INTELLIGENCE SUMMARY.
(*Erase heading not required.*)

Army Form C. 2118.

93rd FIELD AMBULANCE

Place	Date	Hour	Summary of Events and Information	Remarks and references to Appendices
ROLLINCOURT	1917 Nov 17th		Capt. A. MacKinnon proceeded on 1 month's special leave of absence to ENGLAND.	
			Capt. J. MacPhail was evacuated sick to base.	
"	Nov 18th		Sergt MAJOR F. RELF was evacuated sick to 42 CCS.	
"	Nov 19th		The 47th Div. is being relieved by 3rd Div, which will hold temporarily the XIII CORPS front. Under instructions from ADMS 3rd Div. wounded from present left sector of 47th Div. are to be evacuated from R.A.P.s via OUSE TRENCH to ADS. TUNNEL DUMP. There are two RAPs & two relay posts in OUSE ALLEY, to be taken over from 4th LONDON F.A. Relief to be completed by 6 p.m. 20th Nov.	
"	Nov 20th		The new line of evacuation and relay posts were taken over from 4th LONDON F.A.	
"	Nov 21st		ADS. WILLERVAL & ADS on VANCOUVER RD & Relay Post in HUDSON TRENCH were handed over to 4th CANADIAN F.A. today, & party withdrawn. The central R.A.P. at ARLEUX is being retained & will evacuate to ADS. TUNNEL DUMP via TOMMY ALLEY. Various relay posts have been reinforced.	

A5834 Wt. W4973/M687 750,000 8/16 D. D. & L. Ltd. Forms/C.2118/13.

Instructions regarding War Diaries and Intelligence Summaries are contained in F. S. Regs., Part II. and the Staff Manual respectively. Title pages will be prepared in manuscript.

PAGE V.

WAR DIARY
or
~~INTELLIGENCE SUMMARY.~~
(*Erase heading not required.*)

93rd FD. AMBULANCE

Army Form C. 2118.

Place	Date	Hour	Summary of Events and Information	Remarks and references to Appendices
ROCLINCOURT.	1917 Nov 22nd		Under instructions from ADMS 31st DIV. LIEUT. MOORE U.S.M.O.R.C. is attached for duty to 18th Bn. DURHAM L.I. LIEUT. CANTER U.S.M.R.C. will be attached to this unit upon relief.	A.R. [illegible] Lt Col
"	Nov 23rd		Nothing to report.	A.R.
"	Nov. 24th		Capt. L.C. ARTHUR returned from 1st ARMY SCHOOL of INSTRUCTION.	A.R.
"	Nov. 25th		Nothing to report. I inspected ADS. TUNNEL DUMP.	A.R.
"	Nov 26th		LIEUTS. E. NOLAND & R. McHENRY U.S.A. M.O.R.C. joined this unit for duty.	A.R.
"	Nov 27th		Capt. ARTHUR & LIEUT. NOLAND proceeded to ADS. TUNNEL DUMP & Lt. CANTER returned to Hqrs. Capt. R.S. CUMMING M.C. proceeded on 14 days leave of absence to ENGLAND.	A.R.
"	Nov 28th		Capt. W. CRABTREE proceeded to ADS. TUNNEL DUMP, in relief of Capt. L. ARTHUR who is attached to 15th Bn. W. YORKS for temporary duty.	A.R.
"	Nov 29th		Nothing to report.	A.R.
"	Nov. 30th		Nothing to report, except that S.O.S. reported to O.C. 63rd F.A. and was struck off the strength of this unit.	A.R. [illegible] Lt Col O.C. 93rd FA

A5834. Wt. W4973/M687 750,000 8/16 D. D. & L. Ltd. Forms/C.2118/13.

Confidential 23 140/2618 Volume XXIV

Dec. 917

Vol 22

War Diary.

93rd Field Ambulance 31st Division

December 1917.

Instructions regarding War Diaries and Intelligence Summaries are contained in F. S. Regs., Part II. and the Staff Manual respectively. Title pages will be prepared in manuscript.

Army Form C. 2118.

WAR DIARY
or
~~INTELLIGENCE SUMMARY.~~
(Erase heading not required.)

PAGE I. 93rd F.D AMBULANCE

Place	Date	Hour	Summary of Events and Information	Remarks and references to Appendices
1917 ROCLINCOURT	~~Dec.~~ Dec 1st		Under instructions from ADMS 3rd DIV. I detailed a N.C.O. & 20 men to take over and hold stores and Field Ambulance site at HARDEUIL, from 63rd F.A.	[illegible]
"	Dec 2nd.		Nothing to report.	AP
"	Dec 3rd.		I received preliminary warning to be ready to withdraw my bearers from the forward area, and to be ready to hand over the M.D.S. at ROCLINCOURT, at short notice.	AP
"	Dec 4th.		I received RAMC OPERATION ORDER no. 26 from ADMS. 3.4 DIV. The ADS. & relay posts are to be handed over to 2/3 LONDON. F.A. on 6th inst: also the M.D.S. on 9th inst. This unit is to be affiliated to [illegible] INF BDE. and will be prepared to entrain on 9th inst.	AP
"	Dec 5th.		Nothing to report.	AP
"	Dec 6th.		My officers & men were relieved in the forward area by 2/3 LONDON F.A. ADS TUNNEL & relay posts handed over.	AP
			30 gassed cases (Mustard gas) admitted this evening.	

A5834 Wt. W4973/M687 750,000 8/16 D. D. & L. Ltd. Forms/C.2118/13.

Instructions regarding War Diaries and Intelligence Summaries are contained in F. S. Regs., Part II. and the Staff Manual respectively. Title pages will be prepared in manuscript.

PAGE II

WAR DIARY
or
~~INTELLIGENCE SUMMARY.~~
(*Erase heading not required.*)

Army Form C. 2118.

93rd Fd. AMBULANCE

Place	Date	Hour	Summary of Events and Information	Remarks and references to Appendices
ST. CATHERINES.	1917 Dec 7th		We came today under administration of 94th INF. BDE.	
			Unit moved to billets in St CATHERINE, moving off at 11 A.M. Move completed by mid-day.	
			Billets are bad: broken down and damp houses and cellars.	
			The F.A. site at ROCLINCOURT was handed over to 2/3 LONDON F.A. Ambulance	[illegible]
"	Dec. 8th.		Lt. CANTER and 2 N.C.O's reported from temporary duty at 1st ARMY SCHOOL of INSTRUCTION.	AP.
"	Dec 9th		Nothing to report.	AP
HAROEUIL	Dec 10th		Unit moved this morning & took over F.A. site at HAROEUIL. to open for reception of N.Y.D. Gas cases.	AP
"	Dec 11th		Nothing to report	AP.
"	Dec 12th		Nothing to report	AP.
"	Dec 13th		Nothing to report. The men of the unit are mainly engaged in cleaning and clearing the site, which has become very dirty and dilapidated.	AP

A5834 Wt. W4973/M687 750,000 8/16 D. D. & L. Ltd. Forms/C.2118/13.

Instructions regarding War Diaries and Intelligence Summaries are contained in F. S. Regs., Part II. and the Staff Manual respectively. Title pages will be prepared in manuscript. PAGE III

Army Form C. 2118.

WAR DIARY
or
~~INTELLIGENCE SUMMARY.~~
(*Erase heading not required.*)

93rd Fd AMBULANCE

Place	Date	Hour	Summary of Events and Information	Remarks and references to Appendices
	1917			
MAROEUIL	Dec. 14th		Capt. R. CUMMING M.C. returned from leave. Lt. CANTER proceeded on 4 days leave to PARIS.	[illegible]
"	Dec. 15th.		Nothing to report.	[illegible]
"	Dec. 16th		Capt. C. L. ARTHUR returned from temporary duty with the 15th Btn. W. YORKS Regt.	
			I received ADMS. OPERATn. ORDER no. 27. The division returns to the line, in this sector, on 18th-19th inst., for a period of 32 days.	
			This unit will remain in its present position	[illegible]
"	Dec. 17th		Operation order of yesterday cancelled.	
			LIEUTS. NOLAND & McHENRY with 1 tent subdivision proceeded to XIII CORPS REST STATn. for temporary duty.	[illegible]
"	Dec 18th		Nothing to report.	[illegible]
"	Dec 19th.		Nothing to report.	[illegible]
"	Dec. 20th		LIEUT. CANTER returned from leave of absence to PARIS.	[illegible]
"	Dec 21st		The 31st division is now taking over the original divisional line	

A5834 Wt. W4973/M687 750,000 8/16 D. D. & L. Ltd. Forms/C.2118/13.

Army Form C. 2118.

Instructions regarding War Diaries and Intelligence Summaries are contained in F. S. Regs., Part II. and the Staff Manual respectively. Title pages will be prepared in manuscript.

WAR DIARY
or
~~INTELLIGENCE SUMMARY.~~

(Erase heading not required.)

PAGE IV — 93rd Fd AMBULANCE

Place	Date	Hour	Summary of Events and Information	Remarks and references to Appendices
	1917			
MARŒUIL	Dec 21st		(contd). I received operation order no 29. by ADMS 31st Div. The 94th F.A. proceed tomorrow to ROCLINCOURT (M.D.S.) and are also to take over the evacuation of whole front. This unit to remain as at present.	[illegible]
"	Dec 22nd		Nothing to report.	[illegible]
"	Dec 23rd		Nothing to report. Was notified that Capt. R. MacKinnon is struck off the strength as from 19th inst.	[illegible]
"	Dec 24th		Nothing to report.	[illegible]
"	Dec 25th		XMAS DAY. The unit dined at 4.30 p.m. and attended a concert afterwards. Lt. CARTER proceeded on duty to PARIS & is struck off strength.	[illegible]
"	Dec 26th		I proceeded on 14 days leave of absence and handed over to Capt. R.S. CUMMING. M.C. A.S.C personnel held Xmas Dinner which was followed by concert.	[illegible] O.C. 93 F.A.
"	Dec 27th		Nothing to report.	
"	Dec 28th		Unit visited by G.O.C 31st Division who delivered an address wishing all the men on parade the compliments of the season.	R.S. Cumming Capt.
"	Dec. 29th		Nothing to report.	R.S.C.
"	Dec 30th		Nothing to report.	R.S.C.
				R.S.C.

A5834 Wt. W4973/M687 750,000 8/16 D. D. & L. Ltd. Forms/C.2118/13.

Army Form C. 2118.

Instructions regarding War Diaries and Intelligence Summaries are contained in F. S. Regs., Part II. and the Staff Manual respectively. Title pages will be prepared in manuscript.

Page V.

WAR DIARY
or
~~INTELLIGENCE SUMMARY.~~
(Erase heading not required.)

93rd Field Ambulance.

Place	Date	Hour	Summary of Events and Information	Remarks and references to Appendices
MARDEUIL	31st Dec.		Hospital personnel changed and formed drill squad for the week. Unit held Concert and Whist drive in the evening	R.S. Cunningham Capt RAMC for OC 93rd Field Ambulance

A5834. Wt. W4973/M687 750,000 8/16 D. D. & L. Ltd. Forms/C.2118/13.

31

140/2784

No. 93. 7. A.

1

Army Form C. 2118.

Instructions regarding War Diaries and Intelligence Summaries are contained in F. S. Regs., Part II. and the Staff Manual respectively. Title pages will be prepared in manuscript.

PAGE I

WAR DIARY
or
INTELLIGENCE SUMMARY.
(Erase heading not required.)

93rd Fd AMBULANCE

Vol 23

Place	Date	Hour	Summary of Events and Information	Remarks and references to Appendices
MAROEUIL	1st Jan 1918.		New Years Day. Nothing to report as weather still makes all outside work almost impossible. Horse transport has been unable to use the roads owing to shortage of frost cogs Visited by DADMS 31st Division.	R.S.Cumming Capt.
"	2nd Jan.		Capt W. CRABTREE. RAMC returned from leave. New stove made for mess kitchen.	R.S.C.
"	3rd Jan		95th Field Ambulance to admit and evacuate all local hospital sick from Chinese Labour Companies	R.S.C.
"	4th Jan.		Extract from War Office Gazette dated Jan 1. 1918. Capt (A Lt Col) A.M Pollard D.S.O.	R.S.C.
	5th Jan		Nothing to report.	R.S.C
"	6th Jan		O.C. 2/2 (West Riding) Field Ambulance visited site at MAROEUIL to arrange taking over in accordance with RAMC Operation Order. No 30 dated 6.1.18 (ADMS. 31st Div)	R.S.C
	7th Jan		1 tent subdivision (19 O.R) reported to O.C. XIII Corps Rest Station in accordance with RAMC Operation Order No 30 dated 6.1.18 1 Section as advance party arrived from 2/2 (West Riding) Field Ambulance at 5.30 pm	R.S.C

A5834 Wt. W4973/M687 750,000 8/16 D. D. & L. Ltd. Forms/C.2118/13.

Instructions regarding War Diaries and Intelligence Summaries are contained in F. S. Regs., Part II. and the Staff Manual respectively. Title pages will be prepared in manuscript.

PAGE II

WAR DIARY
or
INTELLIGENCE SUMMARY.
(Erase heading not required.)

93rd Fd. AMBULANCE

Army Form C. 2118.

Place	Date	Hour	Summary of Events and Information	Remarks and references to Appendices
	1917			
MAROEUIL } ST. ELOI }	8th	JAN	Handed over Hospital at 9am. Camp handed over at 12.30pm. Unit marched to billets in ST. ELOI at 12.30pm arriving at 2.0pm. Filthy billets with bad accommodation.	R.S. Cumming Capt.
ST ELOI	9th	JAN	Cleaning up the site. Nothing to report. R.S.C. ~~CAPT. W. CRABTREE proceeded [illegible]~~	
ST. ELOI	10th	JAN	Nothing to report. R.S.C.	
"	11th	JAN	I returned from leave today. Took over charge from Capt. R.S. CUMMING. M.C.	A[illegible] Lt Col
"	12th	JAN	With the DADMS 31st Div. I inspected a proposed site for new Field Ambulance Hqrs at ESCOUVRES (F.14.b.3.5)	A.P.
"	13th	JAN	Capt. J. FREW. RAMC joined this unit for duty	A.P.
"	14th	JAN	Nothing to report.	A.P.
"	15th	JAN	Capt. R.S. CUMMING M.C. was evacuated sick to 57 C.C.S.	A.P.
"	16th	JAN	} Nothing to report.	A.P.
	17th	JAN		
	18th	JAN		

A5834 Wt. W4973/M687 750,000 8/16 D. D. & L. Ltd. Forms/C.2118/13.

Instructions regarding War Diaries and Intelligence Summaries are contained in F. S. Regs., Part II. and the Staff Manual respectively. Title pages will be prepared in manuscript.

WAR DIARY
or
~~INTELLIGENCE SUMMARY.~~
(*Erase heading not required.*)

Army Form C. 2118.

PAGE III

92nd Fd Amb.

Place	Date	Hour	Summary of Events and Information	Remarks and references to Appendices
Mt St Eloi	1917 JAN. 19th		Capt W CRABTREE & 2 N.C.O's returned back from the Course at 1st ARMY SCHOOL of INSTRUCTION	AP Appendix 1917
"	JAN 20th		Nothing to report.	AP.
"	JAN 21st		Capt L C ARTHUR proceeded on leave of absence to England	AP
"	JAN 22nd		Nothing to report	AP
"	JAN 23rd		Capt J FREW rejoined at 1st ARMY SCHOOL of INSTRUCTION (22 C.C.S.) from course of instruction	AP
"	JAN 24th		Nothing to report	AP
"	JAN 25th		Lieut A McKENNA returned from XIII CORPS REST STATION	AP
"	JAN 26th		Nothing to report.	AP
"	JAN 27th		Nothing to report	AP
"	JAN 28th		A new kitchen with stove has been erected in a cook-house for patients & personnel. A new kitchen has also been erected for ASC MT and a third is in course of construction for the Horse Transport. A big incinerator is also being built	AP

A5834 Wt. W4973/M687 750,000 8/16 D. D. & L. Ltd. Forms/C.2118/13.

Instructions regarding War Diaries and Intelligence Summaries are contained in F. S. Regs., Part II. and the Staff Manual respectively. Title pages will be prepared in manuscript.

WAR DIARY
or
~~INTELLIGENCE SUMMARY.~~

(*Erase heading not required.*)

PAGE IV

92nd FD AMBULANCE.

Army Form C. 2118.

Place	Date	Hour	Summary of Events and Information	Remarks and references to Appendices
MONT ST ELOI	1917 JAN. 29th		Under instructions from DMS. 1st ARMY, huts etc are being protected against splinters from bomb attacks, by earthen banks built against them. Part of the ground is being dug up for vegetables.	[illegible]
"	JAN 30th		Nothing to report.	[illegible]
"	JAN 31st		LIEUT E. NOLAND returned from temporary duty with 14th Bn. Y. & Lancs. Regt. & proceeded to XIII CORPS Rest Station in relief of LIEUT R. McHENRY, who returned to Hqrs. of the unit.	[illegible] Comm. 92nd F.A.

A5834 Wt. W4973/M687 750,000 8/16 D. D. & L. Ltd. Forms/C.2118/13.

Feb. 1918.

140/2784.

No. 93. F. A.

19

Instructions regarding War Diaries and Intelligence Summaries are contained in F. S. Regs., Part II. and the Staff Manual respectively. Title pages will be prepared in manuscript.

PAGE I

WAR DIARY
or
INTELLIGENCE SUMMARY.
(Erase heading not required.)

Army Form C. 2118.

VR 24

92nd FIELD AMBULANCE

Place	Date	Hour	Summary of Events and Information	Remarks and references to Appendices
Mt St Eloi	1917 Feb	1st	Lieut R. McHenry proceeded to report to O.C. 16th W. Yorks Regt for duty (temporary) in relief of Capt G. Roche	[illegible]
"	Feb	2nd	Under instructions from ADMS 31st Div 92 [illegible] reported to Hqrs 92nd Inf Bde for work in reconstruction of a RAP ARRAS [illegible]. Capt J Frew returned from a course at 1st Army School of Instruction	[illegible]
"	Feb	3rd	Under instructions from ADMS 31st Div Capt J Frew reported to O.C. 2/3 W Riding [illegible] in relief of Capt [illegible] who reported [illegible] for duty	[illegible]
"	Feb	4th	Nothing to report	[illegible]
"	Feb	5th	Nothing to report	[illegible]
"	Feb	6th	Capt C. I. Arthur returned from leave	[illegible]

A5834 Wt. W4973/M687 750,000 8/16 D. D. & L. Ltd. Forms/C.2118/13.

Instructions regarding War Diaries and Intelligence Summaries are contained in F. S. Regs., Part II. and the Staff Manual respectively. Title pages will be prepared in manuscript.

WAR DIARY
or
INTELLIGENCE SUMMARY.
(Erase heading not required.)

Army Form C. 2118.

PAGE II 93rd Fd AMBULANCE

Place	Date	Hour	Summary of Events and Information	Remarks and references to Appendices
MT ST ELOI	1917 Feb. 6th		LIEUT E. NOLAND proceeded to 1st ARMY SCHOOL of INSTRUCTION.	
	(contd).		Capt. M. PURCELL relieved LIEUT. NOLAND at XIII CORPS REST STATION.	[initials]
"	Feb 7th		I attended a conference at DDMS XIII CORPS	
"	Feb 8th		Nothing to report	[initials]
"	Feb 9th		Capt. A.W. FREW from 94th F.A. reported for duty with this unit	
			Capt. C. ARTHUR proceeded to 1st ARMY SCHOOL of INSTRUCTION to take over the duties of Assistant Commandant.	[initials]
"	Feb 10th		Nothing to report	[initials]
	Feb 11th		No. 11585 Pte CASTELL F.J. was killed today whilst working at the R.A.P. ARLEUX SIDING.	[initials]
"	Feb 12th		Under instructions from DDMS XIII CORPS, Capt. CRABTREE proceeded to XIII CORPS Rest Station in place of Capt. PURCELL who rejoined HQrs of the unit. DDMS XIII CORPS inspected the horses.	[initials]
"	13th		Nothing to report	[initials]
"	14th		Nothing to report	[initials]
"	15th		Nothing to report	[initials]
"	16th		LIEUT E. NOLAND rejoined from the SCHOOL of INSTRUCTION. Lieut. H. MCHENRY rejoined from duty with 16th Bn W. Yorks Regt.	[initials]

A5834 Wt. W4973/M687 750,000 8/16 D. D. & L. Ltd. Forms/C.2118/13.

Instructions regarding War Diaries and Intelligence Summaries are contained in F. S. Regs., Part II. and the Staff Manual respectively. Title pages will be prepared in manuscript. PAGE III

WAR DIARY
or
~~INTELLIGENCE SUMMARY.~~
(Erase heading not required.)

93rd FIELD AMBULANCE

Army Form C. 2118.

Place	Date	Hour	Summary of Events and Information	Remarks and references to Appendices
MONT ST. ELOI.	1918 Feb. 17th		Under instructions from A.D.M.S. 31st Div. Capt. W. PURCELL reported for duty to A.D.M.S. 56th Div. & is struck off the strength of this unit	A.W. [illegible]
"	Feb 18th.		Nothing to report	A.B.
"	Feb 19th		I attended a conference at Office of ADMS 31st Div	A.B.
"	Feb 20th		I attended a conference at Office of D.D.M.S. XIII CORPS	A.B.
"	Feb 21st		Capt. R.S. CUMMING. M.C. was today evacuated to the base	A.B.
"	Feb 22nd		Under instructions from ADMS. I proceeded with DADMS. to neighbourhood of COMMANDANT'S HOUSE to select a site for a new rear A.D.S.	A.B.
"	Feb 23rd Feb 24th Feb 25th		} Nothing to report	A.B.
"	Feb 26th		Lieut. E. NOLAND returned from leave.	A.B.
"	Feb 27th.		I sent Capt. FREW and advance party to take over F.A. site at [illegible] from 2/1st W. RIDING F.A.	
"	Feb 28th.		Handed over F.A. site at Mt. St. ELOI to 3/1st W. RIDING F.A. Came under the 93rd I. Bde from today. Unit [illegible] ready to move at [illegible] notice. Unit marched today to VERMIN and occupied [illegible] and F.A. site	A.W. [illegible] Comdg 93 F.A.

A5834 Wt. W4973/M687 750,000 8/16 D. D. & L. Ltd. Forms/C.2118/13.

Mar. 1918.

/

140/2902.

93rd. Field Ambulance.

7

Instructions regarding War Diaries and Intelligence Summaries are contained in F. S. Regs., Part II. and the Staff Manual respectively. Title pages will be prepared in manuscript.

PAGE I

WAR DIARY
or
INTELLIGENCE SUMMARY.
(Erase heading not required.)

Army Form C. 2118.

Vol 25

93rd Fd AMBULANCE

Place	Date	Hour	Summary of Events and Information	Remarks and references to Appendices
HERMIN	1918 March 1st		A scheme of training has been arranged for the unit, whilst in G.H.Q. reserve.	
			Billets are poor – mainly draughty barns. Sanitary arrangements not good, and new latrines have to be dug everywhere. As billets are very scattered, many latrines are needed and this is entailing a lot of time which would otherwise be employed in training	
"			ADMS visited the unit today.	A W Pollard Lt Col
	March 2nd		Capt A.W FREW departed today for duty at 51 General Hospital and is struck off the strength.	
			22 O.R. reported from work in the forward area.	AP
"	March 3rd		Nothing to report	AP
"	March 4th		Capt CRABTREE and 2 [illegible] returned back from temporary duty at XIII CORPS REST STAT^n^	AP
"	March 5th		1st Lieut. Mc [illegible] departed for duty with 18th D.L.I. in place of Capt MOORE, who after a course at [illegible] ARMY SCHOOL is to return for duty with this unit.	AP

A5834 Wt. W4973/M687 750,000 8/16 D. D. & L. Ltd. Forms/C.2118/13.

Army Form C. 2118.

Instructions regarding War Diaries and Intelligence Summaries are contained in F. S. Regs., Part II. and the Staff Manual respectively. Title pages will be prepared in manuscript.

PAGE II

WAR DIARY
or
~~INTELLIGENCE SUMMARY.~~
(Erase heading not required.)

[illegible] Field Ambulance

Place	Date	Hour	Summary of Events and Information	Remarks and references to Appendices
HERMIN	1918		Capt. L. MOORE reported for duty and proceeded to 1st Army School)	
	March 6th		INSTRUCTION for a course.	
			Capt. W. L. SMITH M.O.R.C. USA reported for duty with the unit	
			The D.M.S. 1st ARMY inspected the unit today. Parade at 10 a.m.	
			[illegible] [illegible] [illegible] of unit in line of sections	[illegible]
	March 7th		Nothing to report	[illegible]
	March 8th		Nothing to report	[illegible]
"	March 9th		Nothing to report	[illegible]
"	March 10th		Capt. W. L. SMITH proceeded on leave [illegible] to PARIS	[illegible]
"	March 11th		LIEUT. HOLLAND proceeded to join 2nd GRENADIER Gds for temporary	
			duty.	[illegible]
"	March 12th		Nothing to report	[illegible]
"	March 13th		I attended conference of O.C. 93rd Inf Bgde group, with	
			reference to tactical scheme on 15th inst	[illegible]
"	March 14th		Nothing to report.	[illegible]

A5834 Wt. W4973/M687 750,000 8/16 D. D. & L. Ltd. Forms/C.2118/13.

Instructions regarding War Diaries and Intelligence Summaries are contained in F. S. Regs., Part II. and the Staff Manual respectively. Title pages will be prepared in manuscript.

WAR DIARY
or
~~INTELLIGENCE SUMMARY.~~
(*Erase heading not required.*)

Army Form C. 2118.

PAGE III

93rd Fd AMBULANCE

Place	Date	Hour	Summary of Events and Information	Remarks and references to Appendices
HERMIN	1918 March 15th		The unit took part in a tactical scheme of 93rd Bgde. Dressing Stations were erected and the bearer division practised in keeping touch with regimental units	
"	March 16th		Capt H G MOORE returned from duty at 1st ARMY SCHOOL of INSTRUCTION	
"	March 17th		Capt L C MOORE M.O.R.C. USA proceeded to report to ADMS CALAIS for duty & is struck off the strength. Capt L L ARTHUR returned from duty with 1st ARMY SCHOOL of INSTRUCTION	
	March 18th		Capt W L SMITH returned from leave	
"	March 19th		Nothing to report	
"	March 20th		Received preliminary notice that unit would change back to MAREUIL on 22nd	

A5834 Wt. W4973/M687 750,000 8/16 D. D. & L. Ltd. Forms/C.2118/13.

Army Form C. 2118.

Instructions regarding War Diaries and Intelligence Summaries are contained in F. S. Regs., Part II. and the Staff Manual respectively. Title pages will be prepared in manuscript.

PAGE IV

WAR DIARY
or
~~INTELLIGENCE SUMMARY.~~
(Erase heading not required.)

93rd FIELD AMBULANCE

Place	Date 1918	Hour	Summary of Events and Information	Remarks and references to Appendices
HERMIN	March 21st.		This evening received orders that move to MAROEUIL was cancelled & that	
	MARCH 22nd		Unit [illegible] to BERLES on ARRAS-DOULLENS Rd under orders of 93rd Bde. The unit embussed with Bde and proceeded via St Pol, DOULLENS to BLAIREVILLE. Unit billeted night there at [illegible] CORPS School Camp.	A.P.
BLAIREVILLE	23rd		Took over [illegible] at BLAIREVILLE from 136 F.A. as a MAIN DRESSING STATION. Detailed Capt. W.L. SMITH & [illegible] [illegible] & S.O. [illegible] to proceed to [illegible]COURT [illegible] to O.C. 93rd F.A. [illegible]	A.P.
"	24th		[illegible] [illegible] of all [illegible] [illegible] [illegible] afternoon [illegible] word that Capt. MASON had been severely wounded, Capt SMITH slightly wounded and that 2 O.R. were killed and [illegible] wounded, one dying later. Sgt CROOKS [illegible] [illegible] the billet.	A.P.

A5834 Wt. W4973/M687 750,000 8/16 D. D. & L. Ltd. Forms/C.2118/13.

Army Form C. 2118.

WAR DIARY
or
~~INTELLIGENCE~~ SUMMARY.
(*Erase heading not required.*)

Instructions regarding War Diaries and Intelligence Summaries are contained in F. S. Regs., Part II. and the Staff Manual respectively. Title pages will be prepared in manuscript.

PAGE V

93rd Fd AMBce.

Place	Date	Hour	Summary of Events and Information	Remarks and references to Appendices
BLAIREVILLE	1918 MARCH 25th		L.O. [illegible] returned from work at A.D.S. HAMBLINCOURT. The A.D.S. moved back to ADINFER this evening	[illegible]
BAILLEULMONT	MARCH 26th		Handed over M.D.S. to [illegible] Division [illegible] A.D.S. [illegible] BAILLEULMONT, where [illegible] billeted for the night.	[illegible]
"	MARCH 27th		[illegible] to BIENVILLERS to [illegible] M.D.S. [illegible] Prepared [illegible] DIV [illegible] [illegible] BAILLEULMONT [illegible] M.D.S. [illegible] M.D.S.	[illegible]
LE SUD du BAC	MARCH 28th		The M.D.S. at BAILLEULMONT [illegible] to [illegible] LE SUD du BAC [illegible] M.D.S. [illegible] 43rd C.C.S. [illegible] 350 [illegible]	

A5834 Wt. W4973/M687 750,000 8/16 D. D. & L. Ltd. Forms/C.2118/13.

Army Form C. 2118.

WAR DIARY
or
INTELLIGENCE SUMMARY.
(Erase heading not required.)

Instructions regarding War Diaries and Intelligence Summaries are contained in F. S. Regs., Part II. and the Staff Manual respectively. Title pages will be prepared in manuscript.

[illegible] 93rd RFA Bde

Place	Date	Hour	Summary of Events and Information	Remarks and references to Appendices
	1918			
	MARCH 28th (cont)		between 8. p.m. and 9. p.m. [illegible] from [illegible]	[illegible]
Le Sud du Bois	March 29th		A [illegible] [illegible] [illegible] [illegible] 6 [illegible]	
			FA [illegible] DIV. The [illegible] [illegible] RINSART	[illegible]
"	March 30th		Capt. H. L. GAUNTLETT and Lt. HALL MORROW [illegible] joined [illegible]	
"	MARCH 31st		Received orders to move at [illegible] p.m. to SUS St LEGER [illegible]	
			orders of 93rd Bde. The [illegible] [illegible] [illegible]	
			32nd Div.	
			[illegible] Comdg. 93rd [illegible]	

A5834 Wt. W4973/M687 750,000 8/16 D. D. & L. Ltd. Forms/C.2118/13.

apr. 1918.

140/2902.

93rd. Field Ambulance.

19

Instructions regarding War Diaries and Intelligence Summaries are contained in F. S. Regs., Part II. and the Staff Manual respectively. Title pages will be prepared in manuscript.

PAGE I

WAR DIARY
or
~~INTELLIGENCE SUMMARY.~~

(*Erase heading not required.*)

Army Form C. 2118.

Vol 26

93rd Fd AMBULANCE

Place	Date 1918	Hour	Summary of Events and Information	Remarks and references to Appendices
LE BAC-du-SUD.	APRIL 1st.		Received preliminary notice that the unit would be relieved in line by the 32nd Div. & would carry over only duties at CORPS M.D.S. to 91st F.A. [illegible]	
SUS ST LEGER	April 2nd.		On relief by 91st F.A. the unit marched to billets at SUS ST LEGER, under the orders of 93rd Bde.	AP
BAJUS.	April 3rd		Unit embussed and moved into billets at BAJUS. Transport marched independently under Major ARTHUR	AP
"	April 4th		Nothing to report.	AP
"	April 5th		I attended a conference of O.C. units called by G.O.C. 31st Div.	AP
"	April 6th		Nothing to report	AP
"	April 7th		Capts. H. BOYES M.C., W.C. KIRKWOOD, P.S. MILNE and R.G. BATTERSBY reported for duty. Capt. W. CRABTREE returned from temporary duty with 13th Bn YORK & LANCS Regt.	AP
"	April 8th		Nothing to report.	AP

A5834 Wt. W4973/M687 750,000 8/16 D. D. & L. Ltd. Forms/C.2118/13.

Instructions regarding War Diaries and Intelligence Summaries are contained in F. S. Regs., Part II. and the Staff Manual respectively. Title pages will be prepared in manuscript.

PAGE II

WAR DIARY
or
~~INTELLIGENCE SUMMARY.~~
(*Erase heading not required.*)

93rd FD AMBULANCE

Army Form C. 2118.

Place	Date	Hour	Summary of Events and Information	Remarks and references to Appendices
BAJUS	1918 April 9th		Nothing to report, save that Capt KIRKWOOD proceeded to 95th F.A. for duty	[illegible]
do	April 10th		We got sudden orders at 2-30 pm that unit would move with 92nd I. Bgde to VIEUX BERQUIN by bus. We arrived there at midnight & billeted. Transport proceeded separately.	[illegible]
MERRIS	"	11th	93rd Inf. Bgde went into line on right of 92nd Bgde. GUARDS Bgde arrived and were separated by the 29th Div. from 92nd Bgde. Line held from VIEUX BERQUIN to just W. of STEENWERCK.	
			93rd Bgde attacked during night to strengthen line & [illegible] CARVER [illegible] with 60 bearers to form Collecting Post at NOOTE BOOM. Cars were	

A5834 Wt. W4973/M687 750,000 8/16 D. D. & L. Ltd. Forms/C.2118/13.

Army Form C. 2118.

Instructions regarding War Diaries and Intelligence Summaries are contained in F. S. Regs., Part II. and the Staff Manual respectively. Title pages will be prepared in manuscript.

WAR DIARY
or
~~INTELLIGENCE SUMMARY.~~

(Erase heading not required.)

PAGE IIII

92nd FD. AMBULANCE

Place	Date	Hour	Summary of Events and Information	Remarks and references to Appendices
MERRIS	1918 April 11th		at OUTERSTEEN.	
			Maj. CRABTREE & Capt. BYERS & 40 bearers were stationed at a point 2 miles S. of OUTERSTEEN. Bearers were attached to various battalions. Cars cleared to M.D.S. STRAZEELE (96th F.A.) Bgrs of unit were at a farm just E. of MERRIS.	
"	April 12th		Early this morning 93rd Bgde were driven in by a very heavy counterattack & 92nd Bgde had to fall back in touch with them. Wounded collected in OUTERSTEEN & MERRIS were all cleared.	
			Major ARTHURS party did excellent work in clearing wounded, after the Infantry had been driven back	

A5834 Wt. W4973/M687 750,000 8/16 D. D. & L. Ltd. Forms/C.2118/13.

Army Form C. 2118.

WAR DIARY
or
INTELLIGENCE SUMMARY.
(*Erase heading not required.*)

Instructions regarding War Diaries and Intelligence Summaries are contained in F. S. Regs., Part II. and the Staff Manual respectively. Title pages will be prepared in manuscript.

PAGE. IV   93rd FD AMBULANCE

Place	Date	Hour	Summary of Events and Information	Remarks and references to Appendices
MERRIS	1918 April 12th		The latter cleared back to METEREN evacuated their wounded by lorry & rejoined at STRAZEELE. I formed a Collecting Post at a farm ½ mile NW part of STRAZEELE, as our line was now ½ mile behind MERRIS. Leaving Major CRABTREE in charge, I proceeded to STRAZEELE to warn O.C. 92nd F.A. of change & to use the MDS as an ADS. Just as I arrived there, Lt Col STEWART DSO MC O.C. 92nd F.A. & Lt GIBBS were killed and Major McEWEN was wounded. I assumed temporary command & gave orders for 92nd F.A. to fall back on BORRE, as STRAZEELE was terribly dangerous being blown to bits by shell fire	

A5834 Wt. W4973/M687 750,000 8/16 D. D. & L. Ltd. Forms/C.2118/13.

Instructions regarding War Diaries and Intelligence Summaries are contained in F. S. Regs., Part II. and the Staff Manual respectively. Title pages will be prepared in manuscript.

WAR DIARY
or
~~INTELLIGENCE~~ SUMMARY.

(*Erase heading not required.*)

Army Form C. 2118.

PAGE V — 92nd FD AMBULANCE

Place	Date	Hour	Summary of Events and Information	Remarks and references to Appendices
	1918			
STRAZEELE	April 12th		I had all stretcher cases – 82 in number – carried some half a mile towards PRADELLES from this point they were cleared by lorries and M.A.C. cars.	
			I evacuated STRAZEELE & formed an A.D.S. at PRADELLES with a relay post for cars below the hill leading to STRAZEELE. Capt H. L. GAUNTLETT & Capt Rev. C. Raymond [illegible] att 93 F.A. were wounded 20 O.R. were also wounded.	[illegible]
PRADELLES	April 13th		Hqrs. I moved at PRADELLES with Hqrs. 92nd Inf Bgde. Usual evacuation proceeded into the M.D.S. BORRE (96 FA).	
LARREULE	April 14th		Divn was relieved early this morning by 1st AUSTRALIAN Divn. The bearers rejoined & proceeded with 94th F.A. to LA KREULE where the unit billeted	

A5834 Wt. W4973/M687 750,000 8/16 D. D. & L. Ltd. Forms/C.2118/13.

Instructions regarding War Diaries and Intelligence Summaries are contained in F. S. Regs., Part II. and the Staff Manual respectively. Title pages will be prepared in manuscript.

PAGE VI

WAR DIARY
or
INTELLIGENCE SUMMARY.
(Erase heading not required.)

98th F.A. AMBULANCE

Army Form C. 2118.

Place	Date	Hour	Summary of Events and Information	Remarks and references to Appendices
	1918			
LA KREULE	April 15th		On handing over to COL. BRACKENRIDGE C.M.G., the A.D.M.S. 33rd DIV. COL. BEWLEY C.M.G. visited the unit and said goodbye to the men. Maj. ARTHUR assumed temporary command of 94th F.A.	[illegible]
"	April 16th		Nothing to report. [illegible]	[illegible]
"	April 17th			
	April 18th		Div. being formed into 98th Bgde. & 92nd Comp. Bde. [illegible] with HAZEBROUCK defences.	[illegible]
	April 19th		33rd Div. relieved 5th AUSTRALIAN Bgde. [illegible] front line 92nd Bgde & 98th Bgde holding the line, 93rd Bgde being in support. Wounded evacuated via LA MOTTE – VIEUX BERQUIN Rd to car post at LA MOTTE, & thence to A.D.S. at LE [illegible]. Also by a road 1 mile North to a car post equidistant N of LA MOTTE & thence to A.D.S. M.D.S. (94 F.A.) at Les CINQ RUES 3 miles W of HAZEBROUCK.	

A5834 Wt. W4973/M687 750,000 8/16 D. D. & L. Ltd. Forms/C.2118/13.

Army Form C. 2118.

WAR DIARY
or
INTELLIGENCE SUMMARY.

(*Erase heading not required.*)

Instructions regarding War Diaries and Intelligence Summaries are contained in F. S. Regs., Part II. and the Staff Manual respectively. Title pages will be prepared in manuscript.

PAGE VII

93rd F.A. Amb[ce]

Place	Date	Hour	Summary of Events and Information	Remarks and references to Appendices
	1918			
HAZEBROUCK	April 4th		93rd & 95th F.A.s responsible for evacuation, all 96th F.A. were holding M.D.S. Hqrs. of 93rd F.A. in Western outskirts of HAZEBROUCK	[illegible]
"	April 15th		LA RIESTA was badly shelled last night – luckily only one officer wounded. ADS moved to a farm about 800 yds W. Major CRABTREE in charge. By arrangement with ADMS I move clothing & dressing station in the forest at LA MOTTE & only a small post at this farm.	[illegible]
"	April 21st		The dressing station at LA MOTTE was enlarged today.	[illegible]
"	April 22nd		The dressing station at LA MOTTE was badly shelled with H.E. & gas shells last night & early this morning. I regret to report that Capt P. MILNE of this unit was killed & 2nd Lt Sergt A.W. FRANKLIN M.M. was severely wounded & died on admission into C.C.S. Two O.R. died also ~~were wounded~~; and	

A5834 Wt. W4973/M687 750,000 8/16 D. D. & L. Ltd. Forms/C.2118/13.

Instructions regarding War Diaries and Intelligence Summaries are contained in F. S. Regs., Part II. and the Staff Manual respectively. Title pages will be prepared in manuscript.

WAR DIARY
or
INTELLIGENCE SUMMARY.
(Erase heading not required.)

Army Form C. 2118.

PAGE VIII

92nd Fd AmbCe.

Place	Date	Hour	Summary of Events and Information	Remarks and references to Appendices
HAZEBROUCK	1918		and twelve O.R. wounded.	
	April 22nd		A conjoint ADS was established on the canal bank at D.18.a.2.4.	
"	April 23rd		Nothing to report. Capt. R.L. KITCHING joined this unit for duty.	
"	April 24th		The Guards Bgde did a successful raid last night, although preparations were made for extra bearers casualties only amounted to very few.	
			Capt R. BOYERS M.C. proceeded to 63 C.C.S. for duty & struck off strength.	
"	April 25th		Nothing to report.	
	April 26th		Nothing to report.	
"	April 27th		The 92nd Inf. Bgde did a successful raid last night. Extra stretcher bearers were sent up to reinforce but not required.	

A5834 Wt. W4973/M687 750,000 8/16 D. D. & L. Ltd. Forms/C.2118/13.

Army Form C. 2118.

Instructions regarding War Diaries and Intelligence Summaries are contained in F. S. Regs., Part II. and the Staff Manual respectively. Title pages will be prepared in manuscript.

WAR DIARY
or
~~INTELLIGENCE SUMMARY.~~
(Erase heading not required.)

PAGE R 93rd FD Amb[illegible]

Place	Date	Hour	Summary of Events and Information	Remarks and references to Appendices
	1918			
LA KREULE	April 28th		Division was relieved last night by 29th Div. which moved back to LA KREULE.	
"	April 29th April 30th		} Nothing to report	

[illegible] Lt Col
Cmdg 93rd F.A.

A5834 Wt. W4973/M687 750,000 8/16 D. D. & L. Ltd. Forms/C.2118/13.

Confidential

Volume XXIX

Vol 27

140/2983.

May 1918.

War Diary

93rd Field Ambulance

May, 1918.

Instructions regarding War Diaries and Intelligence Summaries are contained in F. S. Regs., Part II. and the Staff Manual respectively. Title pages will be prepared in manuscript.

Army Form C. 2118.

WAR DIARY
or
~~INTELLIGENCE SUMMARY.~~
(Erase heading not required.)

PAGE I

2/3rd FD. AMBULANCE.

Place	Date 1918	Hour	Summary of Events and Information	Remarks and references to Appendices
LA KREULE.	May 1st		Received instructions from ADMS. 31st Div. that the unit would move into billets at STAPLE.	
STAPLE	"	2nd	Unit moved into billets at STAPLE. Men are accommodated in a barn & in the school rooms. Transport in a good field.	
"	"	3rd		
"	"	4th	Nothing to report.	
"	"	5th		
"	"	6th	Under instructions from ADMS. I detailed 2 marquees, a walking wounded Post at X roads. U. 19.a.4.0. Major ... in charge & party of 8 O.R., with motor ambulance and a water cart.	
"	"	7th	Nothing to report.	
"	"	8th	Capt. KITCHING relieved Major CRABTREE at Walking Wounded Post	
"	"	9th	Nothing to report.	
"	"	10th	I detailed Lt. HALL M.O.R.C. for temporary duty with 12th Bn. K.O.Y.L.I.	
"	"	11th	Nothing to report save that I withdrew Capt. KITCHING from Walking	

A5834 Wt. W4973/M687 750,000 8/16 D. D. & L. Ltd. Forms/C.2118/13.

Army Form C. 2118.

WAR DIARY
or
~~INTELLIGENCE SUMMARY.~~
(Erase heading not required.)

Instructions regarding War Diaries and Intelligence Summaries are contained in F. S. Regs., Part II. and the Staff Manual respectively. Title pages will be prepared in manuscript.

PAGETT   92nd Fd Ambulance

Place	Date	Hour	Summary of Events and Information	Remarks and references to Appendices
	1918		(Wounded post, by authority of ADMS	[illegible signature]
STAPLE	May 12th		Nothing to report	AP
"	May 13th		I have established a post at GOEDERSWELDE for wounded & sick artillery. 1 N.C.O + 3 men	AP
"	" 14th		Nothing to report.	AP
"	" 15th			
"	" 16th			
"	" 17th			
"	" 18th			
"	" 19th			
	May 20th		Capt. H. TAYLOR & Lt. A.L. WASHBURN M.O.R.C. reported for duty.	AP
"	May 21st		Nothing to report	AP
"	May 22nd			
"	May 23rd		Unit took over site from 98th F.A. at LUMBRES – CHATEAU LANNOY and opened a divisional rest station. A post was also formed at the 92nd Bde Camp. VAL de LUMBRES.	AP
LUMBRES				
"	May 24th		Nothing to report	AP

A5834 Wt. W4973/M687 750,000 8/16 D. D. & L. Ltd. Forms/C.2118/13.

Army Form C. 2118.

Instructions regarding War Diaries and Intelligence Summaries are contained in F. S. Regs., Part II. and the Staff Manual respectively. Title pages will be prepared in manuscript.

WAR DIARY
or
INTELLIGENCE SUMMARY.
(*Erase heading not required.*)

PAGE III

93rd F. Amb.

Place	Date 1918	Hour	Summary of Events and Information	Remarks and references to Appendices
LUMBRES	May 25th		Capt. KITCHING proceeded last night on leave	
"	May 26th		Capt. R. BATTERSBY returned from temporary duty with 10th E. YORKS. –	
"			LIEUT. W. WASHBURN was detailed to take his place	
"	May 27th		Nothing to report	
"	May 28th			
"	May 29th		G.O.C. 31st Div inspected the hospital	
"	May 30th		Major W. CRABTREE proceeded on leave	
"	May 31st		Nothing to report	

[signature]
Cmdt. 93rd F.A.

A5834 Wt. W4973/M687 750,000 8/16 D. D. & L. Ltd. Forms/C.2118/13.

June 1918.

140/3076.

93rd. 7. C

29

Army Form C. 2118.

Vol 28

WAR DIARY
or
INTELLIGENCE SUMMARY.
(*Erase heading not required.*)

Instructions regarding War Diaries and Intelligence Summaries are contained in F. S. Regs., Part II. and the Staff Manual respectively. Title pages will be prepared in manuscript.

PAGE I

93rd F. AMBULANCE

Place	Date	Hour	Summary of Events and Information	Remarks and references to Appendices
	1918			
LUMBRES	June 1st.		The 92nd Bgde. including this unit were paraded for inspection by G.O.C. 31st Div. and medals awarded during past 2 months were conferred. Brigade afterwards marched past in line. Transport was inspected by [illegible].	
			Patients admitted during past 24 hrs. O.R. 10.	
			Patients remaining Off. 1. O.R. 52.	
			Prevailing disease P.U.O.	[illegible]
	June 2nd		Patients admitted during past 24 hrs. O.R. 10.	
			Patients remaining Off. 1 O.R. 59.	
			Prevailing disease P.U.O.	[illegible]
	June 3rd		Patients admitted during past 24 hrs. O.R. 53	
			Patients remaining Off. 1 O.R. 68.	
			Prevailing disease Influenza	
			Lt. F. HALL returned from temporary duty with 12th Bn. K.O.Y.L.I.	[illegible]
"	June 4th.		Patients admitted during past 24 hrs. O.R. 28	
			Patients in hospital Off 1 O.R. 80	
			Prevailing disease P.U.O	[illegible]

A5834 Wt. W4973 M687 750,000 8/16 D. D. & L. Ltd. Forms/C.2118/13.

Instructions regarding War Diaries and Intelligence Summaries are contained in F. S. Regs., Part II. and the Staff Manual respectively. Title pages will be prepared in manuscript.

WAR DIARY
or
~~INTELLIGENCE SUMMARY.~~
(Erase heading not required.)

Army Form C. 2118.

PAGE II — 93rd Fd. AMBULANCE

Place	Date 1918	Hour	Summary of Events and Information	Remarks and references to Appendices
LUMBRES.	June 5th		Patients admitted during past 24 hrs. O.R. 14	
			Patients remaining. O.R. 75	
			Prevalent disease. P.U.O.	[illegible]
"	June 6th		Patients admitted during past 24 hrs. O.R. 20	
			Patients remaining O.R. 86	
			Prevalent disease Influenza	A.P.
	June 7th		Patients admitted during past 24 hrs. off. 2 O.R. 13	
			Patients remaining off. 1. O.R. 85.	
			Prevalent disease	
			Lt. Col. W. [illegible] Comdg. 15th Bn. W. Yorks was admitted [illegible]	
			[illegible] Referred [illegible] with 31st Div. [illegible] [illegible] 5/6/18	
			[illegible]	A.P.
			An advance party under Capt. BATTERSBY was sent [illegible] to take over F.A. [illegible]	
			[illegible] 13th F.A.	A.P.
[illegible]	June 8th		[illegible] at 7 a.m. to [illegible] with 93rd Bde. [illegible]	
			moved off at 5 a.m. arrived 11.30 a.m.	

A5834 Wt. W4973/M687 750,000 8/16 D. D. & L. Ltd. Forms/C.2118/13.

Army Form C. 2118.

Instructions regarding War Diaries and Intelligence Summaries are contained in F. S. Regs., Part II. and the Staff Manual respectively. Title pages will be prepared in manuscript.

WAR DIARY
or
~~INTELLIGENCE SUMMARY.~~
(Erase heading not required.)

PAGE III — 93rd Fd AMBULANCE

Place	Date	Hour	Summary of Events and Information	Remarks and references to Appendices
	1918			
RACOWINGIER	June 8th (contd)		1 off. + 99 o.r. were [illegible] [illegible] [illegible] 95th F.A. 13 o.r. were taken over by one from 95th F.A. [illegible] of 70 cases of malaria from 93rd Bgde [illegible] found [illegible] [illegible] [illegible] were [illegible] [illegible] [illegible] [illegible] [illegible]	[illegible]
"	June 9th		Cases admitted during past 24 hrs. Off. 1. o.r. 49. Amongst these MAJ. J. V. KERSHAW D.S.O. 1st E LANCS. was evacuated to 18. C.C.S. Cases remaining Off. 1. o.r. 17. Prevailing disease Malaria.	[illegible]
"	June 10th		Patients admitted during past 24 hrs. o.r. 19. Patients remaining o.r. 42. Prevailing disease Influenza	[illegible]
"	June 11th		Patients admitted during past 24 hrs o.r. 25. Patients remaining o.r. 30. Prevailing disease Influenza. D.D.M.S. XV CORPS visited the camp this afternoon	[illegible]

A5834 Wt. W4973/M687 750,000 8/16 D. D. & L. Ltd. Forms/C.2118/13.

Instructions regarding War Diaries and Intelligence Summaries are contained in F. S. Regs., Part II. and the Staff Manual respectively. Title pages will be prepared in manuscript.

WAR DIARY
or
~~INTELLIGENCE SUMMARY.~~
(Erase heading not required.)

Army Form C. 2118.

PAGE IV.

93rd FD AMBULANCE

Place	Date	Hour	Summary of Events and Information	Remarks and references to Appendices
RAGQUINGHEM	June 12th 1918		Patients admitted during past 24 hrs. 25	
			Patients remaining 30	
			Prevailing disease Influenza	[illegible] H.M.
"	June 13th		Patients admitted during past 24 hrs. O.R. 26	
			Patients remaining O.R. 29	
			Prevailing disease Influenza	A.P.
"	June 14th		Patients admitted during past 24 hrs. ~~[illegible]~~ O.R. 31	
			Patients remaining 36	
			Prevailing disease Influenza	
			Major W. [illegible] returns from leave. Major P. [illegible] proceeds	
			on leave last night.	A.P.
"	~~[illegible]~~		Warning order received that the [illegible] Bde would [illegible] [illegible]	A.P.
"	June 15th		Patients admitted during past 24 hrs. [illegible] O.R. 8	
			Patients remaining O.R. 35	
			Prevailing disease Influenza	A.P.
			(cont'd)	

A5834 Wt. W4973/M687 750,000 8/16 D. D. & L. Ltd. Forms/C.2118/13.

Army Form C. 2118.

Instructions regarding War Diaries and Intelligence Summaries are contained in F. S. Regs., Part II. and the Staff Manual respectively. Title pages will be prepared in manuscript.

PAGE V

WAR DIARY
or
~~INTELLIGENCE SUMMARY.~~

(Erase heading not required.)

93rd FIELD AMB^ce.

Place	Date	Hour	Summary of Events and Information	Remarks and references to Appendices
WALLON CAPPEL.	1918 June 15th		(Contd). 92nd Bgde group moved to area N of WALLON CAPPEL in readiness to [illegible] 2nd Army [illegible] W of HAZEBROUCK.	
			All Influenzal cases of Bgde group were left at [illegible] CAMP [illegible] and one section was left behind to deal with them.	
			Unit arrived at new destination [illegible] in a field at 6.30 p.m.	[illegible]
"	June 16th		Cases admitted during past 24 hrs. Off. 6 O.R. 410.	
			Cases remaining Off. 6 O.R. 422	
			Prevalent disease. Influenza.	
"	June 17th		92nd Bgde group moved back to [illegible] area the evening. [illegible] to a field [illegible] arrived at 9.40 p.m.	[illegible]
			Cases admitted during past 24 hrs. Off. 9 O.R. 442.	
			Cases remaining Off. 15 O.R. 493.	
[illegible]	June 18th		Cases admitted during past 24 hrs. Off. 1 O.R. 74.	[illegible]
			Cases remaining Off. 15 O.R. 552.	
			Prevailing disease. Influenza.	

A5834 Wt. W4973/M687 750,000 8/16 D. D. & L. Ltd. Forms/C.2118/13.

Instructions regarding War Diaries and Intelligence Summaries are contained in F. S. Regs., Part II. and the Staff Manual respectively. Title pages will be prepared in manuscript.

WAR DIARY
or
INTELLIGENCE SUMMARY.
(*Erase heading not required.*)

Army Form C. 2118.

PAGE VI

92nd Fd. AMBULANCE

Place	Date	Hour	Summary of Events and Information	Remarks and references to Appendices
	1916			
RACQUINGHEM	June 14th (contd)		Captns. BATTERSBY & TAYLOR are admitted as patients. Capt. RAINFORD reports for temporary duty from 95th Fd. AMBULANCE.	[illegible]
"	June 19th		Patients admitted during last 24 hrs. Of. 1 O.R. 26.	
			Patients remaining Of. 9 O.R. 320.	
			Prevailing disease [illegible]	[illegible]
	June 20th		A.D.M.S. [illegible]	
			Received orders [illegible] to LES CINQ RUES	
			to take over M.D.S. [illegible] 59th Fd. [illegible]	
			XI CORPS [illegible]	
			Patients admitted during past 24 hrs. of. 2 O.R. 17	
			Patients remaining O.R. 280	
			Prevailing disease [illegible]	
			Capt. RAINFORD returned to 95th F.A.	[illegible]

A5834 Wt. W4973/M687 750,000 8/16 D. D. & L. Ltd. Forms/C.2118/13.

Instructions regarding War Diaries and Intelligence Summaries are contained in F. S. Regs., Part II. and the Staff Manual respectively. Title pages will be prepared in manuscript.

PAGE VII

WAR DIARY

or

~~INTELLIGENCE SUMMARY.~~

(Erase heading not required.)

93rd Fd. AMBULANCE

Army Form C. 2118.

Place	Date	Hour 1918	Summary of Events and Information	Remarks and references to Appendices
RACQUINGHEM	June 21st		Patients admitted during past 24 hrs Off. 2. O.R. 13. Patients remaining O.R. 231. Prevalent disease Influenza. The 31st Div. is relieving 29th Div. in the [illegible]. Sent an advance party under Major [illegible] to take over M.D.S. at LES CINQ RUES from 89th F.A. Capt. RITCHIE [illegible] struck off strength from today.	[illegible signature]
LES CINQ RUES	June 22nd		Took over M.D.S. this morning [illegible] Patients transferred to 89th F.A. O.R. 231. No. of patients admitted during past 24 hrs Sick Off. 1. O.R. 40. Wounded O.R. 9. D.D.M.S. visited F.A. this morning.	
"	June 23rd		Capt. J. DUNN D.S.O., M.C., D.C.M. reported for duty & taken on strength. Patients admitted during past 24 hrs Sick Off. 1. O.R. 6. Wounded O.R. 13. Prevailing disease Influenza.	[initials]
	June 24th		I attended a conference at A.D.M.S. 31st Div. Patients admitted during past 24 hrs. Sick Off. 1 O.R. 16. Wounded O.R. 13. Prevailing disease P.U.O.	[initials]

A5834 Wt. W4973/M687 750,000 8/16 D. D. & L. Ltd. Forms/C.2118/13.

Instructions regarding War Diaries and Intelligence Summaries are contained in F. S. Regs., Part II. and the Staff Manual respectively. Title pages will be prepared in manuscript.

PAGE VIII

WAR DIARY
or
~~INTELLIGENCE SUMMARY.~~
(Erase heading not required.)

92nd Fd. Ambulce

Army Form C. 2118.

Place	Date 1918	Hour	Summary of Events and Information	Remarks and references to Appendices
WALLON CAPPELLE	June 25th		I took over the site of the Div. Rest Camp on MORBECQUE – WALLON CAPPELLE Rd today, ~~and~~ ~~opened~~ as a Main Dressing Station. This did not open today, but will operate from 10 a.m. tomorrow. The 95th F.A. proceeded to EBBLINGHEM. I left Capt. TAYLOR and a[illegible] party at LES CINQ RUES	
			Patients admitted during last 24 hrs. Sick O.R. 17. Wounded O/1. O.R. 9.	
			Prevailing disease Influenza.	
"	JUNE 26th		Opened this morning as a MAIN DRESSING STATION.	
			Patients admitted during past 24 hrs Sick O/1. O.R. 17. Wounded O/1. O.R. 29.	
"	June 27th		Early this morning, the 92nd Bde attacked and ANKLE FARM. Casualties resulting from this raid were about 50.	
			Six wounded German prisoners admitted, of whom one died from G.S.W. head.	
			No. of patients admitted during past 24 hrs. Sick O.R. 14. Wounded O/5. O.R. 47	

A5834 Wt. W4973/M687 750,000 8/16 D. D. & L. Ltd. Forms/C.2118/13.

Army Form C. 2118.

Instructions regarding War Diaries and Intelligence Summaries are contained in F. S. Regs., Part II. and the Staff Manual respectively. Title pages will be prepared in manuscript.

WAR DIARY
or
INTELLIGENCE SUMMARY.
(Erase heading not required.)

PAGE XX

93rd FD. AMBULANCE

Place	Date	Hour	Summary of Events and Information	Remarks and references to Appendices
WALLON CAPPEL	1918 June 28th		Under instructions from A.D.M.S. 31st Div. the following arrangements were made for the Divisional operations today.	
			Sent 18 stretcher squads last night to report A.D.S. 94 Fd. Amb. Also sent the large Motor Ambulances, and the Horse Ambulance to collect walking wounded.	
			Two lorries were stationed here, and fifteen Motor Ambulances by D.S. 16. M.A.C.	
			Division attacked this morning and reached its final objectives at 7.30 a.m. being the line LA BECQUE – GARS BRUGGHE.	
			The casualties were roughly 700. 38 wounded German prisoners were admitted.	
			4 O.R. (British) died in the M.D.S. from wounds received in action.	
			The attack commenced at 6 A.M. Casualties began to come in at 9 a.m. and continued until about 4.15 p.m. after which it was a very small evacuation.	
			Patients admitted during past 24 hrs.	
			Sick Off 1 O.R. 43. Wounded Off 2 O.R. 81.	
			Prevailing disease Influenza.	
			A.D.M.S. & D.D.M.S. XV Corps visited the M.D.S. during the day	
			No. 6357 Pte TAYLOR H.F. was killed in action, & 5 O.R. of this unit were wounded	[signature]

A5834 Wt. W4973/M687 750,000 8/16 D. D. & L. Ltd. Forms/C.2118/13.

WAR DIARY
or
INTELLIGENCE SUMMARY.
(Erase heading not required.)

Army Form C. 2118.

Instructions regarding War Diaries and Intelligence Summaries are contained in F. S. Regs., Part II. and the Staff Manual respectively. Title pages will be prepared in manuscript.

PAGE X

3rd F^d AMBULANCE

Place	Date	Hour	Summary of Events and Information	Remarks and references to Appendices
WALLON CAPPEL	1916 June 29th		Casualties came in steadily during the night, but no rush.	
			Patients admitted during past 24 hrs. — No. 59325 Pte ROTTER T. & No. 133508 Pte FRANCE H. of this unit died of wounds received in action.	
			Sick O.R. 19. Wounded Of. 22 O.R. 672	
			The bearer squads returned this evening.	
"	June 30th		Patients admitted during past 24 hrs	
			Sick Of. 1 O.R. 52. Wounded Of. 2 O.R. 38.	
			~~Total casualties~~ A.D.M.S. & D.D.M.S. VII Corps visited the M.D.S. this morning.	
			Total number of cases admitted during the rush	
			Sick Of. 33 O.R. 1400. Wounded Of. 34 O.R. 981	
			Total number of evacuations ~~Sick~~ Of. 16 O.R. 642 Wounded Of. 32 O.R. 961	
			Number discharged fit for duty Sick Of. 17 O.R. 589 Wounded Of. 1 O.R. 2	

A5834 Wt. W4973/M687 750,000 8/16 D. D. & L. Ltd. Forms/C.2118/13.

July 1918

140/2131.

93rd F. A.

24

Instructions regarding War Diaries and Intelligence Summaries are contained in F. S. Regs., Part II. and the Staff Manual respectively. Title pages will be prepared in manuscript.

WAR DIARY
or
INTELLIGENCE SUMMARY.
(Erase heading not required.)

Army Form C. 2118.

PAGE I — 93rd Fd AMBULANCE — Vol 29

Place	Date	Hour	Summary of Events and Information	Remarks and references to Appendices
WALLON CAPPELL	1918 July 1st		Patients admitted during past 24 hrs: Wounded Of. 2 o.r. 78 Sick. O. o.r. 145.	
			Prevailing disease Influenza.	
			I attended a conference at the ADMS 3rd Divn this morning. Capt. TAYLOR [illegible] 12th [illegible] NORFOLK Regt. for temporary duty whilst M.O. is on leave.	[illegible]
"	July 2nd		Patients admitted during past 24 hrs. Wounded Of. 1 o.r. 12. Sick Of. 4 o.r. 58.	
			Prevailing disease. Influenza.	[illegible]
"	July 3rd		Influenza in the division is most distinctly abating.	
			Patients admitted during past 24 hrs. Wounded o.r. 15. Sick Of. 1 o.r. 32.	[illegible]
"	July 4th		Patients admitted during past 24 hrs. Wounded Of. 2. o.r. 9. Sick Of. 1 o.r. 26.	
			Prevailing disease Influenza	[illegible]

A5834 Wt. W4973/M687 750,000 8/16 D. D. & L. Ltd. Forms/C.2118/13.

Instructions regarding War Diaries and Intelligence Summaries are contained in F. S. Regs., Part II. and the Staff Manual respectively. Title pages will be prepared in manuscript.

WAR DIARY

or

~~INTELLIGENCE SUMMARY.~~

(Erase heading not required.)

Army Form C. 2118.

PAGE II

92nd Fd AMBULANCE

Place	Date	Hour	Summary of Events and Information	Remarks and references to Appendices
WALLON CAPPELL	1918 July 5th		Patients admitted during past 24 hrs. Wounded O.R. 14. Sick O.R. 22. Under instructions from A.D.M.S. [illegible] in the forward area [illegible] C.R.S.	[illegible]
"	July 6th		Patients admitted during past 24 hrs. Wounded Off 2 O.R. 10 Sick Off [illegible] O.R. 36. Lt. Col. A.R. Morse Comdg. 92nd Bn. Norfolk Regt. evacuated wounded G.S.W. leg. Prevailing disease Influenza.	[initials]
"	July 7th		Patients admitted during past 24 hrs. Wounded O.R. 8. Sick Off 1 O.R. 29.	[initials]
"	July 8th		Patients admitted during past 24 hrs. Wounded O.R. 4. Sick Off 1 O.R. 17. Major [illegible] to SCULLY S.C. ([illegible]) also evacuated [illegible] of the strength.	[initials]
"	July 9th		Patients admitted during past 24 hrs. Wounded O.R. 3. Sick Off 1 O.R. 23.	[initials]

Instructions regarding War Diaries and Intelligence Summaries are contained in F. S. Regs., Part II. and the Staff Manual respectively. Title pages will be prepared in manuscript.

PAGE III

WAR DIARY
or
~~INTELLIGENCE SUMMARY.~~
(Erase heading not required.)

Army Form C. 2118.

93rd Fd. AMBULce.

Place	Date	Hour	Summary of Events and Information	Remarks and references to Appendices
WALLON CAPPEL	1918. July 10th		Patients admitted during past 24 hrs. wounded O.R. 4. Sick Off 1. O.R. 18.	
"	July 11th.		Patients admitted during past 24 hrs wounded O.R. 4 sick O.R. 24	[illegible]
"	July 12th		Patients admitted during past 24 hrs. wounded O.R. 1.	
			Sick O.R. 18.	
"	July 13th.		Patients admitted during past 24 hrs. wounded Off 1. O.R. 37	
			Sick Off 1 O.R. 37.	
			The 93rd Bgde made a successful raid last night on left sector.	
			I attended a lecture on Scabies treatment by Major McCORMICK	
"	July 14th		Capt J. DUNN. DSO. M.C. DCM proceeded to take over medical charge of 10th E Yorks. | Patients admitted wounded O.R. 14	
			Sick Off 2. O.R. 24.	
			Prevailing disease of the well Influenza	

Instructions regarding War Diaries and Intelligence Summaries are contained in F. S. Regs., Part II. and the Staff Manual respectively. Title pages will be prepared in manuscript.

WAR DIARY
or
INTELLIGENCE SUMMARY.
(Erase heading not required.)

Army Form C. 2118.

PAGE IV — 93rd Bde. AMBULANCE

Place	Date	Hour	Summary of Events and Information	Remarks and references to Appendices
WALLON CAPPELL	1918 July 15th		Patients admitted during past 24 hrs. Wounded O.R. 2. Sick O.R. 14.	
			Major W. CRABTREE proceeded to Officers Rest Camp LE TOUQUET	
"	July 16th		Patients admitted during past 24 hrs. Wounded O.R. 8. Sick O. 2, O.R. 28	
"	July 17th		Patients admitted during past 24 hrs. Wounded O.R. 3. Sick O. 2. O.R. 15	
			Capt BATTERSBY proceeded to relieve Lt GEORGE M.O.R.C. whilst on leave, with 11th E. LANCS. R.F.	
			Capt. W. L. SMITH M.O.R.C. late of this Unit, rejoined for duty.	
"	July 18th		Patients admitted during past 24 hrs. Wounded O.R. 6. Sick O. 1. O.R. 10.	
			No 41717 Pte NOBLES H. 12th NORFOLK died of G.S.W. chest.	
"	July 19th		Patients admitted during past 24 hrs. Wounded O. 2. O.R. 14. Sick O.R. 21	
			Opened for reception of 20 cases of Scabies.	
"	July 20th		Patients admitted during past 24 hrs. Wounded O. 2. O.R. 90. Sick O.R. 9.	
			An attack was carried out on lines of 93rd Bgde.	

Instructions regarding War Diaries and Intelligence Summaries are contained in F. S. Regs., Part II. and the Staff Manual respectively. Title pages will be prepared in manuscript.

PAGE T

WAR DIARY
or
~~INTELLIGENCE SUMMARY.~~
(Erase heading not required.)

93rd Fd Ambulce.

Army Form C. 2118.

Place	Date 1918	Hour	Summary of Events and Information	Remarks and references to Appendices
WALLON CAPPELL	July 21st		Wounded are still coming in from yesterday. Some difficulty in clearing them.	
			Patients admitted during past 24 hrs. Wounded O.R. 16 Sick O.R. 12	AR
			Prevailing disease during past week is Influenza, though this is decidedly abating.	
"	July 22nd		Patients admitted during past 24 hrs. Wounded O.R. 4. Sick O.R. 12.	AR
"			Major W. CRABTREE returned from Officers Rest camp.	
	July 23rd		Patients admitted during past 24 hrs. Wounded Of. 1 O.R. 8.	
			Sick. Of. 1 O.R. 34.	AR
"	July 24th		Patients admitted during past 24 hrs. Wounded O.R. 6 Sick O.R. 23	AR
"	July 25th		Patients admitted during last 24 hrs. Wounded Of. 2 O.R. 30	
			Sick Of. 3. O.R. 16	
			Severe hostile bombardment last night	AR

A5834 Wt. W4973/M687 750,000 8/16 D. D. & L. Ltd. Forms/C.2118/13.

Instructions regarding War Diaries and Intelligence Summaries are contained in F. S. Regs., Part II. and the Staff Manual respectively. Title pages will be prepared in manuscript.

WAR DIARY
or
INTELLIGENCE SUMMARY.
(Erase heading not required.)

Army Form C. 2118.

PAGE VI

92nd F.D. AMBCE.

Place	Date	Hour	Summary of Events and Information	Remarks and references to Appendices
	1918			
WALLON CAPPEL.	July 26th		Patients admitted during past 24 hrs. Wounded O.R. 8. Sick Off 1. O.R. 30	
			D.D.M.S. XV CORPS inspected the unit & camp to-day. The men and transport were on parade in marching order.	
			Capt H. W. TAYLOR returned last night from temporary duty with 12th Bn NORFOLK Regt.	
"	July 27th		Patients admitted during past 24 hrs. Wounded O.R. 11. Sick Off 2. O.R. 17	
"	July 28th		Patients admitted during past 24 hrs. Wounded Off 3. O.R. 9. Sick Off 1. O.R. 15.	
			Capt W. L. SMITH A.R.S. proceeded for temporary duty with 96th F.A.	
"	July 29th		Patients admitted during past 24 hrs. Wounded Off 2. O.R. 26. Sick O.R. 9.	
			I attended conference at ADMS for purpose of discussing arrangements in case of compulsory withdrawal	

A5834 Wt. W4973/M687 750,000 8/16 D. D. & L. Ltd. Forms/C.2118/13.

Instructions regarding War Diaries and Intelligence Summaries are contained in F. S. Regs., Part II. and the Staff Manual respectively. Title pages will be prepared in manuscript.

PAGE VII

WAR DIARY

or

~~INTELLIGENCE SUMMARY.~~

(Erase heading not required.)

Army Form C. 2118.

3rd Fd. Ambce.

Place	Date	Hour	Summary of Events and Information	Remarks and references to Appendices
	1918			
WALLON CAPPELL	July 30th		Patients admitted during past 24 hrs. Wounded O.R. 18. Sick O.R. 12	[illegible] Maj
"	July 31st		Patients admitted during past 24 hrs. Wounded O.R. 26. Sick Off. 1 O.R. 37	
			Large numbers of N.Y.D. gas cases.	
			No 60433 Pte. S.C. MORETON, No 76650 Pte. H. WORSNIP, No 24968 Pte. J.G. HODGSON } were all awarded Military Medal for conspicuous gallantry on June 28th 1918.	
			Prevailing disease through the month has still been Influenza.	
			Total admissions for Month — Wounded: Off. 20, O.R. 482; Sick: Off. 28, O.R. 807	
			" Evacuations " " — Wounded: Off. 14, O.R. 456; Sick: Off. 28, O.R. 781	
			Discharged to duty " " — Wounded: 2, O.R. 25 (1 Died); Sick: —, O.R. 26	[illegible] Major Comdg. 3/3 F.A.

Aug. 1918.

140/3259

93rd F. Amb.

Instructions regarding War Diaries and Intelligence Summaries are contained in F. S. Regs., Part II. and the Staff Manual respectively. Title pages will be prepared in manuscript.

WAR DIARY
or
~~INTELLIGENCE SUMMARY.~~
(Erase heading not required.)

Army Form C. 2118.

PAGE I

93rd Fd. Amb^ce.

Vol 30

Place	Date	Hour	Summary of Events and Information	Remarks and references to Appendices
	1918			
WALLON CAPPEL.	Aug 1st.		Patients admitted during past 24hrs. Wounded Of. 1. O.R. 5 Sick. O.R. 26	
"	Aug 2nd		Patients admitted during past 24hrs. Wounded O.R. 7 Sick Of 2 O.R. 22.	
"	Aug 3rd		Patients admitted during past 24hrs. Wounded O.R. 18 Sick Of. 1. O.R. 17	
"	Aug 4th		Patients admitted during past 24hrs. Wounded O.R. 22 Sick Of 2 O.R. 12.	
			Capt W.L. SMITH. M.R.C. was evacuated sick to NEW ZEALAND HOSPITAL. CAPT DATTERIBE rejoined the unit	
"	Aug 5th.		Patients admitted during past 24hrs. Wounded. Of 1 O.R. 3 Sick Of 2. O.R. 28	

A5834 Wt. W4973/M687 750,000 8/16 D. D. & L. Ltd. Forms/C.2118/13.

Instructions regarding War Diaries and Intelligence Summaries are contained in F. S. Regs., Part II. and the Staff Manual respectively. Title pages will be prepared in manuscript.

Army Form C. 2118.

WAR DIARY
or
~~INTELLIGENCE SUMMARY.~~
(Erase heading not required.)

PAGE II 93rd F.A. [illegible]

Place	Date	Hour	Summary of Events and Information	Remarks and references to Appendices
	1918			
WALLON CAPPEL	Aug 6th.		Patients admitted during past 24 hrs. Wounded. ~~Off. 1. O.R. 5~~ O.R. 6. Sick Off 2. O.R. 15.	[illegible]
"	Aug 7th		Patients admitted during past 24 hrs. Wounded. Off. 1. O.R. 17. Sick. O.R. 16.	[illegible]
"	Aug 8th.		Patients admitted during past 24 hrs. Wounded. Off. 1. O.R. 5. Sick. Off. 2. O.R. 60. 31 cases of Scabies in Hospital. Proceeded on leave, handed over to Major C.L. ARTHUR.	
"	Aug 9th		2nd Lt H.C. Whilmore 12 Norfolks att. 94 L.T.M.B. died of accidental G.S.W. Patients admitted during past 24 hrs Wounded Off. 3 OR 18 Sick Off 1. O.R. 22 1 patient died G.S.W. back hips & stomach.	[illegible]

[illegible] Major

A5834 Wt. W4973/M687 750,000 8/16 D. D. & L. Ltd. Forms/C.2118/13.

Instructions regarding War Diaries and Intelligence Summaries are contained in F. S. Regs., Part II. and the Staff Manual respectively. Title pages will be prepared in manuscript.

WAR DIARY
or
~~INTELLIGENCE SUMMARY.~~
(Erase heading not required.)

Army Form C. 2118.

93rd Fd Amb

Page III

Place	Date	Hour	Summary of Events and Information	Remarks and references to Appendices
Wallon Cappel	Aug 10th.		Patients admitted during past 24 hrs Wounded Off 4 O.R. 92 Sick Off 1. O.R. 21	[signature] Major
	Aug 11th		Patients admitted during past 24 hrs Wounded Off 0. O.R 16 Sick O.R 14 2 patients died GSW Buttock penet. Abdomen GSW Thigh Fract femur	[initials]
	Aug 12th		Patients admitted during past 24 hrs Wounded Off 1. O.R 19 Sick Off 1 O.R. 25 2 patients died one a P.O.W. of Bayonet wds Chest & abdomen the other of G.S.W. arm & leg Capt H.W. Taylor proceeded to take over Med. Charge of 10th E York Regt in relief of Capt. Dunn DSO MC DCM. returned to England Capt W.L. Smith M.R.C. USA. rejoined from N.Z Stat. Hosp.	[initials]
	Aug 13th		Patients admitted during past 24 hrs Wounded Off 2 O.R 29 Sick Off 3. O.R. 23 Two patients died G.S.W. Legs & G.S.W. Leg & arm G.O.C. 31st Div visited the unit with A.D.M.S. & went round the Camp	[initials]

A5834 Wt. W4973/M687 750,000 8/16 D. D. & L. Ltd. Forms/C.2118/13.

Instructions regarding War Diaries and Intelligence Summaries are contained in F. S. Regs., Part II. and the Staff Manual respectively. Title pages will be prepared in manuscript.

WAR DIARY
or
~~INTELLIGENCE SUMMARY.~~
(Erase heading not required.)

Army Form C. 2118.

93rd F.D Amb^a

Page 17

Place	Date	Hour	Summary of Events and Information	Remarks and references to Appendices
Wallon Cappel	Aug	17	Patients admitted during past 24 hrs. Wounded Off 2 O.R 65. Sick Off 2 O.R 21	[signature] Major
	Aug	15	Patients admitted during past 24 hrs. Wounded Off 3 O.R 31 Sick Off 2 O.R 24	[signature]
	Aug	16	Patients admitted during past 24 hrs. Wounded Off 2 O.R 25 Sick Off 3 O.R. 48 3 Patients died - GSW. Neck, GSW abdomen (penet) GSW. head & chest	[signature]
	Aug	17	Patients admitted during past 24 hrs. Wounded Off 4 O.R. 146 Sick Off 2 O.R. 33 1st Lieut H. Samuel M.R.C. USA proceeded to take over temp med charge of 24th R.W.F. in relief of Lieut Thomas R.A.M.C.	[signature]
	Aug	18	Patients admitted during past 24 hrs Wounded Off 2 O.R 23 Sick Off 1 O.R 16	[signature]
	Aug	19	Patients admitted during past 24 hrs. Wounded Off – O.R 20 Sick Off – O.R 20 One patient died - GSW. R. thigh.	[signature]
	Aug	20	Patients admitted during past 24 hrs Wounded Off 4 O.R 83 Sick Off 1 O.R 17	[signature]

A5834 Wt. W4973/M687 750,000 8/16 D. D. & L. Ltd. Forms/C.2118/13.

Army Form C. 2118.

WAR DIARY
or
~~INTELLIGENCE SUMMARY.~~
(Erase heading not required.)

Instructions regarding War Diaries and Intelligence Summaries are contained in F. S. Regs., Part II. and the Staff Manual respectively. Title pages will be prepared in manuscript.

Page V

93rd Fd Ambce

Place	Date	Hour	Summary of Events and Information	Remarks and references to Appendices
Wallon Cappel	Aug 21st		Patients admitted during the past 24 hrs Wounded Off. nil O.R. 46 Sick Off. nil O.R 27 1 Pat. died G.S.W. abdomen Capt W.L. SMITH. M.R.C. U.S.A. took over temporary med charge of 10th E. York Regt.	[signature]
	Aug 22nd		Patients admitted during the past 24 hrs Wounded Off nil, O.R. 60 Sick Off 2. O.R. 34	[signature]
	Aug 23rd		Patients admitted during the past 24 hrs Wounded Off 1. O.R. 13 Sick Off 1. O.R. 27 Handed over to Lieut-Col A.M. POLLARD D.S.O. on his return from leave	[signature]
"	Aug 24th.		I assumed charge of unit on return from leave Patients admitted wounded Off 1. O.R. 6. Sick Off 2 O.R. 26. I handed over the site to [illegible] Fd A. and moved to [illegible] relieving 95th Fd A. as D.R.S.	[signature]

A5834 Wt. W4973/M687 750,000 8/16 D. D. & L. Ltd. Forms/C.2118/13.

WAR DIARY
or
INTELLIGENCE SUMMARY.
(Erase heading not required.)

Army Form C. 2118.

Instructions regarding War Diaries and Intelligence Summaries are contained in F. S. Regs., Part II. and the Staff Manual respectively. Title pages will be prepared in manuscript.

PAGE VI

9th F.A.

Place	Date	Hour	Summary of Events and Information	Remarks and references to Appendices
EBLINGHEM.	1918 Aug 25th.		No. of cases admitted Sick O.R. 14. Prevailing disease Diarrhoea. Arranged for separate diarrhoea ward and separate dining room.	[illegible]
"	Aug 26th.		No. of cases admitted Sick O.R. [illegible]	
			Capt. W. L. SMITH rejoined from temporary duty with 10th E. YORKS.	[illegible]
	Aug 27th.		No. of cases admitted Sick O.R. 8 Wounded O.R. 11.	[illegible]
"	Aug 28th.		No. of cases admitted Sick O.R. 23	
			Capt. R. McKINNON [illegible] is posted to this unit for duty.	[illegible]
"	Aug 29th.		No. of cases admitted O.R. 6.	
			Lt. SAMUEL returned from temporary duty with 26th R. W. FUSILIERS	[illegible]
	Aug 30th.		No. of cases admitted O.R. 26.	
			H. SAMUEL was evacuated to 58 C.C.S. with Gas shell poisoning, battle casualty, date of casualty 27.8.18. Prevailing disease still DIARRHOEA.	[illegible]
	Aug 31st.		[illegible] Major CRABTREE [illegible] F.A. [illegible] CAESTRE [illegible] A.D.S. Unit moved to CAESTRE. [illegible] 135th F.A. [illegible] 135th F.A.	P.T.O.
			Cases admitted during month Wounded O.R. [illegible] Sick O.R. [illegible]	
			~~37 776 55 35 616.~~	
			~~Totals Wounded O.R. 8 Sick O.R. [illegible]~~ 26 757 33 [illegible]	[illegible]

A5834 Wt. W4973/M687 750,000 8/16 D. D. & L. Ltd. Forms/C.2118/13.

Instructions regarding War Diaries and Intelligence Summaries are contained in F. S. Regs., Part II. and the Staff Manual respectively. Title pages will be prepared in manuscript.

PAGE VII

WAR DIARY
or
~~INTELLIGENCE SUMMARY.~~
(Erase heading not required.)

93rd Fd Ambce.

Army Form C. 2118.

Place	Date	Hour	Summary of Events and Information	Remarks and references to Appendices
EBLINGHEM	1918 Aug 31st (contd).		Monthly statistics. Prevailing diseases Diarrhoea · Influenza	
			WOUNDED. / SICK.	
			ADMITTED: Offs. 38, O.R. 776; Sick: Offs. 35, O.R. 696	
			EVACUATED: Offs. 36, O.R. 757; Sick: Offs. 33, O.R. 530	
			TO DUTY: Offs. 1, O.R. 8; Sick: Offs. –, O.R. 78.	
			Died at A.D.S. (wounded)	
			31st M.G.Btn. Lt. H. CLARKE. 31.8.18	
			(Sick: accidental wound)	
			12th Bn NORFOLK Regt. att'd 94 L.T.M.B.	
			2/Lt. H.C. WHITMORE. 8.8.18.	
			Died at M.D.S. 12 O.R. (wounded)	

[signature] Lt Col

~~Oct.~~ Sept. 1918

140/33.24

93rd Fd. Ambce.

9

Instructions regarding War Diaries and Intelligence Summaries are contained in F. S. Regs., Part II. and the Staff Manual respectively. Title pages will be prepared in manuscript.

WAR DIARY
or
~~INTELLIGENCE~~ SUMMARY.
(Erase heading not required.)

PAGE I

93rd Fd Amb

Army Form C. 2118.

Place	Date	Hour	Summary of Events and Information	Remarks and references to Appendices
	1918			
CAESTRE	Sept 1st		CAPT. W. L. SMITH proceeded on 10 days leave to PARIS.	
			Unit moved to CAESTRE, arriving at 11 A.M.	
			Patients admitted during past 24 hrs. wounded O.R. 14. Sick O.R. 5.	
	Sept 2nd		LIEUT. G. READ proceeded on leave to ENGLAND	
			Patients admitted during past 24 hrs. [illegible]	
	Sept 3rd		Patients admitted during past 24 hrs. [illegible]	
	Sept 4th		Patients admitted during past 24 hrs. wounded [illegible]	
			A.D.M.S. visited the hospital	
	Sept 5th		Patients admitted during past 24 hrs. wounded [illegible] O.R. 44. Sick [illegible] O.R. 20	
	Sept 6th		Patients admitted during past 24 hrs. wounded [illegible]	
	Sept 7th		[illegible]	

A5834 Wt. W4973/M687 750,000 8/16 D. D. & L. Ltd. Forms/C.2118/13.

Army Form C. 2118.

Instructions regarding War Diaries and Intelligence Summaries are contained in F. S. Regs., Part II. and the Staff Manual respectively. Title pages will be prepared in manuscript.

WAR DIARY
or
~~INTELLIGENCE SUMMARY.~~

(Erase heading not required.)

PAGE II — 93rd F^d AMBUL^ce

Place	Date	Hour	Summary of Events and Information	Remarks and references to Appendices
CAESTRE	1918 Sept 7th (Contd)		Patients admitted during past 24 hrs. Wounded O.R. 6. Sick Off. 2. O.R. 18	[illegible]
"	Sept 8th		Patients admitted during past 24 hrs. Sick O.R. 35	[illegible]
"	Sept 9th		Patients admitted during past 24 hrs. Sick O.R. 63 Wounded O.R. 1. ADMS visited the hospital	[illegible]
"	Sept 10th		Patients admitted during past 24 hrs. Sick Off 1 O.R. 32 ~~Patien~~	[illegible]
"	Sept 11th		Patients admitted during past 24 hrs. Sick O.R. 33 Wounded O.R. 6. G.O.C. visited the hospital [illegible]	[illegible]
"	Sept 12th		[illegible] S.R. McKinnon [illegible] G.O.C. 31st Div. ADMS proceeded on leave and I [illegible] his duty temporarily in addition to my own. Capt W.L. [illegible] returned from leave at PARIS	
"			Patients admitted during past 24 hrs. Sick Off. 2 O.R. 44	[illegible]
"	Sept 13th		Patients admitted during past 24 hrs. Sick O.R. 46 Wounded O.R. 2. Prevailing disease diarrhoea.	[illegible]

Army Form C. 2118.

Instructions regarding War Diaries and Intelligence Summaries are contained in F. S. Regs., Part II. and the Staff Manual respectively. Title pages will be prepared in manuscript.

WAR DIARY
or
~~INTELLIGENCE SUMMARY.~~
(Erase heading not required.)

PAGE III

92nd Fd. Amb.

Place	Date 1918	Hour	Summary of Events and Information	Remarks and references to Appendices
CAESTRE	Sept 14th		Patients admitted during past 24 hrs. Sick. Officers 2 O.R. 24	[signature]
"	Sept 15th		Patients admitted during past 24 hrs. Sick O.R. 48.	[initials]
"	Sept 16th		Patients admitted during past 24 hrs. Sick Off. 1 O.R. 44.	[initials]
"	Sept 17th		Patients admitted during past 24 hrs. Sick Off. 4 O.R. 42.	[initials]
			Prevailing disease Diarrhoea and Dysentery.	
"	Sept 18th		Patients admitted during past 24 hrs. Sick O.R. 27.	
			Lt. RAAD rejoined from leave to England	[initials]
"	~~Sept 18~~		Sent an advance party to take over D.R. site from 88th F.A. at BORRÉ.	[initials]
BORRÉ	Sept 19th		Unit moved to BORRÉ. Sick are accommodated in the schoolhouses.	
			Patients admitted during past 24 hrs. O.R. 33. Wounded O.R. 2	[initials]
"	Sept 20th		Patients admitted during past 24 hrs. Sick O.R. 17 Wounded O.R. 1.	[initials]
	Sept 21st		Patients admitted during past 24 hrs. O.R. 15.	[initials]
"	Sept 22nd		Patients admitted during past 24 hrs. Sick O.R. 30.	
			Prevailing disease Pyrexia type	[initials]

A5834 Wt. W4973/M687 750,000 8/16 D. D. & L. Ltd. Forms/C.2118/13.

Instructions regarding War Diaries and Intelligence Summaries are contained in F. S. Regs., Part II. and the Staff Manual respectively. Title pages will be prepared in manuscript.

PAGE IV

WAR DIARY
or
INTELLIGENCE SUMMARY.
(Erase heading not required.)

Army Form C. 2118.

93rd Fd. Amb^ce

Place	Date	Hour	Summary of Events and Information	Remarks and references to Appendices
	1918			
BORRÉ	Sept 23rd		Patients admitted during past 24 hrs. Sick Of 1. O.R. 13.	
			Attended conference at G.O.C. 31st DIV.	Ap. May 21/7
"	Sept 24th.		Patients admitted during past 24 hrs. Sick O.R. 21.	AP.
"	Sept 25th.		Patients admitted during past 24 hrs Sick O.R. 17.	AP.
	Sept 26th.		Patients admitted during past 24 hrs. Sick O.R. 21.	
			A.D.M.S. returned from leave to England.	AP.
"	Sept 27th.		I detailed Capt. BATTERSBY & 64 bearers to report for duty to O.C. 95 F.A. at A.D.S. in front of BAILLEUL. also 1. N.C.O. & 2 O.R. as holding party.	AP.
"	Sept 28th →		Patients admitted during past 24 hrs. O.R. 16. Prevailing disease Diarrhoea. At 4 p.m. Major CRABTREE and party took over present A.D.S. and opened an M.D.S., as the division had attacked and gained ground E of PLOEGSTREET WOOD.	
			Patients admitted during past 24 hrs. O.R. 18.	AP.
"	Sept 29th.		Patients admitted during past 24 hrs. Sick. O.R. 33. Wounded Of. 11. O.R. 218.	
			Capt. BATTERSBY. joined 11th E. YORKS. in relief of Capt. I DUNN DSO. MC. wounded.	

A5834 Wt. W4973/M687 750,000 8/16 D. D. & L. Ltd. Forms/C.2118/13.

P.T.O

Instructions regarding War Diaries and Intelligence Summaries are contained in F. S. Regs., Part II. and the Staff Manual respectively. Title pages will be prepared in manuscript.

WAR DIARY
or
~~INTELLIGENCE SUMMARY.~~
(Erase heading not required.)

Army Form C. 2118.

PAGE 5. 93rd Fd Amb^ce

Place	Date 1918	Hour	Summary of Events and Information	Remarks and references to Appendices
BORRE	Sept 29th (contd)		2 O.R. (11th E YORKS) died at M.D.S. of Gas Shell Poisoning.	
			1 O.R. (14th LONDON Rgt) " " " " G.S.W. Lt Leg.	
			Capt. A.J. THOMAS (24 R.W.F.) " " " " G.S.W. Head	
			2/Lt. R.J. ROSS (5th att 12th R.S.F.) " " " " G.S.W. Chest.	
"	Sept. 30th		Patients admitted during past 24 hrs. Sick Off. 3. O.R. 43.	A.R.[illegible] Lt Col
			Wounded Off. 9. O.R. 142.	
			Division has [illegible] [illegible] [illegible] [illegible] of 48.	
			Total admissions for Month. Sick Off. 23. O.R. 821. Wounded Off. 24 O.R. 461	
			" Evacuations for Month. Sick Off. 23 O.R. 525 Wounded Off. 21 O.R. 451	
			Discharged to duty. Sick O.R. 175 Wounded Off. 1. O.R. 6	
			Died Off. 2 O.R. 3	
			Capt. R.C. LEONARD RAMC joined unit for duty in [illegible] [illegible]	A.R.[illegible] Lt Col

A5834 Wt. W4973/M687 750,000 8/16 D. D. & L. Ltd. Forms/C.2118/13.

Oct. 1918.

140/3401.

93rd. F.A.

6

Instructions regarding War Diaries and Intelligence Summaries are contained in F. S. Regs., Part II. and the Staff Manual respectively. Title pages will be prepared in manuscript.

WAR DIARY
or
~~INTELLIGENCE SUMMARY.~~
(Erase heading not required.)

Army Form C. 2118.

PAGE I

92nd Fd. Amb^ce

Vol 32

Place	Date 1918	Hour	Summary of Events and Information	Remarks and references to Appendices
BORRÉ	Sept. 1st.		Patients admitted during past 24 hrs. Sick o/1. o.r. 45. Wounded o.r. 73	
"			1. O.r. (61st Siege Bty. R.G.A.) died from G.S.W. abdomen.	
		C	91st Fd Amb took over the M.D.S. & Major CRABTREE & party rejoined H.Qrs. of unit.	[illegible]
"	Sept 2nd		Patients admitted during past 24 hrs. Sick ~~o/1~~ o.r. 31. Wounded o/1. 2. o.r. 2.	[illegible]
"	Oct 3rd		Patients admitted during past 24 hrs. Sick o.r. 35 Wounded o.r. 2. A.D.M.S. inspected the D.R.S. [illegible]	[illegible]
"	Oct 4th		Patients admitted during past 24 hrs. Sick o.r. 15. [illegible] [illegible] [illegible] [illegible] [illegible] [illegible] [illegible]	[illegible]
"	Oct 5th		Patients admitted during past 24 hrs. o.r. 10.	Major R. [illegible] proceeded on leave to England. [illegible]
"	Oct 6th		Patients admitted during past 24 hrs. o.r. 14.	[illegible]
"	Oct 7th		Patients admitted during past 24 hrs. o.r. 12. Capt W. L. SMITH proceeded for temporary duty with 12th R.S.F.	Prevailing disease DIARRHOEA. [illegible]

A5834 Wt. W4973/M687 750,000 8/16 D. D. & L. Ltd. Forms/C.2118/13.

A.

Instructions regarding War Diaries and Intelligence Summaries are contained in F. S. Regs., Part II. and the Staff Manual respectively. Title pages will be prepared in manuscript.

WAR DIARY
or
INTELLIGENCE SUMMARY.
(Erase heading not required.)

Army Form C. 2118.

PAGE II

93rd Fd. AMBULANCE

Place	Date 1918	Hour	Summary of Events and Information	Remarks and references to Appendices
BORRÉ	Oct 9th		Patients admitted during past 24 hrs. officers 1. O.R. 4. DDMS XV CORPS inspected the D.R.S. today	
BAILLEUL	Oct 10th		Unit moved today, and opened D.R.S. at LUNATIC ASYLUM, BAILLEUL.	
"	Oct 11th		Patients admitted during past 24 hrs. O.R. 7. Capt. R. J. WAUGH was posted to this unit for duty.	
"	Oct 12th		Patients admitted during past 24 hrs O.R. 7. Prevailing disease DIARRHOEA. No 62581 Pte (a/L/Cpl) A WALKER has been awarded the Military Medal by the CORPS COMMANDER	
"	Oct 13th		Patients admitted during past 24 hrs. O.R. 10.	
"	Oct 14th		Patients admitted during past 24 hrs. O.R. 13. officers 1. ADMS visited the D.R.S. today.	
"	Oct 15th		Patients admitted during past 24 hrs. Off 1. O.R. 16.	
"	Oct 16th		Patients admitted during past 24 hrs Of 2. O.R. 25.	
"	Oct 17th		Patients admitted during past 24 hrs. O.R. 41 Prevailing disease I.C.T.	

A5834 Wt. W4973/M687 750,000 8/16 D. D. & L. Ltd. Forms/C.2118/13.

Instructions regarding War Diaries and Intelligence Summaries are contained in F. S. Regs., Part II. and the Staff Manual respectively. Title pages will be prepared in manuscript.

PAGE III

WAR DIARY
or
~~INTELLIGENCE SUMMARY.~~
(Erase heading not required.)

Army Form C. 2118.

92nd Fd. Ambce.

Place	Date	Hour	Summary of Events and Information	Remarks and references to Appendices
BAILLEUL	Oct. 1918	18th	Patients admitted during past 24 hrs. O.R. 16.	R. Macbeth
"	Oct	19th	Patients admitted during past 24 hrs. Off. 2 O.R. 26. Prevailing disease Influenza	
"	Oct	20th	Patients admitted during past 24 hrs. Off. 1 O.R. 6.	
"	Oct	21st	Patients admitted during past 24 hrs. O.R. [illegible] 5	
"	Oct	22nd	Patients admitted during past 24 hrs O.R. [illegible] 12.	
ARMENTIÈRES	Oct	23rd	Patients admitted during past 24 hrs O.R. 4. Prevailing disease Influenza, Pyrexia. The Division being three days march ahead, the DRS was closed, and the unit moved to billets in ARMENTIÈRES.	
			Capt. R. WAUGH proceeded for temporary duty with 11th E LANCS. yesterday.	
WAMBRECHIES	Oct	24th	Unit moved to billets at WAMBRECHIES	
CUERNE	Oct	25th	Orders for the unit to move to LANNOY were cancelled, and the unit moved to 2nd CORPS area, CUERNE with 92nd Inf. Bgde.	
"	Oct	26th	Major MacKINNON proceeded to take over ADS at STACEGHEM, but ~~[illegible]~~ was withdrawn this evening. Major CRABTREE & Capt. LEONARD took over ADS at VICHTE STATION from 87th F.A. The 92nd Bgde is holding the line with 2 battalions and one in support, a car post is stationed within 500 yds. of each RAP	

A5834 Wt. W4973/M687 750,000 8/16 D. D. & L. Ltd. Forms/C.2118/13.

Instructions regarding War Diaries and Intelligence Summaries are contained in F. S. Regs., Part II. and the Staff Manual respectively. Title pages will be prepared in manuscript.

PAGE IV

WAR DIARY
or
~~INTELLIGENCE SUMMARY.~~
(Erase heading not required.)

93rd Fd Amb^ce

Army Form C. 2118.

Place	Date 1918	Hour	Summary of Events and Information	Remarks and references to Appendices
CUERNE.	Oct 27th		Unit is now stationed at the OLD MILL, in the CUERNE area.	
			Capt. C. MORRELL is posted to the 40th Div. and struck off the strength, never having actually served with this unit.	[illegible]
"	Oct 28th		Capt. W. L. SMITH returned from duty with the 12th R.S.F.	[illegible]
"	Oct 29th		Nothing to report. Visited ADS. RAPs + car post.	[illegible]
"	Oct 30th		Nothing to report.	[illegible]
"	Oct 31st		The Division attacked this morning, and reached its final objective about 1 p.m. The attack was highly successful, and casualties were about 160. Seventy enemy wounded passed through A.D.S., including 1 enemy medical officer who worked at the ADS. German prisoners were employed to help the evacuation.	
			The R.A.P.s were kept clear, and were enabled to move up rapidly; as did also the car post.	
			Capt W. SMITH was in charge of the bearers, who were supplemented by those of 95th FA.	
			I presided over Court of Enquiry to determine the illegal absence of No 33019 Pte F. BOUCHER M.M. of my unit.	

[illegible] M.C.
Cmd 93rd FA.

A5834 Wt. W4973/M687 750,000 8/16 D. D. & L. Ltd. Forms/C.2118/13.

Nov. 1918

140/34 81

No. 93 F. A.

Instructions regarding War Diaries and Intelligence Summaries are contained in F. S. Regs., Part II. and the Staff Manual respectively. Title pages will be prepared in manuscript.

Army Form C. 2118.

WAR DIARY
or
~~INTELLIGENCE SUMMARY.~~

(Erase heading not required.)

Page I. 93rd Field Ambulance.

Vol 33

Place	Date	Hour	Summary of Events and Information	Remarks and references to Appendices
CUERNE	1/11/18		1 O.R. evacuated to C.C.S. Sick.	
—	2/11/18		1 O.R. evacuated to C.C.S, Sick.	
LAUWE	3/11/18		Unit now stationed in LAUWE.	
—	4/11/18		Capt. R.G.BATTERSBY. RAMC, returned from leave of absense to the United Kingdom.	
—	5/11/18		Major W.CRABTREE. proceeded on leave to PARIS from 5.11.18 to 12.111.18 1 O/R evacuated to C.C.S., sick.	
AVELGHEM	6/11/18		Capt R.J.P.WAUGH, proceeded on temporary duty with the 13th YORK and LANCS. Opened A.D.S, in the AVELGHEM area to-day, and also a temporary M.D.S., Bearer party proceed with the 94th Bde, under the charge of M.O. 12th NORFOLKS.	
—	7/11/18		1 O.R. evacuated to C.C.S.,Sick. Patients admitted 1 sick and 5 wounded Other ranks and 1 sick and 4 wounded evacuated to CCS. Prevailing disease. Influenza.	
SWEVELGHEM	8/11/18		The Unit now situated at SWEVELGHEM. Belgian Interpreter joined Unit. 2 sick and 1 wounded O.R. admitted and evacuated. Prevailing disease Influenza.	
—	9/11/18		1 O/R. evacuated to C.C.S. sick. (R.A.M.C).	
AVELGHEM	10/11/18		Unit now situated at AVELGHEM. 1 O.R. posted for duty (R.A.M.C).	
RENAIX	11/11/18		Unit now situated at RENAIX. Opened hospital for sick and wounded. Armistise Peace Terms signed.	
—	12/11/18		27 O.R. admitted and remaining. Sick. Prevailing Disease. Influenza. A.D.M.S., visited the Unit.	

A5834 Wt. W4973/M687 750,000 8/16 D. D. & L. Ltd. Forms/C.2118/13.

Instructions regarding War Diaries and Intelligence Summaries are contained in F. S. Regs., Part II. and the Staff Manual respectively. Title pages will be prepared in manuscript.

Army Form C. 2118.

WAR DIARY
or
~~INTELLIGENCE SUMMARY.~~

Page II. (*Erase heading not required.*) 93rd Field Ambulance.

Place	Date	Hour	Summary of Events and Information	Remarks and references to Appendices
RENAIX	13th		1 Officer and 37 O Ranks admitted Sick, and 1 Off and 56 O.R. ~~xxxxxxx remaining~~.evac to CCS. Prevailing disease Influenza.	
"	14th		1 O.R. RAMC, evacuated to CCS Sick. 2 Officers and 21 O.R. admitted and evacuated to CCS. Prevailing Disease I.C.T.	
SWEVEGHEM	15th		Unit now situated at SWEVEGHEM. 1 Off and 19 O.R. evacuated to CCS. Sick.	
MARCKE	16th		Major W.CRABTREE, rejoined Unit from leave to PARIS. Unit now situated at MARCKE. 3 O.R. admitted and evac to CCS. Sick.Prevailing disease. Influenza.	
"	17th		I carried out an inspection of the Unit to-day, preparatory to the G.O.C's visit on the 18th. 1st Lieut F.M.SMITH. MC.USA posted for duty. 1 O.R. re-inforcement posted for duty (RAMC). 5 O R admitted and evac to CCS sick. Prevailing disease Pyrexia.	
"	18th		The Divisional General visited the Unit for the purpose of presenting Medal Ribbons. 11 O.R. admitted and evac to CCS sick.Prevailing Disease. Influenza.	
"	19th		Opened Divisional Rest Station. 12 O.R. admitted and evac to CCS, Sick. Prevailing disease. Influenza.	
"	20th		1 O.R. RAMC, posted for duty with 104th Field Ambulance. 9 O.R. admitted sick. 4 O.R. evac to CCS. and 5 O.R. remaingig. Prevailing disease. Influenza.	
"	21st		2 O.R.RAMC, rejoined Unit from CCS. 29 O.R. admitted Sick. 5 O.R. evac to CCS. 29 O.R. remainign. Prevailing Disease. Influenza.	
"	22nd		M2/153002 Pte CRYDERMAN. N.W., ASC. MT att 93rd Field Ambce, Awarded Military Medal. Auth 31st Divl.R.O. NO.4128 d/18.11.18. 28 O.R. admitted 24 O.R. evac to CCS. 33 O.R. remaining Sick.	

A5834 W.W.4973 M687 750,000 8/16 D. D. & L. Ltd. Forms/C.2118/13.

Army Form C. 2118.

Instructions regarding War Diaries and Intelligence Summaries are contained in F. S. Regs., Part II. and the Staff Manual respectively. Title pages will be prepared in manuscript.

WAR DIARY
or
~~INTELLIGENCE SUMMARY.~~

Page III. *(Erase heading not required.)* 93rd Field Ambulance.

Place	Date	Hour	Summary of Events and Information	Remarks and references to Appendices
MARCKE	23/11/18		36 O.R. admitted Sick. 38 O.R. evac to CCS sick. 27 O.R. remaining. Prevailing disease. Influenza. Capt. R.J.P.WAUGH RAMC, posted in Medical Charge of 13th YORK & LANCS. and struck off the strength of 93rd F.Ambce. Capt. R.C.LEONARD. RAMC, posted in Medical Charge of 11th EAST YORKS, and struck off the strength of 93rd F.Ambce.	
–	24/11/18		9 O.R. admitted sick, and 22 O.R. evac to CCS. sick and 4 O.R. remaining sick. Prevailing Disease. Influenza. Major R.MACKINNON. RAMC,SR. proceeded to report to War Office for release. Capt. C.C.IRVINE. M.C.,RAMC, posted for duty with 93rd Field Ambce from 11th EAST YORKS, and taken on the strength. 1 O.R. RAMC, evac to CCS Sick. 1 O.R. RAMC, posted for duty from 104th F.Ambce.	
MENIN	25/11/18		Unit now situated at MENIN. 1 Off and 4 O.R. admitted sick. 1 Off and 5 O.R. evac to CCS sick. and 1 O.R. remaining sick. Prevailing disease. Influenza.	
VLAMERTINGHE	26/11/18		Unit now situated at VLAMERTINGHE. 10 O.R. admitted and evac to CCS, sick 1 O.R. remaining Sick Prevailing disease Influenza.	
STEENVOORDE	27/11/18		Unit now situated at STEENVOORDE. 9 O.R. admitted and evac to CCS, 1 O.R. remaining Sick. Prevailing disease. Influenza.	
STAPLE	28/11/18		Unit now situated at STAPLE. 4 O.R.,RAMC, evac to CCS sick. 19 O.R. admitted sick. 7 O.R.evac to CCS sick and 13 O.R. remaining sick. Prevailing disease. I.C.T.	
ST. OMER	29/11/18		Unit now situated in ST.OMER. 6 O.R. admitted sick. 19 O.R. remaining. Prevailing disease. I.C.T.	
–	30/11/18		1 O.R. RAMC, rejoined from CCS. 16 O.R. admitted sick. 34 O.R. remaining. Prevailing disease. Influenza.	

A5834 Wt. W4973/M687 750,000 8/16 D. D. & L. Ltd. Forms/C.2118/13.

Army Form C. 2118.

WAR DIARY
or
~~INTELLIGENCE-SUMMARY.~~
(Erase heading not required.)

Instructions regarding War Diaries and Intelligence Summaries are contained in F. S. Regs., Part II. and the Staff Manual respectively. Title pages will be prepared in manuscript.

Page IV. 93rd Field Ambce.

Place	Date	Hour	Summary of Events and Information	Remarks and references to Appendices
St OMER	30th		A recreation and games room has been provided for the personnel of the Unit.	
			Total admissions for month. Sick. 5 offs. 313 O.R. Wounded 6 O.R.	
			Evacuated for month. Sick. 5 offs. 254 O.R. Wounded 5 O.R.	
			Discharged to duty Sick. 25.O.R. Wounded 1 O.R.	

A5834 Wt. W4973/M687 750,000 8/16 D. D. & L. Ltd. Forms/C.2118/13.

Dec. 1918

14/3481

No. 93. F. A.

9/2

Instructions regarding War Diaries and Intelligence Summaries are contained in F. S. Regs., Part II. and the Staff Manual respectively. Title pages will be prepared in manuscript.

WAR DIARY
or
~~INTELLIGENCE SUMMARY.~~

(Erase heading not required.)

Army Form C. 2118.

93 Fd Amb

N R 34

Place	Date	Hour	Summary of Events and Information	Remarks and references to Appendices
ST OMER	1/12/18		Patients admitted 17 OR sick Remaining 50 OR	Prevailing disease Influenza
			1 OR rejoined unit from CCS	
"	2-12		25 OR admitted 13 OR evacuated Remaining 53 OR	1 C.T.
"	3-12		3 OR rejoined from CCS	Influenza
			1 Off 28 OR admitted 1 Off 10 OR evacuated Remaining 62 OR	
			Major W CRABTREE granted leave to UK. 5/12/18 to 19/12/18	
"	4-12		1 Off 43 OR admitted 1 Off 17 OR evacuated Remaining 84 OR	"
"	5-12		32 OR admitted 18 OR evacuated Remaining 90 OR	"
			Capt. W. L. SMITH M.R.C. U.S.A. awarded Military Cross	
			authority 31st Div R.O. 4156 d/5 12/18	
"	6-12		24 OR admitted 13 OR evacuated Remaining 98 OR	"
			Lt F M SMITH M.R.C. U.S.A. proceeded for temporary duty to ADMS ST OMER	
"	7-12		1 Off 25 OR admitted 1 Off 12 OR evacuated Remaining 108 OR	"
"	8-12		1 Off 34 OR admitted 1 Off 29 OR evacuated Remaining 102 OR	"
			1 OR evacuated to CC	
"	9-12		1 Off 20 OR admitted 1 Off 14 OR evacuated Remaining 96 OR	"
			Major Rev W.J. SCULLY D.S.O. S.C.F. P.C's dept. taken on	
			ration strength from 9/12/18	
			1 OR evacuated to CCS sick	"
"	10-12		21 OR admitted 21 OR evacuated Remaining 86 OR	"
	11-12		9 OR admitted 3 OR evacuated Remaining 85 OR	
			6 OR off strength - continuing sent to dispersal centre	

A5834 Wt. W4973/M687 750,000 8/16 D. D. & L. Ltd. Forms/C.2118/13.

Army Form C. 2118.

Instructions regarding War Diaries and Intelligence Summaries are contained in F. S. Regs., Part II. and the Staff Manual respectively. Title pages will be prepared in manuscript.

WAR DIARY
or
~~INTELLIGENCE SUMMARY.~~

(Erase heading not required.)

Place	Date	Hour	Summary of Events and Information	Remarks and references to Appendices
St OMER	12-12-18		1 Off 30 OR admitted 1 Off 25 OR evacuated Remaining 64 OR 4 OR off strength - coalminers sent to dispersal centre Lt F.M. SMITH MRCUSA struck off strength on proceeding to duty with 80th Labour Corps 1 OR evacuated to CCS sick	Prevailing disease Influenza
"	13-12		24 OR admitted 14 OR evacuated Remaining 68 OR 1 OR evacuated to CCS sick Capt W.L. SMITH MRCUSA proceeded on leave to PARIS 13-20 12/18	"
"	14-12		30 OR admitted 18 OR evacuated Remaining 75 OR 3 OR sent to dispersal centre	"
"	15-12		35 OR admitted 13 OR evacuated Remaining 90 OR 1 OR sent to dispersal centre	"
"	16-12		14 OR admitted 17 OR evacuated Remaining 78 OR 3 OR sent to dispersal centres Lt COL A.M. POLLARD DSO proceeded to 8 (Richelham) Convalescent Home CARMARTIN	"
"	17-12		2 Off 22 OR admitted 2 Off 19 OR evacuated Remaining 80 OR 6 OR sent to dispersal centre 1 OR evacuated to CCS sick	"
"	18-12		8 OR admitted 8 OR evacuated Remaining 60 OR 1 OR rejoined from CCS 1 OR sent to dispersal centre	"
"	19-12		20 OR admitted 19 OR evacuated Remaining 57 OR 1 OR evacuated to CCS sick	"

Instructions regarding War Diaries and Intelligence Summaries are contained in F. S. Regs., Part II. and the Staff Manual respectively. Title pages will be prepared in manuscript.

WAR DIARY
or
~~INTELLIGENCE SUMMARY.~~
(Erase heading not required.)

Army Form C. 2118.

Place	Date	Hour	Summary of Events and Information	Remarks and references to Appendices
ST OMER	20.12.18		1 Off 9 OR admitted 1 Off 9 OR evacuated Remaining 47 OR Prevailing disease Influenza Major W CRABTREE returned from leave to UK Capt. W.L.SMITH returned from leave to PARIS	
"	21.12		~~1 Off~~ 7 OR admitted 4 OR evacuated Remaining 44 OR 2 OR returned to unit from CCS	
"	22.12		18 OR admitted 6 OR evacuated Remaining 57 OR Capt. R G BATTERSBY proceeded for temporary duty to 5th Army Demobilization Staging Camp HONDEGHEM	
"	23.12		1 Off 14 OR admitted 1 Off 10 OR evacuated Remaining 47 OR 1 OR joined unit from RAMC depot Base	
"	24.12		8 OR admitted 4 OR evacuated Remaining 47 OR 1 OR rejoined from CCS	
"	25.12		6 OR admitted 3 OR evacuated Remaining 50 OR Patients were supplied with special diet with seasonable extras RAMC Personnel had Christmas dinner & smoking concert & were visited & addressed by ADMS with acclamation	
"	26.12		1 Off 5 OR admitted 1 Off 6 OR evacuated Remaining 46 OR A concert was given to patients by RAMC personnel	
"	27.12		11 OR admitted 6 OR evacuated Remaining 49 OR	I.C.T.
"	28.12		10 OR admitted 4 OR evacuated Remaining 53 OR 1 OR evacuated to CCS sick 2 OR sent to dispersal centre	

A5834 Wt. W4973/M687 750,000 8/16 D. D. & L. Ltd. Forms/C.2118/13.

Instructions regarding War Diaries and Intelligence Summaries are contained in F. S. Regs., Part II. and the Staff Manual respectively. Title pages will be prepared in manuscript.

WAR DIARY
or
~~INTELLIGENCE SUMMARY.~~
(Erase heading not required.)

Army Form C. 2118.

Place	Date	Hour	Summary of Events and Information	Remarks and references to Appendices
ST OMER	29.12.18		11 OR admitted 2 OR evacuated Remaining 57 OR	Prevailing disease Influenza
"	30.12		9 OR admitted 2 OR evacuated Remaining 59 Capt W.L. SMITH MRC USA proceeded to American Base Hospital Centre SAVERNAY (LOIRE INFERIEURE) in accordance with instructions from American H.Q. + Adjt General British forces	"
	31.12		15 OR admitted 10 OR evacuated Remaining 57 OR 1 OR sent to dispersal centre	"
			Total admissions for month Sick / Wounded – 11 Officers 534 OR	
			" evacuations " " Sick / Wounded 11 Officers 349 OR	
			Discharged to duty Sick / Wounded – 212 OR	

W Aitken
Major RAMC

Field Ambulance Orderly Room No. 251 Date........ R.A.M.C.

A5834 Wt. W4973/M687 750,000 8/16 D. D. & L. Ltd. Forms/C.2118/13.

Jan. 1919

31 DIV

Box 2131

140/3524.

No 93 Field Ambulance

31

Instructions regarding War Diaries and Intelligence Summaries are contained in F. S. Regs., Part II. and the Staff Manual respectively. Title pages will be prepared in manuscript.

PAGE I

WAR DIARY
or
INTELLIGENCE SUMMARY.
(Erase heading not required.)

Army Form C.

93rd Field Ambulance

Vol 35

Place	Date	Hour	Summary of Events and Information	Remarks and references to Appendices
ST OMER	Jan 1/19		11 OR admitted 9 OR evacuated Remaining 55 OR 1 OR sent to dispersal centre	Prevailing disease Pyrexia
"	" 2		11 OR admitted 11 OR evacuated Remaining 55 OR 2 OR sent to dispersal centre 4 OR joined unit from RAMC depot base.	"
"	" 3		2 Off. 15 OR admitted 2 Off 1 OR evacuated Remaining 50 OR 1 OR sent to dispersal centre	"
"	" 4		16 OR admitted 8 OR. evacuated Remaining 52 OR 2 OR sent to dispersal centre 1 OR joined unit from RAMC base depot	"
"	" 5		18 OR admitted 9 OR evacuated Remaining 57 OR 1 OR evacuated to CCS	"
"	" 6		8 OR admitted 3 OR evacuated Remaining 60 OR Capt. C.E MERYON RAMC & Capt. R.J.P. WAUGH joined unit in accordance with ADMS instructions	"
"	" 7		1 Off 16 OR admitted 1 Off & 11 OR evacuated Remaining 58	Scabies
"	" 8		23 OR admitted 16 OR evacuated Remaining 62 1 OR ASC MT posted as reinforcement. 1 OR to dispersal centre	Pyrexia

A5834 Wt. W4973/M687 750,000 8/16 D. D. & L. Ltd. Forms/C.2118/13.

Instructions regarding War Diaries and Intelligence Summaries are contained in F. S. Regs., Part II. and the Staff Manual respectively. Title pages will be prepared in manuscript.

WAR DIARY
or
INTELLIGENCE SUMMARY.

(Erase heading not required.)

Army Form C.2118.

PAGE II

93rd Field Ambulance

Place	Date	Hour	Summary of Events and Information	Remarks and references to Appendices
St Omer	Jan 9		Admitted 16 OR Evacuated 16 OR 83 Remaining	Prevailing disease Pyrexia
			Lt Col [illegible] returned from 1st [illegible] Convalescent Home	
			Capt [illegible] returned from temporary duty at Staging Camp Hondeghem	
			Capt MERRICK proceeded for temporary duty at XIX Corps Concentration Camp Haegebruk	
			12266 Sgt Major PARKER RAMC was awarded Belgian Croix de Guerre authority II Corps [illegible] S 21 dat 7.1.19	
	10		Admitted 2 Offs 21 OR Evacuated 2 Offs [illegible] OR Remaining 57 OR	
"	11		" 9 OR Evacuated 2 OR 55 OR	
"	12		17 OR 14 OR 58 OR	
			1 OR Rejoined for duty	
			3 " to dispersal centre	
"	13		1 Off 23 OR admitted 1 Off 10 OR evacuated Remaining 56	
			3 OR Rejoined to dispersal centre	
	14		15 OR admitted 4 OR evacuated Remaining 60	
			1 OR to dispersal centre	
	15		23 OR admitted 12 OR evacuated Remaining 64	Scabies
			Capt [illegible] proceeded for duty with 95th F Amb	
	16		12 OR admitted 6 OR evacuated " 67	Influenza
			2 OR [illegible] [illegible]	

A5834 Wt. W4973/M687 750,000 8/16 D. D. & L. Ltd. Forms/C.2118/13.

Army Form C. 2118.

WAR DIARY
or
INTELLIGENCE SUMMARY.
(Erase heading not required.)

Instructions regarding War Diaries and Intelligence Summaries are contained in F. S. Regs., Part II. and the Staff Manual respectively. Title pages will be prepared in manuscript.

PAGE III

93rd Field Ambulance

Place	Date	Hour	Summary of Events and Information	Remarks and references to Appendices
St OMER	Jan 17		Admitted 17 OR Evacuated 6 OR Remaining 7[illegible] [illegible]	
			Lt. [illegible] retired from [illegible] 6 OR	
"	18		Admitted 7 OR Evacuated 3 OR Remaining 65	
			6 OR R Dune to dispersal centre	
	19		Admitted 4 OR Evacuated 1 OR Remaining 57	
			5 OR R Dune to dispersal centre	
	20		Admitted 1 Off 5 OR Evacuated 1 Off 3 OR " 56	
			4 OR R Dune to dispersal centre	
			1 OR [illegible]	
"	21		Admitted 7 OR Evacuated 4 OR " 58	
			9 OR R Dune to dispersal centre	
"	22		Admitted 4 OR Evacuated 1 OR " 42	
			5 OR R Dune to dispersal centre	
"	23		Admitted 10 OR Evacuated 5 OR " 44	
			12206 [illegible] awarded Meritorious Service Medal [illegible] 18-1-19	
	24		Admitted 1 Off 6 OR Evacuated 1 Off 4 OR Remaining 42	
"	25		Admitted 3 OR Evacuated 2 OR " 37	
"	26		4 OR Evacuated nil " 40	
"	27		4 OR " 2 " 42	
			Lt Col [illegible] proceeded on leave to UK from 28-1-19 to 27-2-19	

Army Form C. [illegible]

Instructions regarding War Diaries and Intelligence Summaries are contained in F. S. Regs., Part II. and the Staff Manual respectively. Title pages will be prepared in manuscript.

WAR DIARY
or
INTELLIGENCE SUMMARY.
(Erase heading not required.)

PAGE IV — 93 Field Ambulance

Place	Date	Hour	Summary of Events and Information	Remarks and references to Appendices
ST OMER	Jan 28		Admitted 14 OR Evacuated 5 OR Remaining 42 OR	Prevailing [illegible]
"	29		" 1 OR Evacuated 43 OR Remaining Nil —	
			Under orders from [illegible] the unit consisting of 3 officers 80 OR RAMC + 20 OR ASC proceeded to CALAIS with [illegible]	
CALAIS	30		2 OR RAMC 1 OR ASC rejoined from CCS. Lt. [illegible] proceeded [illegible]. Admitted 1 OR Evacuated 1 OR Remaining Nil	
"	31		Admitted 5 OR Evacuated 5 OR " Nil	
			Unit returned to previous station at ST OMER.	
			Total admissions for month 8 off 347 OR sick	
			" evacuations " " 8 off 231 OR "	
			" discharged to duty — 153 OR "	
			Transferred to [illegible] Convalescent Camp 18 OR "	

W [illegible]
Major RAMC

A5834 Wt. W4973/M687 750,000 8/16 D. D. & L. Ltd. Forms/C.2118/13.

Feb. 1919

140/3524

No. 93 Field Ambulance

31

Army Form C. 2118.

Instructions regarding War Diaries and Intelligence Summaries are contained in F. S. Regs., Part II. and the Staff Manual respectively. Title pages will be prepared in manuscript.

WAR DIARY
or
INTELLIGENCE SUMMARY.
(Erase heading not required.)

Page 1

93rd Field Ambulance

Vol 36

Place	Date	Hour	Summary of Events and Information	Remarks and references to Appendices
ST OMER	Feb 1		Admitted 6 OR. Evacuated 4 OR. Remaining 2 OR. Prevailing disease Pyrexia I C T	
"	" 2		" 8 OR " 5 OR " 6 "	
			1 OR Y & L attached sent to dispersal centre	
"	" 3		" 8 OR Evacuated 4 OR Remaining 10 OR. Venereal dis	
			Lt. SCHRAMM J. A. MC USA proceeded for duty (temporary) with 30th Labour Group.	
			Capt. WAUGH R J P returned from temporary duty with 13th Y & L Regt.	
			1 OR R O S C M T evacuated to C C S sick	
			1 OR West Riding Regt attached sent to dispersal centre.	
"	" 4		Admitted 2 Off. 4 OR. Evacuated 2 Off. 3 OR. Remaining 11 OR Influenza	
"	" 5		" 7 OR " 3 OR " 15 OR "	
"	" 6		" 6 OR " nil " 21 OR "	
			1 RAMC + 1 R O S C M T to dispersal centre	
"	" 7		" 1 Off. 10 OR. Evacuated 1 Off 4 OR " 26 " Pyrexia	
			1 OR RAMC to dispersal centre	
"	" 8		" 6 OR Evacuated 3 OR. " 29. "	
			1 OR RAMC. 1 OR Y & L attached. sent to dispersal centre	
"	" 9		" 5 OR Evacuated 5 OR Remaining 27 OR "	
			1 OR RAMC to dispersal centre	
"	"			

A5834 Wt. W4973/M687 750,000 8/16 D. D. & L. Ltd. Forms/C.2118/13.

Instructions regarding War Diaries and Intelligence Summaries are contained in F. S. Regs., Part II. and the Staff Manual respectively. Title pages will be prepared in manuscript.

WAR DIARY
or
INTELLIGENCE SUMMARY.
(Erase heading not required.)

Army Form C. 2118.

PAGE II

93rd Field Ambulance

Place	Date	Hour	Summary of Events and Information	Remarks and references to Appendices
ST OMER	Feb 10		Admitted 1 Off 3 OR. Evacuated 1 Off 6 OR. Remaining 22 OR. Prevailing disease Influenza 2 OR RAMC to dispersal centre	
"	" 11		Admitted 10 OR. Evacuated 7 OR. Remaining 24 OR " Capt R.G. BATTERSBY RAMC proceeded on leave to PARIS from 11/2/19 to 18/2/19	
"	" 12		Admitted 1 Off 12 OR. Evacuated 1 Off 4 OR. Remaining 31 OR. Influenza Major V.J. SCULLY S.C.F. PC 1 dept proceeded on leave to LOURDES from 13.2.19 to 22.2.19 Capt R.J.P. WALSH RAMC proceeded on leave to LOURDES from 13.2.19 to 26.2.19 5 OR RAMC proceeded for temporary duty to No 3 Canadian Stationary Hosp	
"	" 13		Admitted 18 OR. Evacuated 6 OR. Remaining 40 OR. Pyrexia 1 OR RAMC to dispersal centre 1 OR RAMC demobilised whilst on leave & struck off strength from 21.12.18 5 OR returned from temporary duty at No 3 Canadian Stationary Hosp	
"	14		Admitted 1 Off 21 OR. Evacuated 1 Off 6 OR. Remaining 47 OR. Influenza 1 OR RASC MT to dispersal centre 2 OR RASC HT " " " 1 OR Y.M. attached " " " 4 OR RASC HT posted for duty with 22nd Aux. H.T. Coy 1 OR RASC MT rejoined from Hospital Capt J.W. MACFARLANE M.C. RAMC reported for duty	

Army Form C. 2118.

WAR DIARY
or
INTELLIGENCE SUMMARY.
(Erase heading not required.)

Instructions regarding War Diaries and Intelligence Summaries are contained in F. S. Regs., Part II. and the Staff Manual respectively. Title pages will be prepared in manuscript.

PAGE III — 93rd Field Ambulance

Place	Date	Hour	Summary of Events and Information	Remarks and references to Appendices
ST OMER	Feb 15		Admitted 1 Off 11 OR Evacuated 1 Off 9 OR Remaining 47 OR — Prevailing diseases Pyrexia 2 OR RAMC to dispersal centre 1st Lt J. W. SESION M.C.U.S.A. posted for duty	
"	" 16		Admitted 12 OR Evacuated 12 OR Remaining 39 OR " 2 OR RAMC to dispersal centre 12 OR RAMC to No 3 Canadian Stationary Hosp for temporary duty	
"	" 17		Admitted 2 Off 8 OR Evacuated 2 Off Remaining 43 OR Influenza 2 OR RAMC to dispersal centre	
"	18		Admitted 5 OR Evacuated 2 OR Remaining 44 OR Scabies 1 OR RAMC to dispersal centre	
"	19		Admitted 10 OR Evacuated 2 OR Remaining 47 OR Influenza Capt R. G. Batterly returned from Paris Leave Lt QM G Read proceeded on Leave to UK One OR RAMC Leave to UK Appointment to A/Maj of T/Capt CB Irvine MC approved by FM C in C Vide List No 236	

A5834 Wt. W4973/M687 750,000 8/16 D. D. & L. Ltd. Forms/C.2118/13.

Instructions regarding War Diaries and Intelligence Summaries are contained in F. S. Regs., Part II. and the Staff Manual respectively. Title pages will be prepared in manuscript.

WAR DIARY
or
INTELLIGENCE SUMMARY.
(Erase heading not required.)

Army Form C. 2118

PAGE IV

93 Field Ambulance

Place	Date	Hour	Summary of Events and Information	Remarks and references to Appendices
St Omer, Feb	20		Admitted 1 off 9.OR Evacuated 1 off 7.OR Remaining 47.OR Prevailing Disease Influenza. Capt J. W. McFarlane MC RAMC posted for duty with 94th Field Ambulance Capt A. B. R. Swarn RAMC posted for duty from 31st Div Train RASC 2 OR RAMC to dispersal centre.	
	21		Admitted 14.OR Evacuated 4.OR Remaining 54.OR Prevailing disease Scabies 2.OR RAMC and 1 OR York & Lancs attached, to dispersal centre	
	22		Admitted 14.OR Evacuated 5.OR Remaining 57.OR Prevailing Disease Pyrexia	
	23		Admitted 15.OR Evacuated 12.OR Remaining 58 OR Prevailing Disease Pyrexia 1.OR RAMC posted to 3rd A D of M stores, for duty 2 OR RAMC to dispersal centre 1st Lt J.W. Jason MC USA posted for duty with 82nd Labour Group 21/2/19 Major (Rev) V. J. Scully SCF. PC adept attached and Capt R J A Waugh RAMC ~~proceeded on~~ leave to Lourdes returned from	
	24		Admitted 12.OR Evacuated 5.OR Remaining 59.OR Prevailing disease Influenza 1.OR RAMC posted from ADMS 31st Div 22/2/19 1 OR West Riding Regt attached, to dispersal centre	

Instructions regarding War Diaries and Intelligence Summaries are contained in F. S. Regs., Part II. and the Staff Manual respectively. Title pages will be prepared in manuscript.

WAR DIARY
or
INTELLIGENCE SUMMARY.
(*Erase heading not required.*)

Army Form C. 2118.

Page V

93rd Field Ambulance

Place	Date	Hour	Summary of Events and Information	Remarks and references to Appendices
St Omer	Feb 25		Admitted 1. OR Remaining 61 OR Prevailing disease Influenza	
			2. OR. RAMC to dispersal centre	
	26		Admitted 12. OR. Evacuated 9. OR Remaining 57. OR Prevailing Disease Scabies	
"	27		Admitted 1 Officer 12. OR Evacuated 1 Officer & 6 OR. Remaining 52. OR Prevailing Disease Scabies.	
			Major W. Crabtree RAMC proceeded to report War Office for release	
			1. OR RAMC posted for duty with 3 1st A D of Med Stores 27/2/19	
"	28		Admitted 6. OR. Evacuated 3. OR Remaining 26 OR Prevailing Disease Influenza	
			Lt Col Pollard DSO returned from leave to UK	
			1. OR RASC HT attached, to dispersal centre	
			Total admissions for month 11 Officers 265. OR	
			Total Evacuation for month 11 Officers 133. OR	
			Discharged to duty during month 86. OR.	
			Transferred to 95th Field Amb 2. OR	
			[signature] Major RAMC	

A5834 Wt. W4973/M687 750,000 8/16 D. D. & L. Ltd. Forms/C.2118/13.

Mar. 1919.

160/3551

93rd F.A.

Instructions regarding War Diaries and Intelligence Summaries are contained in F. S. Regs., Part II. and the Staff Manual respectively. Title pages will be prepared in manuscript.

WAR DIARY
or
INTELLIGENCE SUMMARY.
(*Erase heading not required.*)

Army Form C. 2118.

37

93rd Field Ambulance

PAGE I

Place	Date	Hour	Summary of Events and Information	Remarks and references to Appendices
St Omer	1/3/19		admitted 9 OR Evacuated 7. OR Remaining 38. OR Prevailing Disease Pyrexia	
	2/3/19		admitted 1 officer 6. OR Evacuated 1 officer 5. OR. Remaining 36. OR Prevailing Disease Pyrexia 1. OR RASC HT att, to dispersal centre	
	3/3/19		admitted 8. OR Evacuated 1. OR Remaining 39. OR Prevailing Disease Pyrexia 2 OR RAMC and 1 OR. RASC. MT to dispersal centre	
	4/3/19		admitted 3. OR Remaining 40. OR Prevailing Disease. Pyrexia	
	5/3/19		admitted 9. OR Evacuated. 1. OR Remaining 43. OR. Prevailing Disease Influenza 1 OR RAMC Leave to UK. No T3/029354 S.M. Harris G. RASC. HT. transferred to 95th Field Ambulance for duty No T2/11301 Sgt Mjr Hilton J. RASC. HT. transferred from 95th Field Amb for duty 1. OR RASC HT leave to UK 1 OR. RAMC to dispersal centre	
	6/3/19		admitted 9. OR Evacuated 5. OR Remaining 43. OR Prevailing disease Influenza 1 OR RAMC to dispersal centre Lt B.M. G Read RAMC rejoined from leave to UK 1 OR RAMC special leave to UK.	

A5834 Wt. W4973/M687 750,000 8/16 D. D. & L. Ltd. Forms/C.2118/13.

Army Form C. 2118.

WAR DIARY
or
INTELLIGENCE SUMMARY.
(*Erase heading not required.*)

Instructions regarding War Diaries and Intelligence Summaries are contained in F. S. Regs., Part II. and the Staff Manual respectively. Title pages will be prepared in manuscript.

Page two

93rd Field Ambulance

Place	Date	Hour	Summary of Events and Information	Remarks and references to Appendices
St Omer	7/3/19		Admitted 6 OR. Evacuated 2 OR Remaining 42 OR Prevailing disease Venereal 1 OR RAMC to dispersal centre	
	8/3/19		Admitted 8 OR Evacuated 23 OR. Remaining 15 OR Prevailing disease Venereal Unit closed down for the admission of sick with the exception of Gonorrhoea cases. DDMS XIX Corps made an inspection of the unit 1 OR RAMC and 1 OR RASC HT to dispersal centre	
	9/3/19		Admitted 1 OR Remaining 16 OR Prevailing disease Venereal 12 OR RAMC transferred for duty with ADMS 3rd Division No 60591 Act L/Cpl Peart R.C. RAMC appointed Cpl from 15/1/19	
	10/3/19		Admitted 2 OR Evacuated 17 OR Remaining 1 OR Prevailing disease Venereal 1 OR RAMC transferred to the MF Police from 6/3/19	
	11/3/19		Admitted 4 OR Remaining 5 OR. Prevailing disease. Venereal 2 OR RASC HT Posted for duty 3 OR RAMC to dispersal centre 1 OR RAMC Leave to UK.	
	12/3/19		Admitted 1 OR. Remaining 6 OR. Prevailing disease. Venereal 1 OR RAMC to dispersal centre. Capt J B Alexander RAMC posted for duty	

A5834 Wt. W4973/M687 750,000 8/16 D. D. & L. Ltd. Forms/C.2118/13.

Army Form C. 2118.

WAR DIARY
or
INTELLIGENCE SUMMARY.
(Erase heading not required.)

Instructions regarding War Diaries and Intelligence Summaries are contained in F. S. Regs., Part II. and the Staff Manual respectively. Title pages will be prepared in manuscript.

Page III — 93rd Field Ambulance

Place	Date	Hour	Summary of Events and Information	Remarks and references to Appendices
St Omer	13/3/19		Admitted Nil. Remaining 6.O.R. Capt A.B.R. Swotn RAMC proceeded to report for duty with DMS Second Army 13/3/19 3.OR RAMC to dispersal centre Capt R.J.P. Waugh RAMC to War Office for demobilisation	
	14/3/19		Admitted 2.OR Evacuated 1.OR. Remaining 7.OR Prevailing Disease Venereal Lt Col A.M. Pollard DSO RAMC relinquished command 93rd F Amb on being posted in command of 95 Field Amb Major V.J. Scully DSO SCF ? C of E dept proceeded to UK for demobilization 5.OR RAMC to dispersal centre	
	15/3/19		Admitted 3.OR Evacuated 2.OR Remaining 8 OR. Prevailing disease Venereal 2.OR RAMC & 4.OR RASC HT for dispersal centre Major C.C. Irvine MC RAMC assumes command of 93rd Field Amb Capt S.A. Williams RAMC posted for duty	
	16/3/19		Admitted 1.OR Evacuated 8.OR. Remaining 1. Prevailing disease Venereal 2 OR RAMC to dispersal centre 1 OR RAMC leave to UK	
	17/3/19		Admitted Nil. Remaining 1.OR	
	18/3/19		Admitted 3.OR Remaining 4.OR Prevailing disease Venereal Capt R.G. Battersby RAMC posted for duty with 94th Field Amb 1OR RASC MT to dispersal centre	

A5834 Wt. W4973/M687 750,000 8/16 D. D. & L. Ltd. Forms/C.2118/13.

Army Form C. 2118.

WAR DIARY
or
INTELLIGENCE SUMMARY.
(*Erase heading not required.*)

Instructions regarding War Diaries and Intelligence Summaries are contained in F. S. Regs., Part II. and the Staff Manual respectively. Title pages will be prepared in manuscript.

Page IV — 93rd Field Ambulance

Place	Date	Hour	Summary of Events and Information	Remarks and references to Appendices
St Omer	19/3/19		Admitted Nil Remaining 4 OR.	
			2 OR RASC MT posted to 31st Div MT Coy	
			1 OR RASC HT posted to 31st Div Train	
	20/3/19		Admitted 2 OR Remaining 6 OR Prevailing disease Venereal	
			Capt E A Williams RAMC posted for duty with 65th Labour Group	
			Capt G D Fairley RAMC posted for duty	
			Capt J B Alexander RAMC to War Office for demobilization 18/3/19	
			1 OR RASC HT struck off strength from 19/11/1918 on admission to hospital in England whilst on leave	
	21/3/19		Admitted 3 OR Remaining 9 OR Prevailing disease Venereal	
	22/3/19		Admitted 3 OR Remaining 12 OR Prevailing disease Venereal	
	23/3/19		Admitted 1 OR Remaining 13 OR Prevailing disease Venereal	
			1 OR RAMC posted to 95th Field Amb	
	24/3/19		Admitted Nil. Remaining 13 OR	
			2 OR RASC MT to dispersal centre	
	25/3/19		Admitted 3 OR Evacuated 14 OR Remaining 2 OR Prevailing disease Venereal.	
			No 9866 Sgt A A Popworth RAMC awarded (Belgian) Decoration Militaire (2nd Class. 1 Croix de guerre)	
	26/3/19		Admitted Nil. Remaining 2 OR.	

A5834 Wt. W4973/M687 750,000 8/16 D. D. & L. Ltd. Forms/C.2118/13.

Army Form C. 2118.

Instructions regarding War Diaries and Intelligence Summaries are contained in F.S. Regs., Part II. and the Staff Manual respectively. Title pages will be prepared in manuscript.

WAR DIARY
or
INTELLIGENCE SUMMARY.
(Erase heading not required.)

Page V

93rd Field Ambulance

Place	Date	Hour	Summary of Events and Information	Remarks and references to Appendices
St Omer	27/3/19		Admitted 2. OR. Remaining 4. OR. Prevailing disease Venereal 1. OR RAMC for temporary duty with OC Concentration Camp Marris	
	28/3/19		Admitted 1. OR. Remaining 5. OR. Prevailing disease Venereal	
	29/3/19		Admitted 1. OR Evacuated 5. OR. Remaining 1. OR. Prevailing disease Venereal	
	30/3/19		Admitted 1 Officer 2. OR. Evacuated 1 Officer 3. OR. Remaining Nil. Prevailing disease Venereal 1. OR RAMC demobilised whilst on leave 25/1/19	
	31/3/19		Admitted Nil. Remaining Nil Total admission sick 2 Officers 93 OR. Total Evacuation sick 2 Officers 94 OR Total Patients to duty 45. OR OC Irwin Major RAMC	

A5834 Wt. W4973/M687 750,000 8/16 D. D. & L. Ltd. Forms/C.2118/13.

Apr. 1919

140/3550

No. 937.a.

Instructions regarding War Diaries and Intelligence Summaries are contained in F. S. Regs., Part II. and the Staff Manual respectively. Title pages will be prepared in manuscript.

Page I

WAR DIARY
or
INTELLIGENCE SUMMARY.
(Erase heading not required.)

93rd Field Ambulance

Army Form C. 2118.

V R 38

Place	Date	Hour	Summary of Events and Information	Remarks and references to Appendices
St Omer	1st April 1919		Admitted 1.O.R. Remaining 1.O.R. Prevailing Disease Venereal	
	2nd April		Admitted Nil Remaining 1.O.R.	
	3rd April		admitted 1.O.R. Remaining 2.O.R. Prevailing Disease Venereal	
	4th April		admitted 2.O.R. Evacuated 2.O.R. Remaining 2.O.R. Prevailing disease Venereal	
	5th April		admitted 1.O.R. Remaining 3.O.R. Prevailing Disease Venereal	
	6th April		admitted 2.O.R. Evacuated 3 O.R. Remaining 2.O.R. Prevailing Disease Venereal	
	7th April		admitted Nil Remaining 2.O.R.	
	8th April		admitted 1.O.R. Remaining 3.O.R. Prevailing Disease Venereal Capt G I Laisley RAMC posted to 95th F Amb 6/4/19	
	9th April		admitted 2.O.R. Evacuated 3 O.R. Remaining 2.O.R. Prevailing Disease Venereal	
	10th April		admitted 3.O.R. Remaining 5.O.R. Prevailing Disease Venereal Lt & QM G Reed evacuated to No 4 Stationary Hospital 1 O.R. RAMC admitted to hospital sick.	
	11th April		admitted 1.O.R. Evacuated 4.O.R. Remaining 2.O.R. Prevailing disease Venereal	
	12th April		admitted 3.O.R. Evacuated 1.O.R. Remaining 4.O.R. Prevailing disease Venereal Capt J N MacCormack RAMC reported for temporary duty	

A5834 Wt. W4973/M687 750,000 8/16 D. D. & L. Ltd. Forms/C.2118/13.

Instructions regarding War Diaries and Intelligence Summaries are contained in F. S. Regs., Part II. and the Staff Manual respectively. Title pages will be prepared in manuscript.

Page II

WAR DIARY
or
INTELLIGENCE SUMMARY. 93rd Field Ambulance
(Erase heading not required.)

Army Form C. 2118.

Place	Date	Hour	Summary of Events and Information	Remarks and references to Appendices
St Omer	13/4/19		Admitted 3. O.R. Remaining 7. O.R. Prevailing Disease Venereal	
	14/4/19		Admitted 1 Officer 2. O.R. Evacuated 1 Officer 7. O.R. Remaining 2. O.R. Prevailing disease Venereal	
	15/4/19		Admitted 2. O.R. Evacuated 4. O.R. Prevailing disease Venereal	
	16/4/19		Admitted 3 O.R. Evacuated 1. O.R. Remaining 2. O.R. Prevailing disease Venereal	
	17/4/19		Admitted 1. O.R. Remaining 3. O.R. Prevailing disease Venereal	
	18/4/19		Admitted 1 O.R. Remaining 4 O.R. Prevailing disease Venereal	
	19/4/19		Admitted 2. O.R. Remaining 6. O.R. Prevailing disease Venereal	
	20/4/19		Admitted Nil. Evacuated 6. O.R.	
	21/4/19		Admitted 2. O.R. Remaining 2. O.R. Prevailing disease Venereal Lt & Qm G. Read rejoined from 4 Stationary Hospital 1. O.R. RASC M.T. demobilised whilst on leave 17/1/19	
	22/4/19		Admitted 2. O.R. Evacuated 1. O.R. Remaining 3. O.R. Prevailing disease Venereal	
	23/4/19		Admitted 1 O.R. Remaining 4. O.R. Prevailing disease Venereal	
	24/4/19		Admitted 1. O.R. Remaining 5. Prevailing disease Venereal Capt J. N. MacCormack RAMC proceeded to report to OC 39 Stationary Hospital for duty.	

Army Form C. 2118.

Instructions regarding War Diaries and Intelligence Summaries are contained in F. S. Regs., Part II. and the Staff Manual respectively. Title pages will be prepared in manuscript.

WAR DIARY
or
INTELLIGENCE SUMMARY.
(*Erase heading not required.*)

Page 3 93rd Field ambulance

Place	Date	Hour	Summary of Events and Information	Remarks and references to Appendices
St Omer	25/4/19		Admitted 3 OR. Remaining 8 OR Prevailing disease Venereal	
	26/4/19		Admitted Nil. Remaining 8 OR.	
	27/4/19		Admitted 1 OR. Evacuated 8 OR Remaining 1 OR Prevailing disease Venereal	
	28/4/19		Admitted 1 OR Remaining 2 OR Prevailing disease Venereal	
	29/4/19		Admitted 1 OR Remaining 3 OR Prevailing disease Venereal	
	30/4/19		Admitted Nil Remaining 3 OR.	
			Total admissions sick 1 officer 43 OR.	
			Total Evacuations sick 1 officer 40 OR.	
			[illegible] Major RAMC	
			OC 93rd Field Amb	

A5834 Wt. W4973/M687 750,000 8/16 D. D. & L. Ltd. Forms/C.2118/13.

May 1919

No 93 Field Ambulance

Instructions regarding War Diaries and Intelligence Summaries are contained in F. S. Regs., Part II. and the Staff Manual respectively. Title pages will be prepared in manuscript.

Page I

WAR DIARY
or
INTELLIGENCE SUMMARY.
(*Erase heading not required.*)

Army Form C. 2118.

93rd Field Ambulance

VR 39

Place	Date	Hour	Summary of Events and Information	Remarks and references to Appendices
St Omer	1/5/19		NIL Remaining in Hospital 2 OR	
–	2/5/19		Patients admitted 1 OR Remaining 3 OR. Prevailing disease V.D.S. 1 OR RASC MT Special leave to UK.	
–	3/5/19		Admitted 2 OR Remaining 5 OR Prevailing disease Venereal	
–	4/5/19		Admitted NIL Remaining 5 OR	
–	5/5/19		Admitted 4 OR Evacuated 4 OR Remaining 5 OR Prevailing disease V.D.S.	
–	6/5/19		Admitted NIL Evacuated 5 OR. Remaining NIL	
–	7/5/19		Admitted 2 OR. Remaining 2 OR Prevailing disease Venereal.	
–	8/5/19		Admitted 3 OR Remaining 5 OR Prevailing disease Venereal.	
–	9/5/19		Admitted NIL Evacuated 1 OR Remaining 4 OR Prevailing disease Venereal 7 OR Rame 1 OR RASC MT to dispersal centre for demobilization.	
–	10/5/19		Admitted NIL Evacuated 4 OR. Remaining NIL.	
–	11/5/19		Admitted 1 OR Remaining 1 OR Prevailing disease Venereal.	
–	12/5/19		Admitted 1 OR Evacuated 2 OR Prevailing disease Venereal	
–	13/5/19		Admitted 4 OR Remaining 4 OR Prevailing disease Venereal 1 OR RASC MT leave to UK.	

A5834 Wt. W4973/M687 750,000 8/16 D. D. & L. Ltd. Forms/C.2118/13.

Instructions regarding War Diaries and Intelligence Summaries are contained in F. S. Regs., Part II. and the Staff Manual respectively. Title pages will be prepared in manuscript.

Army Form C. 2118.

WAR DIARY
or
INTELLIGENCE SUMMARY.
(Erase heading not required.)

Page II — 93rd Field Ambulance

Place	Date	Hour	Summary of Events and Information	Remarks and references to Appendices
St Omer	14/5/19		Admitted 1 OR Remaining 5 OR, Prevailing disease Venereal	
–	15/5/19		Admitted 1 OR Evacuated 6 OR Remaining Nil Prevailing disease Venereal	
			Capt (A/Major) CC Irvine MC RAMC relinquished acting rank of Major from 2/5/19	
			Capt CC Irvine MC RAMC granted leave to UK 15/5/19 to 29/5/19.	
–	16/5/19		Received orders for Cadre to entrain at WIZERNES 19/5/19 for the UK. All transport taken to WIZERNES.	
–	17/5/19		NIL	
–	18/5/19		1 OR [illegible] to Dispersal Camp for demobilization	
–	19/5/19		Left St Omer for WIZERNES 12 noon.	
WIZERNES	19/5/19		Entrained at WIZERNES 5.15 pm. Arrived DUNKERQUE	
DUNKIRK	19/5/19		Detrained and entered Camp	
–	20/5/19		Unit passed through disinfection process & then proceeded to No 1 Camp MARDYCK	
–	21/5/19		NIL	
–	22/5/19		NIL	

A5834 Wt. W4973/M687 750,000 8/16 D. D. & L. Ltd. Forms/C.2118/13.

Instructions regarding War Diaries and Intelligence Summaries are contained in F. S. Regs., Part II. and the Staff Manual respectively. Title pages will be prepared in manuscript.

WAR DIARY
or
INTELLIGENCE SUMMARY.
(*Erase heading not required.*)

Army Form C. 2118.

Page III 93 Field Ambulance

Place	Date	Hour	Summary of Events and Information	Remarks and references to Appendices
DUNKIRK	23/5/19		Nil Awaiting embarkation orders	
–	24/5/19		Unit embarked at Dunkirk for Southampton at 5pm. Unit composed of 1 off 44 OR (Cadre unit) on SS MOGILOFF	
			Patients admitted 20 OR	
			– Evacuated 22 OR	

G [illegible]
Lieut. RAMC
OC 93 Field Ambulance
(Cadre)

93rd FIELD AMBULANCE ORDERLY ROOM No. Date 24/5/19 R. A. M. C.

A5834 Wt. W4973/M68 750,000 8/16 D. D. & L. Ltd. Forms/C.2118/13.

www.ingramcontent.com/pod-product-compliance
Lightning Source LLC
Chambersburg PA
CBHW080817010526
44111CB00015B/2568
* 9 7 8 1 4 7 4 5 1 5 6 7 2 *